THE OIL PRINCE'S LEGACY

油王

THE OIL PRINCE'S LEGACY

ROCKEFELLER PHILANTHROPY IN CHINA

MARY BROWN BULLOCK

WOODROW WILSON CENTER PRESS
Washington, D.C.

STANFORD UNIVERSITY PRESS
Stanford, California

EDITORIAL OFFICES

Woodrow Wilson Center Press
One Woodrow Wilson Plaza
1300 Pennsylvania Avenue, N.W.
Washington, D.C. 20004-3027
Telephone: 202-691-4029
www.wilsoncenter.org

ORDER FROM

Stanford University Press
Chicago Distribution Center
11030 South Langley Avenue
Chicago, IL 60628
Telephone: 1-800-621-2736; 773-568-1550

The Library of Congress has cataloged the hardcover edition of this book as follows:

Bullock, Mary Brown.
    The oil prince's legacy : Rockefeller philanthropy in China / Mary Brown Bullock.
    p. cm.
    1. United States—Foreign relations—China—History.   2. China—Foreign
relations—United States—History.   3. Rockefeller Foundation—History.
4. Endowment of research—China—History.   5. Science and state—China—
History.   6. Medicine—China—History.   I. Title.
E183.8.C5B84 2011
327.73051—dc22   2011003078

paperback ISBN: 978-0-8047-8503-7

Dedicated to my parents,
Mardia Hopper Brown and G. Thompson Brown

CONTENTS

Figures

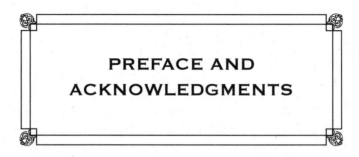

PREFACE AND ACKNOWLEDGMENTS

This book reflects my experience as a participant in United States–China cultural relations since the mid-1970s as well as my long-standing scholarly interest in the history of the Rockefeller Foundation in China. I served as director of the Committee on Scholarly Communication with the People's Republic of China of the National Academy of Sciences, the Social Science Research Council, and the American Council of Learned Societies from 1977 to 1988, and I have been a trustee of the China Medical Board since 1981. My association with both organizations provided many opportunities to witness the renewal of scientific and medical relations between the United States and China during the last three decades. I learned much about the nature of modern scientific and medical institutions, and the importance of capacity building, which dominated the Rockefeller international strategy. These experiences prompted many of the questions and issues that are addressed in this study. I am grateful to my many colleagues who shared Asia travel and their observations with me over the years. This book, however, reflects my own views and is independent from any organization with which I have been or am associated.

My first book, *An American Transplant: The Rockefeller Foundation and Peking Union Medical College* (University of California Press, 1980), concentrates on the period before 1951 and was primarily written before I visited China and before the Rockefeller Archives were fully open. Few writing thirty years ago saw many linkages between Republican and Communist China. As the Cultural Revolution persisted, even fewer viewed the earlier American cultural presence as having a lasting legacy. Reflecting the intellectual issues of the 1970s I, too, was skeptical about the Rockefeller mission, especially its focus on elite scientific medicine. However, writing now, after yearly access to China since 1974 and the benefit of many studies that trace institutions and ideas across the twentieth century's *longue durée*, my views have moderated. One purpose of this second study is to update and refine that earlier record, including the history of Peking Union Medical College (PUMC) since 1951.

I am especially grateful to the many PUMC graduates, faculty, and administrators who have entertained me and shared personal and institutional memories over many years. They are named in appendix B, but I must here acknowledge the five presidents of PUMC whom I have met: Huang Jiasi, Wu Jieping, Gu Fangzhou, Ba Denian, and Liu Depei (photographs of them are in chapter 4). From each, I gained a sense of the many issues PUMC faced during their tenure. Theirs is an inspiring story. Also, Wang Anyou and Jiang Yuhong helped to arrange my interviews in 2007 and 2008, and Zhang Xia assisted me in using the PUMC Archives.

A second purpose of this study is to place the PUMC story in the larger context of multidisciplinary and multi-institutional Rockefeller China philanthropy across the twentieth century. Such a synthesis is only possible because of the many monographs and articles on Rockefeller philanthropy and American science and medicine in China published in recent decades. These rich sources are cited in the notes and bibliography. This literature has been made possible by growing access to historical archives in China and to the Rockefeller Archive Center in Sleepy Hollow, New York. I and many others owe a deep debt of gratitude to Tom Rosenbaum, whose archival knowledge and inquisitive mind made the search for materials so rewarding. I was also ably assisted by Mindy Gordon and Michele Hiltzik.

A third purpose of this book is to chronicle the relationship between the Rockefeller family members and their China philanthropy. The discovery of the China diaries and letters of John D. Rockefeller Jr. and John D. Rockefeller 3rd opened my eyes to the depth of their personal engagement with China. Robert Oxnam, a former president of the Asia Society and a trustee of the Rockefeller Brothers Fund, urged me to "follow the art," which led to a second discovery: the very considerable interest of Abby Rockefeller, Rockefeller matriarch, in Asian art and culture. Cynthia Altman, the curator of Kykuit, the family residence, gave me a guided tour of its China collection. David Rockefeller shared memories of his mother, Abby, while giving me a tour of her Chinese garden in Seal Harbor, Maine. Other members of the Rockefeller family have also been generous in sharing memories with me. Peter Johnson, the Rockefeller family biographer and adviser to David Rockefeller, responded quickly to my many questions and requests for assistance.

Rockefeller philanthropies with a continuing interest in China include the Rockefeller Foundation, the China Medical Board, Inc., the Rockefeller Brothers Fund, the Asia Society, and the Asian Cultural Council. Senior officers as well as China-related staff of each shared both documents and time. They, too, are acknowledged in the notes.

I began the research for this book in the fall of 2006 as a Public Policy Scholar at the Woodrow Wilson International Center for Scholars in Washington. This provided uninterrupted time, wonderful colleagues, and extraordinary research assistance. A sojourn at the Rockefeller Foundation's Bellagio Conference Center in 2007 provided the ideal setting for writing. An early version of chapter 1 benefited from the critique of my Bellagio colleagues. I also benefited from the discussion of chapter 2 at Harvard University's conference on transnational histories of public health in Asia, in May 2008. A summary of this book was presented at a seminar on Rockefeller medicine in China at Peking University's Institute of the History of Western Medicine in June 2009.

Many colleagues have encouraged and assisted me. Joe Brinley, the director of the Woodrow Wilson Center Press, has been interested in this project from the start. I greatly appreciate his support and that of his staff. Warren Cohen, John Israel, Zhou Haicheng, and Li Changsheng read the manuscript in its entirety, while Lincoln Chen, Laurence Schneider, Tom Rosenbaum, Jan Berris, and Jesse Huang read portions. Susan Rabiner and Elizabeth Gallo made helpful comments on an early proposal. Each reader raised important questions, which I have endeavored to address. Student interns helped keep my research interests alive during my many years of academic administration: Li Zhao and Daniel Rosen at the Woodrow Wilson Center; Katy Rosenbaum at Agnes Scott College; and Huaye Dong, Ellie Tang, and Zhou Haicheng at Emory University. Jiling Yang assisted with materials from Cleveland newspapers. Agnes Scott College's Board of Trustees encouraged and funded my research travel to China while I served as president, and Emory University provided research and translation support.

My family has been closely involved with this project from the beginning. My husband George's interest and uncommon patience are deeply appreciated. Graham and Ashley provided editorial, technological, and methodological assistance. All three visited PUMC with me and read and commented at length on the entire manuscript. My parents, G. Thompson and Mardia Brown, who were born in China and Korea, respectively, and took me to Korea and Japan to live as a young girl, were themselves missionary participants in the era about which much of this book is written. Their love of Asia and lifelong interest in United States–Asia cultural relations influenced my worldview from an early age. It is to them that this book is dedicated.

A Note on Names

Rockefeller Names

Four John D. Rockefellers are featured in this book. To distinguish between them, I have followed conventional usage, as follows:

John D. Rockefeller Sr. (1839–1937) is JDR Sr. or Senior.
John D. Rockefeller Jr. (1874–1960) is JDR Jr. or Junior.
John D. Rockefeller 3rd (1906–78) is JDR 3rd or JDR.
John D. Rockefeller IV (1937–) is Jay.

Romanization

I have used the standard pinyin for all Chinese names and places, with the common exceptions of Sun Yat-sen and Chiang Kai-shek, and I have not changed the spelling of Chinese names in quotations. If the individual was well known by a different name or Romanization, that is rendered in parentheses—for example, "Kong Xiangxi (H. H. Kung)"—but only for the first mention. The Chinese characters for Chinese names can be found in appendix C.

I have also opted to retain "Peking" instead of "Beijing" because the key institution in this book, Peking Union Medical College, continues to use "Peking" in its Romanized name today. Using "Peking" for the post-1949 period as well as the pre-1949 period (when the city was also known as "Peiping," from 1927 to 1949) also standardizes the Romanization across the nineteenth and twentieth centuries.

油王

THE OIL PRINCE'S LEGACY

INTRODUCTION

A Century of Rockefeller Philanthropy in China

The Rockefeller name is not often associated with China—Asian art and Japan perhaps, but not China. And yet, during the first half of the twentieth century, China was the primary foreign beneficiary of Rockefeller philanthropy, and Standard Oil was the most successful American company in China. The first three John D. Rockefellers were engaged with China from the time of the American Civil War until Deng Xiaoping's reform era. Today, multiple Rockefeller philanthropies continue China programs in science, medicine, and the arts that began a century ago. Across the twentieth century, the Rockefeller investment in China's science, medicine, and higher education—close to $800 million—far outpaced that of any other American source.[1]

The Rockefeller family's philanthropic involvement in China mirrors a century and a half of American cultural relations with China. The Rockefellers' interests in commerce, religion, science, and art epitomize the multidimensional, nongovernmental forces that have shaped Sino-American relations.

A century ago, American scientists looked to Europe for training and inspiration. Few imagined an era when scientific collaboration with China would become a priority, or that American-educated Chinese might one day dominate China's scientific elite. Today, far-reaching intellectual ties between China and the United States are becoming as important as the educational ties between the United States and Great Britain in the eighteenth and early nineteenth centuries and the scientific ties between the United States and Germany in the late nineteenth and early twentieth centuries. How did this happen? What forces brought about this close encounter between the knowledge communities of the world's largest developing country and its greatest twentieth-century power? And looking ahead, how will China's rise as a global power change the nature of its cultural relations with America?

The core thesis of this book is that the Rockefellers' sustained philanthropic emphasis on elite science and medicine in China legitimated a secular American scientific presence and nurtured a tradition of professional relationships that survived even the upheavals of Mao Zedong's era. The success of the Rockefeller agenda was due in no small part to the convergence of Chinese and Rockefeller priorities. Unlike the Jesuits centuries before them, the Rockefellers were lucky in their timing. Modern science became an important component of China's twentieth-century revolutionary ideology—from the 1919 May 4th movement to the Guomindang's nation building to Deng Xiaoping's "four moderniza-tions." Throughout the century—even, in some respects, during the 1950s and 1960s, when China was isolated from the Rockefellers and the rest of the world—the Rockefellers' philanthropic mission was compatible with China's broader quest to harness science in support of its national pursuit of "wealth and power."

This book focuses primarily on science and medicine, but it also illustrates how the Rockefeller philanthropic network promoted the American understand-ing of Asian culture during many decades. The Chinese art collections of John D. Rockefeller Jr. and his son, John D. Rockefeller 3rd, became part of Ameri-ca's national museums. Abby Aldrich Rockefeller, John D. Rockefeller Jr.'s wife, embraced Asian art, landscapes, and religion, passing these interests on to friends and family alike. The earliest American philanthropic support for China stud-ies, including language and libraries, came from the Rockefeller Foundation in the late 1920s, more than two decades before the Ford Foundation initiated its significant support. The evolving nature of America's cultural encounters with China—including the arts and humanities as well as the sciences—was often led by, and always reflected, the Rockefellers' engagement.

The China story of the Rockefeller family and philanthropic foundations has heretofore only been told in fragments. Access to family diaries and let-ters, institutional archives, and interviews with Chinese medical leaders and several generations of Rockefeller family members now enables a more complete and intimate look at how America's wealthiest family encountered China. The progression of the Rockefeller family's interests, from commerce to religion to medicine and science, as well as its growing affinity for Asian culture, is not only intrinsically interesting but also important for increasing America's awareness of China over the years. As early as the 1920s, John Jr. and Abby's worldview encompassed an appreciation of Chinese religion and art—and even the con-viction that China mattered, not just culturally but also politically. And their embrace of Asian civilization, passed down to their six children—Abby, John 3rd, Nelson, Laurence, Winthrop, and David—filtered American perceptions of China because of the family's prestigious social and political position, but even more because their values helped to shape the institutions they created, which are still influential today. These Rockefeller institutions are numerous, but those that have been most involved with China are the Rockefeller Foundation; the China Medical Board, Inc.; the Rockefeller Brothers Fund; the Asia Society; and the Asian Cultural Council.

The scale and longevity of the Rockefellers' involvement in China raises questions for the historian. The Rockefeller Foundation and the China Medical Board celebrate their one-hundredth anniversaries in 2013 and 2014, respectively. Are there unifying themes that can assist our interpretation and tie this century-long, transpacific narrative together? "Robber baron" and "cultural imperialist" are the two prevailing tropes for the first John D. Rockefeller and his international philanthropy—and not without reason. Most biographies of him, even the most recent and sympathetic, give more attention to his monopolistic business ventures than his philanthropic ones—although his philanthropic legacy has been arguably far more enduring. During the first half of the twentieth century, no other American institution's intellectual reach better exemplifies "cultural imperialism" than that of the Rockefeller Foundation. Adopting a seemingly benevolent motto—"To promote the well-being of mankind throughout the world"—the foundation used the ideologies of American science and medicine as a template for its engagement with countries as different as the United Kingdom and Ceylon (today Sri Lanka). The concepts of atonement and hegemony give insight into the early period of this study—including the Rockefeller family's initial philanthropic motives; the parallel engagements of Standard Oil and the Rockefeller Foundation in China; and the creation of Peking Union Medical College, known as "the Johns Hopkins of China."

However, "robber baron" and "cultural imperialist" are time-bound, unidimensional caricatures that would preclude an exploration of the many layers of Rockefeller family and institutional involvement, especially the diverse ways in which Chinese culture, science, and politics influenced them. Therefore, I have chosen an alternative, more neutral lens through which to view the Rockefellers' China philanthropy across the turbulent twentieth century. This perspective, drawn from Akira Iriye's concept of cultural internationalism, centers on non-state actors that influence the character of foreign relations as much as or sometimes more than traditional state relations. Iriye defines cultural internationalism as "an idea, a movement, or an institution that seeks to reformulate the nature of relations through cross-national cooperation and exchange."[2] This nuanced concept values the world of ideas and the importance of institutions in which knowledge is embedded. It recognizes that culture is not always the handmaiden of the state and that patterns of cultural relations do not necessarily depend on political or economic relationships. Thus, Iriye explains about cultural internationalism and China: "The further growth of education and scholarly exchanges with China and other countries demonstrated that power and culture were not entirely identical, that power did not always determine culture, and that culture did not necessarily seek the support of power."[3] Cultural internationalism provides a frame within which to explore the changing roles and embedded views of several generations of the Rockefeller family and their institutional philanthropy in China. Most important, the "inter" in "cultural internationalism" signifies the role that China and its peoples, cultures, and institutions have played in shaping both the Rockefeller agenda and its legacy.

Art is one domain of twentieth-century cultural internationalism. Even in the late nineteenth and early twentieth centuries, when the Qing Dynasty was weak and United States–China political relations were relatively unimportant, Asian art and aesthetics profoundly influenced American culture.[4] Abby Rockefeller and John D. Rockefeller Jr. were among the Americans who embraced Asian art well before they became involved in philanthropy in China. In fact, their appreciation of Asian culture directly affected their philanthropic imagination. Science is another domain of cultural internationalism. Exporting Western science and medicine to China dominated the Rockefellers' institutional agenda. The first Rockefeller advisers believed that the transmittal of Western scientific values would lead to shared cultural and political norms.[5] Some writers have characterized this as cultural imperialism.[6] But these analysts may have missed something equally fundamental to the Rockefeller agenda: attention to the science itself, and the desire to share cutting-edge American science with China and to include Chinese scientists in a global scientific family.

At the heart of the Rockefeller scientific agenda throughout the twentieth century was the aim to create a scientific community unbounded by national or political boundaries. This agenda exemplifies Eugene Rabinowitch's concept of scientific internationalism, an idealized view of science rooted in a universal scientific community. As he writes:

> At its core were a set of ecumenical traditions and ideals common to the scientific
> profession: that scientific knowledge was universally valuable, that the methods
> and practice of science must remain unaffected by culture or politics, that
> unrestricted scientific exchange among professionals of all nations or peoples was
> critical to the progress of science and human civilization, and that science itself
> was a kind of *lingua franca* that promoted a cosmopolitan perspective, unified
> goals, and an order based on merit that crossed international boundaries.[7]

The notion of a global scientific profession has been a powerful concept throughout much of Western history. Even as European nations vied for scientific primacy in the early days of the Enlightenment, they formed academies and professions that shared scientific knowledge across national boundaries. The concept of "unrestricted" scientific exchange that emerged during the twentieth century was intended to promote science across political boundaries. Through its work on global epidemics and its close ties with the League of Nations, the Rockefeller Foundation became the most important American organization to promote and finance transnational scientific communities, extending the prevailing transatlantic scientific community to the Pacific. That China was from the first included in this new orbit has made a significant difference in the scientific life of both China and the United States.

This book presents Rockefeller philanthropy as a case study of multilayered cultural internationalism, weaving together four narrative themes. The first is the Rockefeller family's China story, beginning in 1863 with John D. Rockefeller's $10 donation to China missions and concluding in 2007 with the improbable dedication of the "Oil Prince's" commemorative statue in Peking. The China views and experiences of John D. Rockefeller Sr. and his son and grandson introduce a narrative thread that links chapter 1, "Origins," chapter 3, "Politics," and chapter 5, "Renewal." Their encounter with Asian culture and continuing involvement in China policy across five decades shed light on the family's intergenerational interest in China and on the role of the founder and his progeny in their foundations' decisionmaking. Of particular interest are John D. Rockefeller Jr.'s and John D. Rockefeller 3rd's encounters with both Chinese Nationalism and Chinese Communism. In these years, the family business, Standard Oil, not only provided the resources that funded the Rockefellers' philanthropies but also was an ever-present backdrop for Rockefeller family activities in China.

The second narrative theme introduces professional philanthropists—presidents, officers, and China-based staff—who join Rockefeller family members as dramatis personae. It was the vision of these career officers—including Frederick Gates, Raymond Fosdick, and John Knowles in New York and John Grant, Roger Greene, Sheldon Segal, and Roy Schwarz in China—who determined the specific philanthropic projects. Chapter 2, "Agenda," and chapter 3 feature Greene and Grant, nearly twenty-year veterans of service in China. Each became an independent actor significantly altering the Rockefeller Foundation's China agenda during the Republican era. Chapter 5, which focuses on the last three decades of the twentieth century, examines the return of Rockefeller philanthropy to China starting in 1980. During this recent period, China programs have not been sui generis but rather have fit into a broader international agenda. Even so, there has been remarkable continuity in the Rockefeller philanthropic mission; the Rockefeller Foundation and the China Medical Board embraced medicine and science as their primary agenda, developing a style of institution building and global research networks that continued throughout the twentieth century.

Chinese intellectuals and institutions—tested by war, revolution, and persecution—are the protagonists in the third narrative theme. Several hundred Chinese institutions and many thousands of Chinese scholars and practitioners have received Rockefeller support over the century. With countless variations, they absorbed, adapted, and reinvented American learning, and sometimes they rejected it altogether. The origins of these institutions, the early role of young Chinese intellectuals, and the expansion of the Rockefellers' China networks are introduced in chapter 2. The fate of these institutions in Mao's China is explored in chapter 4, "Survival," which presents a case study of Peking Union Medical College (PUMC), the Rockefellers' flagship institution. Over the course of many years, I have interviewed PUMC personnel, who enabled me to construct a collective biography of PUMC faculty and graduates during this tumultuous period. This case study of an identifiable cohort enables us to evaluate one layer of the Rockefeller philanthropic enterprise long after Rockefeller financial support ended.

The book's overall sequencing is primarily chronological. It opens with Americans seeking to both exploit and reform China, the "sick man of Asia," and it concludes with Americans recalibrating their agenda as China is becoming a competitive global power. Thus, the fourth and final narrative theme reveals the persistence of American cultural impulses toward China across four wars (World War I and World War II, the Chinese civil war, and the Korean War), during three revolutions (the Nationalist Revolution, the Communist Revolution, and the Cultural Revolution), and into the first decade of the twenty-first century. Contemporary United States–China cultural relations are depicted in the sixth and final chapter, "Legacy," in which PUMC's ninetieth-anniversary celebration in 2007 and the Asia Society's fiftieth anniversary in 2006 illustrate the continuing but changing China interests of the Rockefeller family and Rockefeller philanthropy.

We learn of the involvement of the fourth and fifth generations of Rockefellers in China, as well as the new ways in which China's rise as a global power is changing the nature of Rockefeller philanthropy. From the late nineteenth century to the early twenty-first century, Rockefeller family perceptions and philanthropic priorities have been a bellwether of Sino-American relations.

These four narrative themes do not complete the story. Just as my first book— *An American Transplant: The Rockefeller Foundation and Peking Union Medical College*—reflected the intellectual themes and available materials of the 1970s, the coming decades will bring the progressive opening of more Chinese institutional archives and an increasing number of medical and scientific memoirs. The extensive archives of PUMC were only partially open to me. The pre-1949 materials are expected to be opened soon, and perhaps one day, the post-1950 records will also be available. A more complex picture of the interactive relationship between the Rockefeller Foundation and the Nationalist government and Standard Oil may emerge from work currently under way by Chinese scholars in Chinese archives. Missionary medicine, including studies of individual hospitals, is currently receiving new attention in both Chinese and American historical circles. A growing body of American scholarship seeks to understand the societal implications of Western medicine and its encounter with traditional Chinese culture and medicine. And the recent return of Rockefeller philanthropy to China, sketched very generally here, awaits serious scrutiny.

For now, historians in both the People's Republic of China and the United States have concluded that the causes espoused by the Rockefellers and the Chinese people and institutions funded by their philanthropies have made a significant contribution to the intellectual landscape of both countries. Of course, they all also recognize that this did not happen without great controversy. This is that story. Today, the United States and China are knit together by deep ties in medicine, the arts, the natural and the social sciences, the humanities, and higher education, as well as commerce and geopolitics. Understanding the origin, evolution, interregnum, and renewal of Rockefeller philanthropy in China can bring new clarity to our understanding of the nature and tenacity of these relationships. In the end, we find—perhaps surprisingly—that the Rockefellers' China story is also America's China story.

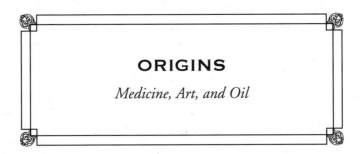

CHAPTER 1

ORIGINS

Medicine, Art, and Oil

In 1863, John D. Rockefeller sold his first kerosene to China and made his first gift to China missions.[1] He was twenty-four years old. Young Rockefeller could not have dreamed that both his oil company and future foundation would one day dominate the American cultural and commercial presence in China. Nor could he have envisioned that his fortune would contribute to internationalizing modern science and medicine. But even at this young age, he had the imagination to see well beyond the environs of Cleveland.

In the 1860s, both the United States and China were in the midst of devastating civil wars. Only with the battle of Gettysburg in 1863 was it clear that the Union would eventually triumph. Likewise the Taiping Rebellion, led by the Christianity-inspired Hong Xiuquan, threatened the collapse of the Qing Dynasty. Although the *Cleveland Morning Leader* reported almost daily on the Civil War, it also chronicled the course of the Taipings, "the terrible destruction of human life," along with details of the Battle of Hangzhou, suggesting that the devastation in China appeared far greater than the bloody American Civil War.[2]

Rockefeller's awareness of this wider domestic and international scene—the human condition of both the American slave and the heathen Chinese—is reflected in his early philanthropy. Called "fantastically charitable" by Ron Chernow, his most recent biographer, this young Baptist enthusiast was an eclectic donor; he gave to a black church and a Catholic orphanage as well as to Methodist and Baptist missions alike.[3] His youthful charity stemmed from his mother Cettie's emphasis on stewardship and his membership in the Erie Street Baptist Church, the focus of his extracurricular life during his early twenties. He attended not only three Sunday services but also midweek prayer meetings. His affiliation with the Young Men's Christian Association, which he joined as a teenager in

1857, expanded his religious and international perspectives.[4] The YMCA, established in England in 1844, was an ecumenical Christian fellowship group with an international orientation. It later introduced both Rockefeller and his son to social reform movements in China.

Calls to support Baptist foreign missions were a regular part of his church life. Still, 1863 is early for support of China missions. The China Baptist mission was then tiny indeed. The first missionaries, arriving in the 1830s, had been limited to Macao and Hong Kong; but with the Treaty of Nanjing (1842), they expanded their presence to Shanghai, Ningbo, and Guangzhou. The first Baptist church opened in 1847 in the coastal city of Ningbo. The Treaties of Tianjin (1858) and the Peking Convention (1860) concluded the Opium Wars and forced China to open its hinterland to both missionaries and merchants. By the early 1860s, there were still fewer than ten Baptist missionaries in the country.[5] Nonetheless, Rockefeller's religious community was aware of missionaries in China; the son of a prominent Cleveland citizen was a Presbyterian missionary, and at least one other missionary, D. J. McGowan, spoke publicly about his China work.[6]

Although China was certainly not very present in the popular imagination of a nation still in the midst of civil war, Rockefeller's early knowledge of China was not limited to missionary sources. Cleveland may have been a town of only 25,000, but it was not a backwater. It was located on Lake Erie, an important railroad stop by midcentury, and had already become a regional transportation center. By the early 1860s, more than 50,000 Chinese immigrants, mainly in the West, were working on the construction of American railways, and commercial shipping to China was well under way. During the 1850s and early 1860s, the *Cleveland Morning Leader* included periodic references to China, including advertisements for tea seed from Hong Kong and sugarcane from China. Twelve Cleveland vessels were expected to ply the Pacific in 1859. Curiosity about Chinese people was expressed: "The Chinese are a strange as well as an old people, and still regard the world outside the great wall as 'outside barbarians.'" When an Ohio delegation was hosted by the "six Chinese companies of San Francisco," they were feted with a dinner of 336 dishes in 130 courses, including the famous "bird nest soup." In 1865, the press acclaimed "the establishment of a monthly mail service between San Francisco and leading ports in the Chinese empire and Japan. . . . The importance of this measure cannot be overestimated."[7] China's millions were viewed with awe: "The almost countless multitudes of the 'Celestials.' The aggregate population is 400,000,000! . . . the mind cannot grasp the real import of so vast a number—*four hundred million*! What does it mean?"[8]

It meant, of course, 400 million souls to be saved and 400 million lamps to be lit. The advent of regular transpacific shipping made possible the global reach of the oil that had just been discovered in Cleveland's backyard. Rockefeller's China mission benefactions coincidentally paralleled his entry into the oil business and his first exports of kerosene to China. His first job in Cleveland was as a clerk and accountant, but in 1858—at the age of eighteen—he went into business for himself with Maurice Clark. Their firm was a commission house, buying and selling a wide range of produce. A year later, oil was discovered in Titusville, Pennsylvania, not far from Cleveland, and the rest, one might say, is history. Although Rockefeller was initially dubious about oil's prospects, he and Clark bought into their first refining business in 1863; it was the cleansing of oil, refining, that produced the first kerosene. According to historians of the Standard Oil Company, some of that first kerosene made its way via New York to China.[9]

The opening of China to both missions and oil accelerated during the 1860s and 1870s. The U.S. minister to China, Anson Burlingame, made a public visit to Cleveland in 1865, promoting the new and expanded treaty system, which provided a more predictable legal structure for United States–China relations. As one of the most promising young businessmen in Cleveland, Rockefeller may have met him and heard him speak. Certainly the significance of Burlingame's visit was noted in the Cleveland newspapers.[10] Burlingame had played an important role in incorporating the United States into the treaty framework hammered out by the British and French upon their victory in the Second Opium War. He had also persuaded the Europeans to limit further encroachments on Chinese sovereignty, winning the United States some initial gratitude from the Chinese officials.

For missionaries and merchants, the three most important treaty provisions were extraterritoriality, unrestricted access to all of China, and a guaranteed ad valorem tariff of only 5 percent. Extraterritoriality ensured that American citizens would be exempt from Chinese law and prosecution; it would become the most contentious of all treaty provisions and was not rescinded until the early 1940s. The low tariff structure also remained unchanged for nearly seventy years, although Standard Oil eventually accepted some additional tariffs in the 1920s in order to negotiate more favorable Chinese market concessions. For the Chinese, this structure of "unequal treaties" would become the rallying point for Chinese nationalism in the years to come. Local opposition to both missionaries and merchants was frequent during the last half of the nineteenth century, but the Qing court was too weak to redress the imposed semicolonial relationship.

Selling kerosene to China was a minor aspect of Rockefeller's growing oil business until the late 1870s. By that time foreign trade in oil was primarily managed by Standard Oil of New York, one of the multiple Standard Oil trusts, led by his brother, William. Rockefeller was kept abreast of international as well as domestic issues; by the 1880s, he was well aware of the growing importance of the China market. A Standard Oil employee, William H. Libby, traveled extensively in China in 1882, assisted by the American vice consul, J. J. Bandinel. Together they recommended a great expansion of Standard's China presence. This was in part to offset the growing role of the Dutch, British, and Russian oil companies in Asia and China.[11]

Years later, Rockefeller would remember well this fierce international competition for the Asia oil business and the origin of the *mei-foo*, the kerosene lamp for China:

> The Standard is always fighting to see the American product against the oil produced from the great fields of Russia . . . and the Burma Oil, which largely affects the market in India. In all these various countries we are met with tariffs which are raised against us, local prejudices, and strange customs. In many countries we had to teach the people—the Chinese, for example—to burn oil by making lamps for them.[12]

To promote the very inexpensive kerosene-burning lamp, Standard Oil advertised with thousands of Chinese brochures and ads, appealing to Chinese culture:

> If a person wishes luck, longevity, health and peace, he should live in a world of light. He should use the recently manufactured Standard Oil lamp. . . . The Standard lamp . . . is as bright as the moon. . . . People are happy when they use it. . . . Late night work will not tire the eyes. . . . If there is a child who studies at home, he will work harder in the light. Who would not want a child of his to progress?[13]

Standard Oil's lamps were made famous in the 1930s by Alice Tisdale Hobart's best-selling novel, *Oil for the Lamps of China*, which was also made into a movie. The phrase "oil for the lamps of China" has become a metaphor for the endless frustrations of the China market, but in fact Standard Oil became the largest and most successful American company in China in the first half of the twentieth century. In China, with the ubiquity of the cheap but effective lantern, *mei-foo* (beautiful confidence) passed into the vernacular.

Cleveland continued as an important base for Rockefeller's enterprises, but his burgeoning oil business required that he move his family to New York City in 1883. By this time, monopolistic practices resulted in Standard Oil's control of nearly 90 percent of the oil refined in the United States and 80 percent of the world's oil market. Rockefeller was already among the top twenty wealthiest men in the country. As his wealth accumulated and as he became better known, his charitable contributions—and the claims upon him—also grew. Baptist causes, especially foreign missions, continued to have a favored spot in his heart, and he made hundreds of miscellaneous donations to individual missionaries. As in his youth, his giving continued to have no sectarian boundaries. Education increasingly captured his imagination, with ongoing gifts to Denison College and what is today Bacone College.

Rockefeller's special attention, however, was reserved for Negro education. During their honeymoon in upper New York State in 1864, he and his wife, Cettie, first met two Baptist educators, Sophia B. Packard and Harriet E. Giles, who had begun to educate young black women in the South. They remained in touch, with Packard and Giles visiting Cleveland almost twenty years later in 1882. Rockefeller responded to their appeal and began his support of their new school for black women in Atlanta. Two years later, he took his entire family by train to celebrate the school's third anniversary. Packard and Giles wanted to name it for him, but he instead chose Spelman, his wife Cettie's family name, in honor of her family's commitment to the abolitionist movement.[14] Spelman College became the best college for black women in the nation, and representatives of the Rockefeller family sit on its board to this day.

During the 1880s, Rockefeller began to turn his attention toward underwriting a great Baptist university. After almost a decade of negotiations with many Baptist religious and intellectual leaders, he rather surprisingly chose to support William Rainey Harper, an Old Testament theologian, in establishing the University of Chicago. Assisting with the final negotiations was Frederick T. Gates, secretary of the American Baptist Education Society, who was to greatly influence Rockefeller's subsequent philanthropy. The University of Chicago embodied Rockefeller's own signature philanthropy, reflecting his growing interest in higher education and large-scale philanthropic projects.

Much credit is given to Gates, who came to work directly for Rockefeller in 1891, for the growth and institutionalization, the "scientific giving" that characterized Rockefeller's mature philanthropic style. By this time, however, Rockefeller himself had established several key trends in his giving. His religious contributions were not limited to Baptists. And higher education, rather than theology, was beginning to claim his resources. Through funding such different institutions as Spelman College and the University of Chicago, he exemplified his lifelong conviction that educational institutions should be problem-solving institutions, enabling individuals of all rank and ethnicity to work and spread American values. As he wrote about the University of Chicago: "Following the principle of trying to abolish evils by destroying them at the source, we felt that to aid colleges and universities, whose graduates would spread their culture far and wide, was the surest way to fight ignorance and promote the growth of useful knowledge."[15]

Building on these principles, Gates's first major contribution was to organize Rockefeller's extensive philanthropy; his second was to introduce Rockefeller to scientific medicine; and his third was to create several large charitable trusts. Gates remembered his initial exposure to Rockefeller's philanthropy:

Mr. Rockefeller had been accustomed to give a few thousand dollars annually to the Baptist Foreign Mission Society. But, quite outside this, he had conducted a small foreign mission society, if I may so call it, of his own, necessarily without adequate knowledge of the field. He was in daily receipt of appeals from individual Baptist missionaries in every region of Baptist missionary endeavor: France, Germany, Russia, Africa, China, Japan, and other nations of the distant East. They asked small sums and great, for educational institutions, hospitals, edifices, compounds, equipment, evangelization. His office, his home, his table were beset with returned missionaries, each comparatively eager for the largest possible aid for his personal field.[16]

Gates began to provide order to Rockefeller's philanthropies, consolidating support to Baptist missionaries through several main organizations. Then, in 1897, Gates read William Osler's monumental *Principles and Practices of Medicine* and became convinced that scientific medicine possessed the keys to discover the cause of illness and alleviate suffering. He repeatedly made the case to Rockefeller that he should focus his philanthropy on medicine.

Understanding John D. Rockefeller's embrace of scientific medicine, and his partial shift away from religious movements, is key to understanding most of his subsequent philanthropies, including his China initiatives. Rockefeller himself never attended college but by the 1890s had become well acquainted with men of letters. He personally never fully accepted modern scientific medicine, preferring to continue his personal treatment with homeopathic medicine. But he determined that all his philanthropies would focus on "enlarging the boundaries of human knowledge," and that "the best philanthropy is constantly in search of the finalities, . . . a search for cause, an attempt to cure evils at their source."[17] Scientific medicine was a perfect fit. Late-nineteenth-century advances in medicine had brought it to what many have called the heroic age of modern medicine. For the first time, it was possible to speak of eradicating disease and even curing disease, not just treating disease.

The death of Rockefeller's grandson from scarlet fever in 1901 personalized the need and provided the final impetus. In that same year, the Rockefeller Institute for Medical Research (today's Rockefeller University) was established. It brought together William Henry Welch, dean of the Johns Hopkins School of Medicine, as its chair, and Simon Flexner, a pathologist and bacteriologist, as its first director. These two leaders of American medicine became the most important medical advisers to the Rockefeller group, eventually becoming trustees of the Rockefeller Foundation.

The early years of the twentieth century were promising for Rockefeller philanthropy, but they were disastrous for Rockefeller's oil empire. As Standard Oil—and its scores of affiliates—dominated the domestic and international oil market, Rockefeller's personal wealth had grown exponentially; he was worth approximately $200 million in 1897. Under Gates's tutelage, Rockefeller initiated the large-scale giving for which he is justly famous. Controversies over his personal wealth and Standard Oil's monopolistic practices, however, also peaked during this period. Rockefeller had amassed control of the industry through a mix of strategies, many considered illegal, including railroad rebates, which gave Standard significant transportation discounts; the control of pipelines; the aggressive purchase of competitors; and the bribery of regulating officials. As a result, integrated vertical control had been established—from production to refinement to transportation to marketing.

Public concern over growing monopolistic companies, including Standard Oil, led first to the Sherman Antitrust Act in 1890. Although the Antitrust Act was relatively ineffective, state and federal investigations and lawsuits against Standard Oil began to proliferate. Critiques of Rockefeller personally also increased during the last decade of the nineteenth century, culminating in Ida Tarbell's exposé in a series of magazine articles published by the popular *McClure's*. Rockefeller was pilloried for his violation of business ethics and Standard Oil for its intimidating, aggrandizing control of oil production in the United States. The many lawsuits against Standard Oil culminated in 1909 with a unanimous decision by a federal court in St. Louis that Standard Oil and thirty-seven affiliates had violated the Sherman Antitrust Act. This decision was upheld by the Supreme Court in 1911, resulting in the immediate dismembering of the Standard Oil empire.

The Rockefeller family weathered this antitrust storm fairly well, continuing to be associated primarily with the Standard Oil Company of New York. Unexpectedly, Rockefeller's personal fortune was not affected negatively; rather, it increased significantly. Public interest in the new diversified oil companies (and the growing importance of gasoline for the automobile) drove the stock price higher. Rockefeller continued to hold a significant percentage of Standard Oil equities; by 1913, his net worth was $900 million, an all-time high. The U.S. national budget that year was less—only $715 million.[18]

JOHN D. ROCKEFELLER JR., CHINA, AND THE ROCKEFELLER FOUNDATION

John D. Rockefeller's only son, John D. Rockefeller Jr., joined the Rockefeller office in 1897, fresh out of college, and it would be JDR Jr. who would lead the Rockefeller philanthropic work until World War II. Most studies of the early years of Rockefeller interest in China have emphasized the influence of Frederick Gates in conceptualizing the China medical program (see chapter 2). In fact, in 1917 Gates abandoned the Rockefeller work in China, before it had hardly begun, leaving JDR Jr. as the primary China advocate within Rockefeller Foundation circles. Because this is a longitudinal study of the Rockefeller family's China interest, the focus here is on understanding the evolution of JDR Jr.'s engagement with China.

Junior was born in Cleveland, but his formative youth was spent in New York, where he grew up in both a pious and cosmopolitan environment. His horizons were broadened during his college years at Brown University by the social action philosophy of President E. Benjamin Andrews and by the rising Progressive Movement.[19] Like his father, John had systematically tithed to a Chinese Sunday school in New York during his teenage years. The church they both attended, the Fifth Avenue Baptist Church, had an active Bible school that included forty "Chinamen" in 1882, twelve of whom were received as members of the church.[20] Like his father, he had joined the YMCA, having been exposed to its new China work while at Brown. JDR Sr., who knew John R. Mott, the charismatic student secretary of the International YMCA, was already giving substantial support to the YMCA, especially its international activities. Mott also forged a friendship with Junior during his several visits to Brown in the mid-1890s. When young John began work at Standard Oil's headquarters at 26 Broadway in Manhattan, he was immediately given responsibility for coordinating his father's philanthropic relationship with Mott. JDR Sr. funded Mott's second trip to Asia in 1902 (the first was in 1896), and his son read the reports with great interest. These dramatic turn-of-the-century China narratives emphasized the importance of education and social reform as well as evangelism. Mott, who was only ten years older than Junior, became a long-term confidant and adviser.[21]

It is not surprising that a China educational initiative followed the Rockefeller Institute as one of the Rockefeller group's first big projects. China was on the mind of progressive America. In addition to the increased numbers of missionaries and the rise of both the YMCA and the Student Volunteer Movement for Foreign Missions, the early twentieth century witnessed the Boxer Rebellion, the Open Door Policy, and an expanding awareness of things Chinese.

The challenge of work in China was dramatized for the American public by the Boxer massacre of China missionaries, the siege of Peking, and the rescue by the military forces of Europe, Japan, and the United States. These events also reinforced the political conviction that continued European expansion of territorial and colonial prerogatives in China was not in America's interest. President William McKinley's secretary of state, John Whitney Hay, formulated the "Open Door Policy," which sought to persuade Europe and Japan not to expand their holdings or violate China's sovereignty. The goal was to secure for the United States, which had no territories, both equal commercial access and a role in changing the balance of power in Asia. The United States was also concerned about the exorbitant size of the indemnity imposed on China because of the Boxer

Rebellion—more than $300 million. The Chinese authorities and American missionaries were among those who lobbied for the United States to return some portion of these indemnity funds.

During the decade after the Boxer Rebellion, the Qing court began to institute educational and political reforms, suggesting to some Americans that new opportunities for influencing China were at hand. The slowness of evangelical work in the nineteenth century had convinced many, including some missionaries, that education could both promote Christianity and hasten China's reforms. Education received particular attention in the congressional debate over how to handle the remission of excess Boxer indemnity funds; scholarships for young Chinese and the establishment of an American college in China were both proposed. Even President Theodore Roosevelt addressed the matter in his 1907 Annual Message to Congress: "This Nation should help in every practicable way in the education of the Chinese people, so that the vast and populous Empire of China may gradually adapt itself to modern conditions."[22]

All these interests were reflected in correspondence to JDR Sr., JDR Jr., and Frederick Gates.[23] Most influential, however, was a 1906 letter from Harry P. Judson, president of the University of Chicago, which captured the attention of both Gates and JDR Jr. In this letter, Judson argued for a comprehensive university in China: "We have become deeply impressed with the desirability that there should be established in China as early as possible a University, distinctly Christian, but wholly undenominational in character, and of the highest ideals and broadest catholicity."[24] This, of course, was the Chicago model, and JDR Jr. and Gates wholeheartedly embraced both the concept and an exploratory trip to China. Several months later, Gates reported to Arthur H. Smith, a well-known missionary publicist, that future Rockefeller funds for China were more likely to go toward education than evangelization: "Moreover, important as evangelization may be, any organization which we at this office could create, would be better fitted to handle education than evangelization."[25]

Characteristically, JDR Sr. was not immediately enthusiastic about the proposed survey expedition to China. He worried about the amount of funding required and the project's open-ended character. It took several letters from his son to convince him. Junior linked the proposed China trip to planning for a large-scale new foundation. In 1907, Senior had concurred with the Junior-Gates proposal to set aside a large sum of money for a new charitable trust, the Rockefeller Foundation, which would hopefully be chartered by the U.S. government. Because the work of this new trust was to be international in scope, Junior argued that "we should have fuller and more accurate data regarding educational and religious conditions in these distant lands before undertaking to inaugurate any such educational or civilizing works as are possible under the new and broad charter."[26] This persuaded his father to allocate the needed

$20,000. Going even further, Gates authorized informing the Chinese government that Rockefeller was prepared to commit $10 million for an American university in China.

The year-long trip in 1908–9 to Asia and the Middle East was led by two University of Chicago professors, Ernest Burton (theology) and Thomas Chamberlain (geology). This exploratory mission on behalf of the Rockefellers became known as the Chicago Commission and the Oriental Education Commission. Although the commission's report covered educational developments in multiple countries, its primary focus was China. The recommendations from this commission shaped the direction of Rockefeller philanthropy in China for the next two decades. Burton concluded that the unsettled political and educational conditions in China argued against trying to create a university like that in Chicago. Missionaries were opposed to a secular university, and the Qing government, which had just begun to create its own modern educational institutions, was not inclined to give carte blanche to a foreign university. As Gates put it, "not even Mr. Rockefeller's promise of ten million for a foundation could tempt the Chinese government to tolerate our proposed institution, freed though it were from all religious bias, unless we would consent that it be controlled and run by appointees of the Chinese government."[27] At even its weakest moment, two years before the Qing Dynasty was overthrown, Chinese officials would not turn over higher education to a foreign enterprise.

Burton was not completely deterred, and his report is full of detailed ideas for possible American or American-British or missionary-secular universities in China. Nonetheless, when reporting on conversations with a former Baptist missionary, Timothy Richard, Burton reflected the changing educational context for Americans in China. He came to two far-reaching conclusions. The first was that a break from contemporary missionary education was needed. Burton quoted Richard verbatim: "Missionaries in past times had done the best they could, but to pursue further the policy of educating from the bottom up is foolish in the extreme. Education at the top, at the very top, and the rest will take care of itself. The highly educated will educate others a little lower down, those still further down and so on." The second conclusion was that the time was ripe for scientific medicine in China: "Though Dr. Richard did not himself throw his thought into that form, what he really suggests is a Johns Hopkins for China."[28]

Burton's lengthy report was read avidly by Gates and JDR Jr., and it became standard background reading for all subsequent Rockefeller meetings related to China. Two years later, Gates returned to Burton's recommendation and wrote: "Might we not do in medicine in China what we had failed in our attempt to do in University education? Might we not indeed at once attempt scientific medicine in China?"[29] As he and JDR Jr. continued with plans for the new foundation, both China and medicine were on their mind.

The Rockefellers originally sought a federal charter for the new Rockefeller Foundation, but this request coincided with the controversy over the Supreme Court's decision to dismember the Standard Oil conglomerate. After three years of public debate, the U.S. Senate rejected a federal charter for the new Rockefeller Foundation. Instead, the Rockefellers turned to the State of New York, which formally incorporated the foundation in 1913. JDR Sr.'s total capitalization of the Rockefeller Foundation was $241 million, including the 1929 transfer of funds from the Spelman Memorial (see chapter 2). Many then, and later, concluded that Rockefeller had decided to create the new foundation in order to gain much-needed public approval. Senior always denied any guilt in amassing his fortune, and his charitable giving long predated his corporate vicissitudes. For Junior, how-ever, the public critique and pressures of being a Rockefeller had a huge effect: Behind his lifelong embrace of the Rockefeller philanthropic tradition was a desire to redeem the Rockefeller reputation.[30]

JDR Jr. became the first president of the Rockefeller Foundation, which selected "the well-being of mankind" as its charter statement. Not unexpectedly, the new foundation embraced global health as its first priority, convinced, as Gates put it, that "disease is the supreme ill of life, and it is the main source of almost all other human ills—poverty, crime, ignorance, vice, inefficiency, hereditary taint, and many other ills."[31] The Rockefeller Foundation's first two programs, the Inter-national Health Board (1913) and the China Medical Board (1914), represented two competing streams of Rockefeller medical philanthropy—public health and scientific medicine. Interest in public health had grown out of the Rockefeller-funded Sanitary Commission, which had tackled hookworm in the South and now sought a global mandate with the creation of the International Health Board. Interest in scientific medicine, with its emphasis on research and curative health care, emerged from Rockefeller support of the Rockefeller Institute and the reforms of American medical education promulgated by Abraham Flexner. The China Medical Board became the institutional vehicle for promoting scientific medicine in China. These differing approaches reinforced the conceptual and institutional separation between public health and medicine, and between pre-ventive and curative medicine, that continues to characterize not only American medicine but also many aspects of global health practice.

Wickliffe Rose led the public health effort, serving as the first director of the International Health Board. By the time it was terminated in 1951, the board had spent $94 million creating schools of public health and managing research and disease control campaigns against such endemic diseases as yellow fever and malaria in more than seventy countries in North America, Europe, Latin Amer-ica, and Asia. Only 8 percent of its budget, however, was spent in Asia.[32]

The China Medical Board expended more than $44 million in one coun-try during the same period.[33] (Other Rockefeller Foundation divisions expended approximately $10 million more.) This attention to one country and emphasis on scientific medicine and not public health was not the only difference with the International Health Board. The close personal attention of JDR Jr. (who became the first chair of the China Medical Board) well into the 1950s was another important difference.

JDR Jr.'s intense involvement began with the very first Rockefeller Foundation meeting on China, in January 1914, which he personally chaired. The two-day meeting included the presidents of Harvard and the University of Chicago, leading China missionaries, and foreign policy specialists. When several participants suggested that the Chinese government would support a Rockefeller educational venture, Junior pressed them on this point: "Your idea is that the government would cooperate in such a scheme? Could it do that?" And later, he sought further clarification: "And the advantage of the cooperation with a foundation is, perhaps that it would be an incentive to the Chinese government, if it had some outside help to come in on such terms?" Also later, he asked the group about the relative role of Chinese versus foreigners: "Is it better to have a large university comprised of mission schools or a solely Chinese university? . . . To be manned by foreigners?" When the group divided over whether a university or a medical school was the appropriate vehicle, Rockefeller tried to smooth the discussion with humor: "Now, gentlemen, the understanding is that each man has in his inside pocket the absolute solution of this difficult problem, which the world thus far has not been able to solve."[34] Although advocates for a Rockefeller university in China persisted, the consensus was in favor of introducing scientific medicine to China, a "virgin field," rather than a university that would be in competition with Chinese universities.

This conference was followed by two additional survey commissions to China, in 1914 and 1915, both of which confirmed that medicine, not higher education, was the appropriate vehicle for Rockefeller philanthropy. The 1914 commission published a survey titled "Medicine in China" that still stands as the best review of medicine in China at that time. The 1915 commission, which included Simon Flexner and William Welch, recommended that the Rockefeller Foundation create two medical centers in China, one in Peking and one in Shanghai. This recommendation was formally approved by the Rockefeller Foundation in 1915.[35]

The American experts who surrounded JDR Jr. and Frederick Gates in formulating plans for what became Peking Union Medical College (PUMC) were the leading American educators and medical specialists of their day. In addition to Flexner and Welch, the presidents of Harvard and the University of Chicago were key members of the China Medical Board. Religious leaders were not absent, at least at the beginning. Both Robert Speer, secretary of the American Presbyterian Mission Board, and John R. Mott were involved in some of the earliest meetings. As the planning process continued, the more secular aspects of science and higher education prevailed. As Ron Chernow put it, "For many of the men associated with the early Rockefeller philanthropies, Science seemed to beckon as a new secular religion as the old spiritual verities waned."[36] Timothy Richard's plea to "educate at the top" also suggested that those who educated needed to be "at the top." Welch and Flexner, who recruited the first PUMC faculty, identified promising young American medical specialists from top-ranked universities. This emphasis on bringing the cutting edge of American medicine to China eventually extended to the natural and social sciences as well.

Roger S. Greene, resident director of the China Medical Board in Peking, was responsible for overseeing the building program. Greene was the brother of Rockefeller Foundation secretary Jerome Greene and had served in China as a U.S. Foreign Service officer. His appointment in 1914 brought a seasoned China specialist to guide the Rockefeller Foundation's work in China. This was needed because the creation of a modern medical college in China was such a huge undertaking that its progress was even chronicled by the *New York Times*.[37] As chair of the China Medical Board, JDR Jr. was intimately involved in all the decisions involving this major project—from the survey commissions, to the purchase of property in both Shanghai and Peking, to the abandonment of the Shanghai property, to the selection of an architect and approval of an impressive plant, the debates over escalating building costs, the selection of the first PUMC director—Franklin McLean—and so on.[38] Even after he stepped down as Rockefeller Foundation president and China Medical Board chair in 1917, JDR Jr. continued to pay close attention to budgets and PUMC issues by staying in close touch with George Vincent and George Buttrick, who had succeeded him as president of the Rockefeller Foundation and chair of the China Medical Board, respectively. At that time, Rockefeller became chair of the Rockefeller Foundation, a position he held until 1940.[39]

The attention given by the Rockefeller Foundation to PUMC in its early years is impressive, especially given the war with Germany, not to mention the foundation's worldwide health initiatives on hookworm, yellow fever, and malaria. For example, President Vincent made a three-month trip to China in 1919, traveling extensively to inspect missionary and Chinese hospitals, work on staffing and curriculum plans for PUMC, and continually inspecting the building progress of PUMC's *fifty-seven* buildings. Roger Greene included the following in his diary of Vincent's visit:

> Mr. V. and I inspected the various designs for the painting of the eaves. It was decided to paint red the panel which sets back above the decorated beam, but to carry a decorative band up each end of the panel and to put in the middle of the panel a medallion something like that previously painted on the round wooden beam which supports the rafters. This round beam is to be left a plain green.[40]

As this detail from the building program suggests, the creation of the PUMC became such an important (and expensive) symbol of the Rockefeller Foundation's new global thrust that a grand international medical meeting was planned for its dedication. Given his intimate involvement in the planning of PUMC from its outset, it is not surprising that JDR Jr. decided to personally attend the dedication. Still, a three-week trip to cross the United States and the Pacific for what became a three-month tour was a major international expedition, even for the well-traveled Rockefeller family. Even for one of New York's most prominent citizens, such an Asian journey was so unusual that the *New York Times* announced plans for the trip three months before it actually took place.[41]

THE ROCKEFELLER TRIP TO ASIA: MEDICINE, ART, AND OIL

Reflecting the depth and breadth of his growing interest in Asia, Rockefeller's 1921 trip to China was a family affair, including his wife Abby and daughter Abby, known as Babs. The Rockefellers had already become patrons of Asian art, with an extensive collection of books related to Asian art, landscape, and religion.[42] Abby, the daughter of Senator Nelson Aldrich of Rhode Island, had traveled to Paris in the 1890s while still a teenager. Exhibitions of Japanese woodblock prints caught her interest, and while in Paris she purchased several prints. Before they were married, both Abby and John visited Japan's Phoenix Villa at the Chicago World's Fair in 1898. When they began planning for Kykuit—the grand residence in Pocantico, outside Tarrytown in Westchester County north of New York City, for JDR Sr.—John proposed to his father that a Japanese garden be incorporated into the design. Meandering down a hillside—and including pine trees, azalea, moss, stone lanterns, and running water—this garden opens onto a flat, walled Japanese rock garden styled after the famous Ryoanji Garden in Kyoto. The garden, completed in 1907, was among the early American residential Japanese gardens.

Abby also encouraged her husband's interest in Chinese art, giving him a book on Chinese ceramics in 1908. John had already been introduced to Chinese porcelain; as a young man, he had often visited the home of the department store magnate Benjamin Altman, whose magnificent collection of Chinese porcelain graces the Metropolitan Museum of Art today. In 1913, John and Abby purchased two "black hawthorns" from the Kangxi Era for their mantel. In 1915, after the death of J. P. Morgan Sr., his entire collection of Chinese vases, comparable to that of Altman, was put up for sale. Although Rockefeller was thirty-nine years old at the time, he had to ask for a loan from his father to make the purchases, primarily of the *famille noir*, *verte*, and *jaune* of the Kangxi Era. In justifying the $2 million request, Rockefeller wrote his father:

A fondness for these porcelains is my only hobby—the only thing on which I care to spend money. I have found their study a great recreation and diversion, and I have become very fond of them. This hobby, while a costly one, is quiet and unostentatious and not sensational. . . . Is it unwise for me to gratify a desire for beautiful things, which will be a constant joy to my friends and to my children as they grow to appreciate them?[43]

JDR Sr. registered initial disapproval but relented with an outright gift after receiving this unusually passionate request. A number of the large Qing vases were put on permanent display in both Senior's office at Kykuit and Junior's office at 26 Broadway. Between 1915 and Rockefeller's trip to China in 1921, his interest in collecting Chinese art intensified. He was in regular communication with the major Chinese art dealers, including C. T. Loo, Sadjiro Yamanaka, Edgar Gore, and the Duveen brothers. Most of his purchases were Chinese ceramics—an art form that he found accessible despite the intricacy of the designs *(figure 1.1)*.[44]

FIGURE 1.1. John D. Rockefeller Jr.'s office with Chinese porcelain vases, circa 1925. *Photograph courtesy of the Rockefeller Archive Center.*

Many decades later, JDR Jr.'s son David remembered Junior's preoccupation with these Chinese vases (his collection grew to more than four hundred pieces, many of which were donated upon his death to the Metropolitan Museum of Art):

Father's pride and joy was his comprehensive collection of Chinese porcelains from the Ming and K'ang-hsi dynasties. He had acquired a significant portion of J. P. Morgan's enormous collection in 1913 and maintained his intense interest in these beautiful objects for the rest of his life. Many of the K'ang-hsi's pieces were huge beakers, taller than I was as a boy *(see figure 1.2)*. To this day I have a picture of him in my mind, examining the porcelains he was thinking of buying with a magnifying glass to ensure that they had not been broken or restored.[45]

FIGURE 1.2. Abby Rockefeller and a Kangxi porcelain vase, circa 1921. *Photograph courtesy of the Rockefeller Archive Center.*

As plans for the Rockefeller trip unfolded, it is clear that this keen interest in Asian art, landscape gardens, and religion was one of the incentives for such an arduous journey. Abby's sister Lucy—even more of an Asian art aficionado—had traveled to Asia several years earlier. Her letters to Abby in 1919 and 1920 from

Asia described her great enthusiasm for Asian culture and art. A letter in 1919 conveys her discovery of a kinship with Buddhism: "I'd much rather be a Buddhist than a Baptist anyway—the whole thing appeals so much more to my temperamental, or is it emotional, love of color: the gold and lacquer, the beat of the drums, and even the smell of incense. I love it all."[46] Abby herself read avidly about Asia, writing Lucy several times in 1919 about her interests in Korean prints and paintings, which had been stimulated in part by a *National Geographic* article.[47] Lucy repeatedly encouraged Abby to make the China trip, which would include Korea, even offering to take care of the Rockefellers' five sons so that Abby might experience her own Asian odyssey.[48]

The extensive presence of Standard Oil in China and Japan provided a further incentive for the Rockefeller journey. JDR Jr.'s biographers indicate that after about 1910, he had little role in the Standard Oil enterprise, and yet he was closely involved with some of the subsequent challenges faced by his father, most notably the Ludlow Massacre in 1915. Although JDR Jr. had divested himself of most Rockefeller corporate interests, he had remained on the board of Colorado Fuel and Iron, which owned twenty-four coal mines in Colorado. Poor living conditions and inadequate wages, coupled with management's refusal to permit a union, inevitably resulted in a strike of 11,000 out of 14,000 workers and conflict with the state's militia; 2 women and 11 children were killed. This disaster became known as the Ludlow Massacre. Representing his family's antilabor policy, Junior persisted in supporting the management of Colorado Fuel and Iron. This led to widespread protests against the Rockefellers, including a very public congressional inquest and demonstrations at Kykuit. This was certainly the nadir of Junior's business career. In the aftermath, and with the advice and counsel of MacKenzie King, a Canadian mediator between labor and management, JDR Jr. turned away from the antilabor tradition of his family to become a moderate advocate of labor-management mediation and worker's rights. In doing so, he began to chart a course distinct from his father, even as Senior finally began to turn over his wealth to his son. By 1922, Junior's personal wealth topped $500 million. Although Junior continued to consult with his father about the Rockefeller philanthropies, from this time on he was the undisputed Rockefeller at the helm of an ever-expanding philanthropic enterprise.[49]

The junior Rockefeller's ongoing awareness of his father's business interests also derived from the location of the Rockefeller Foundation office—in the same building as Standard Oil at 26 Broadway. Standard Oil routinely assisted the Rockefeller family with their international ventures. For example, in Shanghai, Standard Oil provided Roger Greene, the resident director of the China Medical Board, with banking and shipping support during the construction of PUMC.[50] JDR Jr. would certainly have been well aware of Standard Oil's business success in China and the complex negotiations over oil exploration rights in Shanxi Province.

Standard Oil's kerosene market in China, which had grown steadily between the 1880s and the 1910s, was seen by some as a partial hedge against the anticipated breakup of the Standard Oil monopoly in the United States. Standard Oil deployed scores of Chinese and American agents as it developed a marketing infrastructure throughout China, reaching as far inland as Chongqing as early as 1908. In that year, the *New York Times* carried an article titled "Standard Oil Makes the World Its Market: No Land Too Remote, No Community Too Inaccessible for Its Agents—China Is Last to Yield."[51] By 1914, 50 percent of all American exports to China were Standard's petroleum products. Standard's total profits for Guangdong Province alone in that year were $33.9 million. Although it was not exempt from periodic Chinese boycotts of foreign products and friction over taxes and land use rights, the company appears to have been relatively well regarded in China: Kerosene was cheap, sold by Chinese merchants, and needed by all.

Despite this success, transporting oil from the United States to China resulted in long supply lines. Hoping to discover oil in China, Standard began to seek prospecting rights in both Shanxi and Zhili (today Hebei) provinces. The agreement provided for the formation of a joint "Chino-American" company, in which "Standard would have a controlling interest, the Chinese Government receiving a certain percentage of the shares."[52] By 1917, efforts to implement this agreement had come to naught, and it was abandoned by both sides. Standard had concluded that the resources were not worth developing, and the Chinese fear of a foreign company controlling their oil resources had intensified. This Standard Oil effort to acquire the first joint exploration rights in China received widespread public attention, including reportage in the *New York Times*.[53]

JDR Jr.'s identification with Standard Oil in China was never in doubt; the company was the primary logistical host of the Rockefeller family throughout its Asia trip. Standard organized the trip, and Junior made extra efforts to meet and communicate with Standard employees. As he wrote to his father, Standard men met the traveling party at their first stop, Yokohama: "The representative for Japan met us at the steamer and traveled with us until we reached the Chinese border, at which place the representative for China met us and has had us in tow ever since. It is a great convenience to have all traveling and hotel arrangements made for us by those familiar with the ways of the country. Then, too, we enjoy the opportunity of coming to know the company men." In Suzhou, Standard representatives spent days planning a several hour Grand Canal trip for the Rockefellers, including a trial reconnaissance: "It is also planned at this time to have various pearl, jade, and curio merchants in attendance with their wares, should any of the (Rockefeller) party desire to purchase such things. . . . The trip between the various points through the city has been so arranged that it follows the best streets, passing the stores of greatest interest such as, the famous red wood furniture shops, oil shops, etc."[54]

After all this preparation, Junior's diary does not record any purchases, only "took native house boat through city canals."[55] Here, as elsewhere, JDR Jr. made a point of going to the Standard Oil offices "to shake hands not only with the heads of departments but with all of the staff, natives as well as foreigners."[56] And, not unmindful that his wealth came from Standard stock, he was not hesitant to remind a Standard official in Hong Kong that "although your largest stockholders are so far away from you, I want you to know that my father and I are constantly mindful of the splendid service rendered the company by its able and trusted leaders."[57]

The Asia trip may have been long, but the Rockefellers traveled in style. Abby had a personal staff of four, and the president of Mount Holyoke College, Mary G. Wooley, was also along as a companion. George Vincent, president of the Rockefeller Foundation, and William Henry Welch, dean of the Johns Hopkins Medical School, were among those who constituted the official party. A private railroad car took them across the United States, and they traveled with sixty pieces of luggage. The Rockefellers took their trip seriously, reading assiduously about Asia on their two-week trip across the Pacific on the *Empress of Asia*. In Peking, they stayed in a traditional Chinese courtyard mansion and were entertained by business leaders, diplomats, missionaries, and the president of China. In Guangzhou, they dined with Sun Yat-sen and his wife.

The China that the Rockefellers encountered was politically unsettled but intellectually vibrant. Sun Yat-sen had briefly served as the president of the new Republic of China after the downfall of the Qing Dynasty in 1911. By the time the Rockefellers met him ten years later, the political control of his Guomindang Party was limited to South China, and regional warlords held sway throughout a divided China. In the north, Peking continued as the nominal capital, governed by a succession of military and civilian leaders with shifting warlord allegiances. In part because of such weak government, China was in the midst of iconoclastic intellectual movements that repudiated the old Confucian order and made way for both the Nationalist and Communist eras. Two years before the Rockefeller trip, the May 4, 1919, student demonstrations in Peking protested the dismemberment of China at the Versailles Treaty and also ushered in a philosophical debate between "Mr. Science" and "Mr. Democracy." Just two months before the Rockefellers arrived, the first clandestine meeting of the Chinese Communist Party was held in Shanghai. This fluid intellectual and political situation is one reason that the large-scale Rockefeller China project encountered no political obstacles in its beginnings. And prominent Chinese political and intellectual leaders of the day had already embraced modern medicine. Sun Yat-sen and Lu Xun, a prominent writer, were both trained in modern medicine in Japan, and Mao Zedong himself had called for the abolition of superstitious and ineffective traditional medicine.

In any case, the Rockefellers were not deterred by the chaos of Chinese politics. They ventured out into the countryside in China as well as Japan. There was the obligatory two-day trip to the Ming Tombs and the Great Wall, with an overnight in a Chinese guest house. Writing to his eldest son John, JDR Jr. drew parallels with biblical history, noting that the Great Wall had been built around the time of Christ and "took 25 years to build and when one thinks of the thousands and thousands of human lives that must have been sacrificed. . . . One is reminded of the work of the Israelites under the cruel Pharaoh." He also described the peasants threshing grain: "Children were naked, men working with uncovered upper bodies, . . . and Oh, what swarms of people there."[58] Despite the crowds, Rockefeller seemed charmed by the Chinese people. When writing his son Nelson, he observed: "We find the Chinese people a constant source of interest, there are so many of them, they are so different, and while not as picturesque as the Japanese still are very picturesque."[59] He also sought to introduce Nelson to the international reach of the family company. Writing from Shanghai, where all the Standard Oil launches were festooned with banners and flags in honor of his visit, he wrote: "Mei Foo is the Chinese name for the Standard Oil Company, meaning beautiful and bright."[60]

Abby's letters to her children are short, warm descriptions of Chinese scenery and the people. She even sends a postcard with a picture of the omnipresent Standard Oil cans to her son John *(see figure 1.3)*. To the youngest, David, she describes the young Chinese boys with "split pants" working in the fields: "Just now the farmers are harvesting their crops so they are very busy culling the rice and millet and carrying it to the threshing floors where it is all taken care of by hand just the way it was done when Christ was alive 2,100 years ago. Boys even as young as Laurence work very hard. I see them carrying very heavy loads, weaving at looms, and helping their fathers everywhere at all work in the fields."[61] To the eldest, John, she gives more details on their reception in China: "Dearest Johnnie boy. We are kept so busy being entertained or having people here that when we have a minute, we fall asleep from fatigue. . . . I find Peking one of the most interesting cities I have ever been in. I love the people. . . . They all seem friendly and kindly." And when she describes the people traveling with them, notably George Vincent and William Welch, she reminds John of his future role: "Some day you will have a chance to associate with this type of man. Like papa, you will have great responsibilities but also real opportunities. I think that you will enjoy it all, just as I do."[62]

JDR Jr. seems to have been especially impressed by Japanese culture and scenery, writing to son John about the temples and gardens of Nikko and the night train from Kyoto to Tokyo: "About five in the morning, knowing that we were passing in sight of Mount Fuji, the extinct volcano which is covered with snow and is dear to the hearts of every Japanese, I looked out of the stateroom window and

FIGURE 1.3. A Korean water carrier using a Standard Oil container. This postcard, sent by Abby Rockefeller to her son John from Korea, and postmarked September 3, 1921, reads: "Here are some Standard Oil cans being used as water carriers." *Photograph courtesy of the Rockefeller Archive Center.*

12 DRAWING WATER, CHOSEN　　汲　水　(俗風鮮朝)

there in the early twilight saw the snow covered mountain, wonderful to behold."[63] During their five weeks in Japan, the last leg of their trip, the Rockefeller party visited scores of temples and gardens and also spent several days in one of Japan's most isolated monasteries. While in Kyoto, the Rockefellers called on Yamanaka and Company twice, and Sadjiro Yamanaka personally escorted them to Nara and the outlying Horyuji Temple.[64] The Rockefellers subsequently became regular customers, and Yamanaka opened a special American outlet in Seal Harbor, Maine, where the Rockefeller summer residence, the Eyrie, was located.

The Rockefellers spent two weeks in Peking, much of it exploring the new PUMC and presiding over meetings related to its operations. Costs were a major issue. The decision to build a stand-alone medical school in China solely funded by the Rockefeller Foundation turned out to be the biggest international financial commitment ever made by the foundation. PUMC still ranks third, behind Rockefeller University and the University of Chicago, as the largest institutional recipient of Rockefeller funding. By the time of the nationalization of PUMC in 1951, more than $40 million had been expended on PUMC. JDR Jr. was defensive about the 1921–22 operating budget of more than $500,000 in a letter to his father from Peking, but he also wrote enthusiastically: "It seems hardly possible that there should now be in existence here, in the midst of the Chinese Republic, a medical school and hospital with buildings, equipment and a faculty second to none in any part of the world, and yet that is actually what is in operation here today."[65] Chinese and American newspapers extolled the modern scientific plant, but a story of destruction and re-creation lay behind PUMC and its green-tiled roofs.

To create space for PUMC, the Rockefeller Foundation first bought the property of the missionary-owned Union Medical College and then added to it several adjacent properties, including a Qing palace, lake, and garden surrounded by a twenty-foot-high wall. This property had been the site of Duo Duo's (Prince Yu's) mansion since the early seventeenth century. As the fifteenth son of the first Manchu emperor, Nurhachi, Duo Duo had led the Manchu bannermen in their conquest of Korea, defeat of the Ming imperial forces, and establishment of the Qing Dynasty.[66] With the collapse of the Qing Dynasty in 1911, Prince Yu's Manchu family lost all its prerogatives and was forced to sell the valuable property. The Rockefeller Foundation purchased it for $125,000.

PUMC's Peking-based American architect, Harry Hussey, described his first visit to Prince Yu's palace. He was received by the destitute widow of the Manchu Yu family, who asked to be allowed to spend a few additional weeks in her historic home. Hussey records the beauty of the Manchu palace:

> It was a wonderful plot of about twelve acres, surrounded by a twenty-foot wall built of the same large brick that were used in the Great Wall of Peking. I was amazed at the many buildings; the palaces with their beautifully carved, white marble balustrades and steps; the beautiful gardens with small lakes crossed by white marble bridges, and the great number of old trees, all in a remarkably good state of preservation.[67]

Writing decades later, Hussey lamented the destruction:

> The thought has never left me that in destroying the Yu Wang Fu we destroyed greater and more beautiful and more important buildings than we built. It was vandalism; we should have built elsewhere and kept the beautiful Yu Wang Fu, equal to any residence in the imperial city, as a national monument.[68]

Hussey also records that Zhu Qiqian, minister of the interior, asked him to design PUMC in the Chinese style, incorporating characteristics which would evoke Prince Yu's palace *(figure 1.4)*. Zhu requested that the Rockefeller Foundation not "build another foreign city, like the Legation Quarter in Peking so close to the beautiful buildings of their Forbidden City."[69] Hussey reported that Zhu, a well-regarded traditional Chinese architect, was apparently pleased with the final plans. Hussey met with him frequently in order to learn "the proper pitch of a Chinese roof, the amount of overhang for the cornice, the details of the huge ornaments on the ridge of the roofs, the proper design of the little figures, . . . and the other mysteries of Chinese architecture."[70] Craftsmen who had worked on the Imperial Palace were hired to carve the decorated green roofs, an imperial kiln was reopened to make the roof tiles, and some remnants of the former estate were incorporated into the plan, including the marble guardian lions. Faced with the difficulty of obtaining high-quality new brick, Hussey was delighted to discover that he could reuse the traditional Peking grey bricks from Prince Yu's wall to make the walls of the new complex.

FIGURE 1.4. The Peking Union Medical College cornerstone-laying ceremony, 1917. Note Prince Yu's pavilion, which was destroyed a few months later, in the background. *Photograph courtesy of the Rockefeller Archive Center.*

There is no record of a debate within the China Medical Board circles about the destruction of Prince Yu's palace. Hussey did remember, however, that JDR Jr. took great interest in the Chinese architectural details of the new complex and urged him to "spare no cost." Not everyone admired the final result. Liang Sicheng,

China's most famous twentieth-century architect, wrote in 1935: "A Chinese-style roof with four upturned eaves awkwardly covers a Western building; its upper and bottom structures carry completely different purposes. Except for the glazed tiles which apparently represent characteristics of Chinese art, all other parts can be seen as Western architecture."[71] The PUMC compound continued to be referred to by its original property name, the Yu Wang Fu, Prince Yu's palace—but with a twist. A Chinese word pun quickly turned this around to the Oil Prince's Palace: the Chinese word for oil (you) was similar in pronunciation to Yu. The PUMC alumni association, to this day, is called the Yu Wang Fu Association.

Rockefeller's passion for Chinese art had exposed him to China's high cultural heritage, a recognition that echoed in many of his speeches during this trip (although he sometimes attributed these thoughts to his father): "As my father's interest in human betterment widened, . . . his attention was naturally directed to the great Chinese Nation, with its history running back thousands of years; its early achievements in industry; its literature and art, so rich and beautiful; and its population, greater than that of any nation on earth."[72] This respect, even awe, of Chinese civilization was one of the reasons that the Rockefeller family and the Rockefeller Foundation felt incumbent to bring the finest in American science and medicine to China. As Raymond Fosdick put it decades later: "All this elaborate and somewhat expensive design was employed . . . as a symbol of the desire of the Board to make the College not something imposed from an alien source, but an agency which would fit naturally and harmoniously into the picture of a developing Chinese civilization. It reflected, too, the anxiety of the Board, in this first gesture to the Far East, to give China nothing but the best."[73] The Rockefeller respect for Chinese civilization did not, however, extend to traditional Chinese medicine. Given their confidence in Western science, it did not occur to them that Western medicine might appear "alien" or that traditional Chinese medicine, like Chinese architecture, might also be incorporated into the Rockefeller presence in China.

The challenge of educating Chinese medical leaders, hiring Chinese faculty, and ensuring that PUMC's influence extended throughout China constituted Rockefeller's public message in Peking. At the dedication ceremony, he made it clear that by itself PUMC was not, primarily, a humanitarian institution: "A grateful service which the college will be glad incidentally to render to the community through the hospital and dispensary, is the alleviation of suffering. But the number thus reached will of necessity be relatively small for it must be borne in mind that the hospital is primarily a teaching institution, which while affording the best care for patients, exists, first of all, for instruction and research." For Rockefeller, PUMC was a scientific institution, designed as a model for China's medical education system, and he emphasized that Chinese themselves would soon lead the institution, create similar ones, and provide medical care for the people: "We must look forward to the day when most, if not all, of the positions on the Faculty . . . will be held by Chinese, when the Board of Trustees . . . will include leading Chinese." He went on to state: "Above all it was hoped that this new medical centre might so commend itself to the Chinese people that it would stimulate them to develop similar institutions in various parts of China."[74]

It is not difficult to see how Richard Brown, author of *Rockefeller Medical Men* and a strong critic of Rockefeller philanthropy, came to the conclusion that the Rockefeller educators "were more concerned with building an elite professional stratum to carry out cultural and technological transformation than with meeting the health needs of the country."[75] Certainly there was a definite contradiction between Rockefeller aspirations and the essential nature of PUMC, founded, as JDR Jr. also put it, "to develop in China a medical school and hospital of a standard comparable with that of the leading institutions known to Western civilization."[76] Although JDR Jr. never appeared to seriously question the validity of using an American model of medical education for a poor, developing country like China, over the years he did become more critical of PUMC's elitist nature. His personal China philanthropy became more socially oriented, and he supported subsequent Rockefeller Foundation initiatives that addressed the economic and social needs of rural China.

THE IMPACT OF CHINA ON THE ROCKEFELLERS

When John and Abby returned to New York, they did not forget China. Both gave public talks on their impressions of China. Abby discussed the educational needs of China and the thoughtfulness of its people and showed slides of the Ming Tombs, the Summer Palace, and various temples.[77] John's handwritten outline for a talk at Brown University in 1922 includes a list of the problems of China—transportation, provincial government, competing northern and southern governments, foreign concessions, and spheres of influence. He also noted the encouraging features—population, thrift, industriousness, respect for family life, ancestors, graves, patience, intelligence, and honesty.[78]

John and Abby's personal participation in PUMC's beginnings and exposure to both Chinese and Japanese culture left a lasting impact on them and their family: The 1921 trip became a touchstone memory for their descendants. Four successive generations have traveled to Peking and had their pictures taken at PUMC. Wendy O'Neill, John's great-granddaughter, was inspired by the trip and has written of her discovery of her grandmother's (Babs's) letters written while in Peking.[79] His son David Rockefeller, who was left home with his brothers, reflected in his *Memoirs* on the significance of the trip for his parents:

It was a consequential trip for both of them: their interest in Asian art deepened. And they became collectors of ceramics, textiles, prints, paintings, and sculptures from all three of the cultures they encountered. More important, Father was persuaded that while American philanthropy had an important role to play in the modernization of China, traditional American missionary work had become outmoded and irrelevant to the needs of the country. The lessons drawn by each of my parents had not only an enduring impact on them but also on the lives of my brothers and me.[80]

Two years after the Asia trip, the Rockefeller family's attention to China was galvanized again by an episode involving Abby's sister, Lucy Aldrich, who was quite the intrepid traveler and had already visited China and India several times. On this occasion, in May 1923, Lucy was on a train from Shanghai to Peking when the train was hijacked by bandits. All the foreign passengers, including Lucy, were kidnapped by bandits at gunpoint and taken by foot and donkey to a Chinese village. She befriended her captors and was treated reasonably well. The foreign hostages were released two days later, almost as abruptly as they had been taken. Most valuables were confiscated, but Lucy's mother's rings, hidden first in her bedroom slipper and then under a stone near the village, were retrieved sometime later. Her letter to her sister Abby describing this incident in great detail was published in the *Atlantic Monthly*. In responding to Lucy, Abby was disinclined to blame the bandits, who were "probably driven to do this by poverty, perhaps hunger," and went on to affirm: "I am sure that it will not kill your love of China any more than it does ours."[81] This incident became part of the China folklore of the Rockefeller family.

For Abby Rockefeller, the experience in China, Korea, and Japan visiting Buddhist temples and gardens had an immediate aesthetic impact. She had already been a student of Buddhist influence on East Asian art, and now she began collecting statues and artifacts from all three countries, creating what her family called "Buddha" rooms on two floors of their house on West Fifty-Fourth Street (the site was donated in 1937 to create the Museum of Modern Art) and in Maine. In his written memoirs, son David remembered the rooms being "dimly lit and mysterious, and Mother burned incense in these rooms" *(figure 1.5)*.[82] When interviewed in 2008, he recalled his mother's genuine appreciation of Buddhist spirituality, which was sometimes frowned upon by his more devout Baptist father, and that it was her aesthetic taste for early Buddhist sculpture and not his father's passion for Qing porcelain that was passed down to him and his siblings.[83]

Abby was not content with just Buddha rooms, however. In 1926, she commissioned an eclectic Asian garden at their summer home, the Eyrie, in Maine. The design was executed by Beatrix Farrand, a well-known landscape architect, but the vision was Abby's. In selecting her architect, Abby wrote: "Farrand would

FIGURE 1.5. Abby Rockefeller's Buddha rooms, The Eyrie, Mount Desert Island, Maine, 1960. Photograph by Ezra Stoller. © Esto. All rights reserved. *Courtesy of the Rockefeller Archive Center.*

respect my desire to create an authentic Oriental garden, not as a mere ornamental adjunct to the garden but as a spiritual retreat."[84] The garden incorporates statues and garden motifs from all three of the Asian countries she visited—Japan, Korea, and China—with an adjacent and linked European floral garden. Abby's own sense of Chinese aesthetics continually influenced the garden design; for example, she rejected a statue that evoked the eighteenth-century Qianlong Period because it was "not in harmony" with her favored, much earlier Song Dynasty figures.[85] The result, as one critic later noted, was an Asian influence that was "organic, not mere chinoiserie embellishments." Again, son David provides intriguing details. The garden wall seeks to capture the "mottled hue of the walls of the Forbidden City," and it is capped by "yellow tiles made in the eighteenth century for the Forbidden City. They became available to my parents in the mid-1920s and add a great deal to the quality and character of the garden."[86]

The acquisition of roof tiles from the Forbidden City proved to be quite controversial. In 1928, JDR Jr. cabled Roger Greene asking him to confirm the rumor that the tiles were available and to purchase a significant quantity. Greene responded: "Tiles poor purchase not recommended mailing details."

His letter elaborated, "I am not certain that undesirable publicity might not be given to the purchase of material of this sort. It would be easy for rumor to spread that articles of artistic value were being surreptitiously exported from the country." In a letter to the architect, Farrand, Rockefeller asks that the tiles be purchased in her name, avoiding adverse Rockefeller publicity. In her response, she notes that "the matter seems to be rather a delicate one" but proceeds with the transaction. The complexity of purchasing, shipping, and paying for fragile tiles involved years of accounting disagreements between Rockefeller, Farrand, and Yamanaka and Company, which made the arrangements.[87] Although there is no record that the tile purchase created negative publicity for the Rockefellers, several years later the *New York Times* did report a rumor that JDR Jr. and Henry Ford planned to spend $20 million for "old imperial treasures" to protect them from the Japanese.[88]

JDR Jr.'s biographer, Raymond Fosdick, has called the decade after his 1921 China trip his "internationalist" era. With the end of World War I and the U.S. rejection of the League of Nations, Rockefeller plunged into a host of internationalist endeavors—from becoming a founder of the Council on Foreign Relations to urging informal American participation in many of the League of Nations' programs. Having confirmed plans to underwrite the International House at Columbia University shortly before going to China, Rockefeller tried to meet young students from around the world, especially those from China. He and Abby held periodic teas at their elegant town home for Chinese students. Convinced that foreign students were "a great force for the promotion of international understanding and good will for building up right relationships in commerce, industry and trade," Rockefeller went on to personally fund two more International Houses, at the University of California, Berkeley, and the University of Chicago.[89] With immigration laws severely restricting foreign students, especially those from China, such internationalist sentiment was not widespread. Protests marked the opening of the Berkeley International House in 1931; many were opposed to American students socializing with Asians.[90]

During the 1920s, Rockefeller's personal China philanthropy also intensified, encompassing new directions in social work, foreign missions, and historic preservation. The YMCA had long provided both father and son with a China perspective that differed from that of both foreign missions and the Rockefeller Foundation. JDR Jr. had followed in his father's footsteps by contributing to this ecumenical religious and social movement. In 1910, even before he went to China, the YMCA held a fund-raising event for its China programs at the White House. Rockefeller's personal pledge to match up to $400,000 from other donors galvanized the YMCA's wealthy donor community. John R. Mott was named a trustee of PUMC and continued to keep the Rockefellers informed about YMCA programs in China. In 1924, Junior began to fund a YMCA program designed to "promote better industrial standards and conditions in the rapidly developing industries of China."[91] For several years, the YMCA operated a model village in what was then a Shanghai suburb, Pudong, which tried to improve working and living conditions for the common laborer. Surveys of labor unions were also undertaken in Guangzhou. These YMCA programs were plagued by leadership and political problems, and Rockefeller support was discontinued in the early 1930s. Nonetheless, the YMCA China influence on Rockefeller was significant. The Pudong program exposed him to the many economic challenges facing China as it gradually modernized its economy. Also, YMCA contacts introduced Rockefeller to Yan Yangchu (James Y. C. Yen), the founder of China's Mass Education Movement and one of Republican China's most prominent rural reformers.

Rockefeller was quite taken by Yan when they met in New York, perhaps because he was a Christian. In 1928, he invited the young Chinese social reformer and his wife to spend a week with his family at their summer home in Seal Harbor, Maine. Yan was convinced that literacy was essential to raise the social and economic level of China's rural population, and he had developed an impressive reading program in Dingxian, a county south of Peking. This literacy program was subsequently expanded to include a range of social and economic services, and PUMC graduates introduced a rural health care delivery system. Rockefeller's personal contributions totaled approximately $100,000, and "Jimmy" Yan became a family friend. Almost a decade later, the Rockefeller Foundation would follow JDR Jr.'s lead and base its rural reconstruction program in Dingxian.[92] Rockefeller family connections with Yan persisted until at least the late 1940s; in 1948, Nelson gave $10,000 to Yan toward his postwar Sino-American Joint Commission on Rural Reconstruction.[93]

Perhaps surprisingly, Rockefeller's perspective on missionaries changed as a result of his travel in China. As David's remembrances point out, his father returned from China with the view that "traditional missionary work had become outmoded and irrelevant to the needs of the country." Although his commitment to PUMC as a secular institution, but one influenced by Christianity, remained firm, he had apparently reacted against the evangelical fervor and denominational friction of some China missionaries. Rockefeller's own religious convictions were becoming more liberal, moving away from the sectarian faith of his family to a more ecumenical perspective. His wife's interest in Buddhism exposed him to the art and spiritual teaching of a different religion. And he deplored the many rifts in Protestant denominations. Unlike Frederick Gates, however, who had completely abandoned his Christian faith by the early 1920s, Rockefeller remained a devout Christian, committed to the renewal of its many institutions, not their repudiation.

These concerns took the philanthropic form of the Institute of Social and Religious Research, which JDR Jr. personally created and funded and which was managed by several of his closest advisers. The institute endeavored to apply the new social science survey methodology to religious institutions, first to explore the problems of urban and rural churches in the United States but later to the work of foreign missions. In this, Junior continued to be influenced by Mott, who reported on a discouraging trip to review China missions in 1929. Junior gathered a group of influential Baptist leaders to meet with Mott, and they decided to undertake a comprehensive review of missionary work in Asia.

This several-year venture—which was fully funded by Rockefeller, acting as something like a self-appointed critic of the missionary movement—became known as the Layman's Foreign Missionary Inquiry. Its final report, "Rethinking Missions," was published in 1932 and came as a shock to the missionary establishment. It called for a total reorienting of Christian missionary work in Asia: to identify more with Chinese culture, to discover common elements in Chinese religions, and to give more responsibility to Chinese nationals. Because Rockefeller supported the "one world, one church" movement and was avowedly ecumenical by the 1930s, he was in full agreement with the controversial report. But most missionary groups, including his own denomination, the Northern Baptist Convention, were opposed. When he learned that it was not going to implement the recommendations, he withdrew his support from Baptist missions, writing to his father: "I reached the conclusion that there was nothing left for me to do but to discontinue giving through the Northern Baptist Convention and to make gifts directly to those missionary efforts—whether Baptist, or other denominations, inter-denomination, or non-denominational—that have proved themselves to us as vital, effective, Christian agencies."[94]

JDR Jr.'s exposure to the social work of the YMCA, the Mass Education Movement, and the Layman's Inquiry broadened his knowledge of social and religious conditions in China. His personal China philanthropies reflect a broader China interest than the Rockefeller Foundation's medical preoccupation. By the 1930s, these perspectives contributed to the foundation staff's decision to look beyond PUMC and its medical ivory tower toward a more culturally sensitive and populist approach to China's social and economic challenges.

The preservation of traditional Chinese architecture was a third area of Rockefeller's interest, one that echoed his significant contributions to the restoration of Versailles, the Athens Agora, and of course, Colonial Williamsburg. During his visit to Peking, JDR Jr. was distressed by the condition of both the Ming Tombs and the Forbidden City, and he made an immediate contribution toward the restoration of the Ming Tombs. This interest was rekindled when his son John traveled to China in 1929. Like his father, young John was struck by the beauty of Chinese architecture. After visiting the Forbidden City, he wrote:

> You are awed by the stillness of it all; you are thrilled by the beauty of the tiled
> roofs, the painted timbers, the white marblework, and the general effect of the

ensemble; you are quite overcome by the vastness—the feeling that time, labor and expense were as nothing. I can't describe it but all is wonderful and I wish I could spend a whole month at the least right here in Peking just browsing around these places at my leisure.[95]

Remembering his father's earlier descriptions, JDR 3rd also came away troubled by the condition of the Forbidden City and decided to pursue the matter when he returned to the United States.

Between 1929 and 1931, father and son consulted with Roger Greene in Peking and Orientalists at Yale and the University of Chicago, laying the groundwork for a major Rockefeller investment in historic restoration in China.[96] Never one to shown much emotion, JDR Jr. expressed his passion for the restoration of Chinese buildings in an unusual letter to George Vincent: "When in China, I almost cried to think of the beautiful temples and palaces slowly going into decay, with no hope of their being restored and preserved."[97] In 1929, he made an anonymous donation for the preservation of several small temples within the Forbidden City. By September 1931, he was ready to move the project forward, informing Greene of his "growing interest in preservation of architectural monuments," and commissioning a Yale professor, Charles P. Howland, to travel to China to make a study of preservation options. In the instructions to Howland (probably written by JDR 3rd), it is clear that a large-scale project was envisioned: "Organization and work not to be confined to Peking area. While probably centered at Peking would hope to go anywhere in China, including Manchuria, where monuments of importance are located. . . . It might be best to have central committee or organization located in Peking or some other center and then have local organizations in outlying districts."[98]

Howland was also asked to ascertain how the Chinese government would feel about foreign assistance and how a joint Chinese-American project with "possibly some foreign control" could be designed. Greene's responses were always cautionary, suggesting that the Rockefellers begin in a modest way, and in mid-1931 he warned JDR Jr. of a potential obstacle: "We again have a small war in our vicinity."[99] The Japanese invasion of Manchuria was beginning, and Howland's visit was eventually canceled. One can only imagine what might have been the result had the Rockefellers been involved in the restoration of the Forbidden City.

THE ROCKEFELLERS AS CULTURAL INTERNATIONALISTS

Because the China role of JDR 3rd was then just beginning, it is good to pause here and reflect on the distinctive China viewpoints of his father and grandfather.

The first two John D. Rockefellers experienced China in quite different ways. For John D. Rockefeller Sr., China was a distant country filtered through the impressions of missionaries and later oil traders. China was a country where Americans were selling both Christianity and kerosene. For him, there was no conflict between the evangelizing goal and the commercial one, and there was little to gain from China except profits and a converted nation. Nonetheless, even this limited exposure to China widened his view of the potential U.S. role in the world. If one could sell kerosene to Chinese or convert them, why not educate them as well? As first, higher education and then medical science came to dominate his American philanthropies, so it seemed fairly natural to take these themes to a wider international stage.

The significance of JDR Sr.'s gradual philanthropic shift from his early emphasis on religion and foreign missions to education and scientific medicine cannot be overstated. Rockefeller philanthropy in China, as in the United States, came to emphasize the secular rather than the spiritual, science rather than theology. This made a huge difference in pre–World War II higher education and scientific research in the United States. Rockefeller funding also began a new era in United States–China cultural relations. JDR Sr. himself may not have been aware of the long-term implications. Other than a few grand principles, he rarely reflected upon the impact of his philanthropies. Little in the written record suggests what he really thought of China or the Rockefeller Foundation's flagship institution in China, PUMC. We only have a letter written to his son at the time of PUMC's dedication: "We are full of gratitude for all the good reports which have been received from you. How wonderful it all is! We have feasted on your letters, . . . with numerous articles from Chinese newspapers, all of which have been read and enjoyed greatly."[100]

However, for JDR Sr.'s son, JDR Jr., China became a real place, not as close as Europe, to be sure, but one that inspired him aesthetically and in which he took an abiding philanthropic interest. His ongoing role in shaping and sustaining the Rockefeller Foundation's China programs—which lasted fifty years—has been overlooked by his biographers and studies of Rockefeller philanthropy. JDR Jr. never lost the paternalistic feeling about PUMC that he described at its opening celebration, experiencing both pride and anxiety as the institution matured. He believed that Americans had an important role in China—as educators, scientists, explorers, and, if the work was ecumenical, missionaries. He was also confident that these activities would strengthen the overall U.S. role in China. As was clearly evident from his 1921 trip, JDR Jr. was also completely comfortable with his dual identity as both the Standard Oil heir and the first global philanthropist. Appearing before the Chinese Chamber of Commerce in Shanghai, he noted that business and philanthropy were his two ties to China:

> The first is the tie of business. It was my father who founded the Standard Oil Company, which is doing business all over the world. Most pleasant have been the relations of the company with the merchants of China, while its contact generally with the businessmen and officials of the Republic have been equally agreeable. My father and I are glad to have a part in helping build up the commerce of this great Republic. The second tie which binds me to China is humanitarian or philanthropic.[101]

His Chinese hosts, early Shanghai entrepreneurs, were not willing to cede the role of capitalist-philanthropist to the American Rockefeller. Ever polite and respectful, they nonetheless rejoined with a litany of examples of Chinese business support for education and medicine.[102]

Standard Oil's business success in China was certainly not dependent upon the goodwill fostered by Rockefeller philanthropy. It had been the most successful American company in China since at least the 1890s. In the 1910s, Standard's efforts to secure petroleum exploration rights and the Rockefeller Foundation's medical commissions did overlap in time, raising the question whether the Rockefeller medical initiative was intended to influence the Chinese decision about oil exploration. A study of Chinese records related to Standard might reveal official Chinese awareness of a possible linkage between Rockefeller oil and philanthropic interests, but there is no documentary evidence in the Rockefeller archives of such a quid pro quo, and the rationale and the momentum for each had a separate internal logic. Ironically, it is even possible that the Chinese receptivity to Rockefeller philanthropy was conditioned, in part, by China's recognition of Rockefeller's success in international business. Nonetheless, for Chinese, as well as Americans of the same period, the two roles must have blurred. Rockefeller's courtesy calls in Guangzhou on Sun Yat-sen, the titular leader of the opposition Guomindang Party, as well as to Xu Shichang, the president of the Republic of China, inevitably were perceived as solidifying both Rockefeller's commercial and philanthropic enterprises *(figure 1.6)*. Indeed, several years after Rockefeller's lunch with Sun, Standard secured a preferential sales relationship with the Guomindang, one that continued well into the 1930s *(see chapter 3)*.

This parallel role of Standard Oil and Rockefeller philanthropy supports the traditional cultural imperialism literature, according to which the export of American culture went hand in hand with its economic aspirations. Still, imperialism—both economic and cultural—does not adequately explain the early Rockefeller interest in China. Rockefeller China philanthropy emerged from, and was sustained over many decades by, the complex mix of the commercial, cultural, and religious interests of the Rockefeller family in China. It is here that Akira Iriye's concept of "cultural internationalist" contributes a more nuanced explanatory power, one that can encompass art, religion, and science as well as commerce.

FIGURE 1.6. John D. Rockefeller Jr. and President Xu Shichang of China, Peking, 1921.
Photograph courtesy of the Rockefeller Archive Center.

For their own times, each Rockefeller can be said to have had a distinct "international imagination," a phrase coined by Iriye to characterize the nature of cultural internationalism. He observed that before World War I, "Americans had no clear concept of internationalism that embraced different races and people." Iriye especially noted the difficulty Americans had in "assimilating non-Western people (Asia) into the internationalism movement philosophically."[103] Here the Rockefellers were ahead of their times—in part because of Standard Oil's global trading role. Awareness of the lands and peoples and the economic potential of countries around the world gave them a cosmopolitan as well as mercantilist worldview.

In 1908, both John D. Rockefeller Sr. and John D. Rockefeller Jr. could imagine building a world-class American university in China. They even considered appointing an American ambassador for education in China. Embellished in Frederick Gates' typical hyperbolic language, such an individual "will represent the Western learning. He will be a man of tact, of address, of manner, of culture. . . . We will even venture to hope that he may ultimately so far ingratiate himself with Chinese educational officialdom as to secure a powerful influence over their whole educational system and bring it under the influence of our own."[104] Even though Gates allowed that he probably carried this idea further than the Rockefellers would approve, nonetheless theirs was not a modest dream. The fact that Qing Dynasty officials rejected this "gift" of an American university bears repeating. From the very beginning, Chinese national interests conditioned the role of the Rockefellers. And so the Rockefellers moved on to medicine, and later to the natural and social sciences, the humanities, and rural reconstruction—almost a university, but never a controlling role in China's higher education as once envisioned.

Abby and John clearly were cultural internationalists, supporting scores of internationally oriented institutions and nurturing a family whose international cultural influence on the United States eventually surpassed its economic influence. Asia and China were integral to their international vision. One manifestation of this was, of course, art itself. Their early embrace of Asian art was complex—both as a couple and as individuals. Both preferred three-dimensional sculptural forms to Chinese painting (perhaps because it was so different from Western masters), although Abby's collection of Japanese *ukiyo-e* prints, mainly birds and flowers, remains the largest in the world. Abby's love of early Buddhist figures and immersion in Buddhist studies was in marked contrast to John's narrow focus on decorative Qing porcelain. Like others of their era, neither seemed troubled by the provenance of the art that they collected. Although his pursuit of a grand restoration project in China indicates that he was not insensitive to the importance of national cultural ownership, John apparently acquiesced in the destruction of Prince Yu's palace and proceeded with the purchase of tiles from the Forbidden City, despite admonitions from Roger Greene to do otherwise.

For her part, Abby exemplified the affluent American women of the early twentieth century for whom the collection of Asian objects and study of Asian aesthetics enabled the creation of exotic living spaces, one aspect of American Orientalism.[105] But Abby's interests were deeper than most, including her husband. Her appropriation—and assimilation—of landscape design and sculptures from three Asian countries led her to create a unique garden—not a replica. Her six children—Babs, John 3rd, Nelson, David, Winthrop, and Laurence—and many grandchildren grew up frolicking in the family's two Asian gardens, at Kykuit and in Maine, seeking refuge in the mysterious Buddha rooms, and regularly dining on priceless antique Asian china. They remember being exposed to so much from Asia that it ceased to be exotic but instead constituted a comfortable and familiar environment. This daily familiarity with Asian culture influenced several generations of family members. The extended Rockefeller family not only became major collectors of Chinese, Japanese, and Korean art but also, through their great wealth, extended this appreciation to the American public. Their eldest son is but one example; John D. Rockefeller 3rd acquired an important private American Asian art collection, bequeathing it to the Asia Society, which he also founded.[106]

John Jr.'s religious engagement with China was likewise complex. In 1915, he made a pledge to the former missionary owners of PUMC that the new institution, though secular and without religious requirements for faculty or students, would retain a Christian influence. In subsequent years, his growing ecumenism, liberal theology, and skepticism about the missionary movement were influenced to some degree by his knowledge of Asian culture and experience in China. His personal credo, carved into the portal of the Rockefeller Center in New York in the mid-1930s, includes this universalist statement: "I believe in an all-wise and all-loving God, named by whatever name."[107] In China, however, well into the 1930s and early 1940s, JDR Jr. tried to ensure that PUMC remain faithful to its missionary Christian origins, for him a still vital residual value.

For John D. Rockefeller Jr., aesthetic appreciation and religious mission were two sides of the same coin; both deepened his interest in China and his commitment to what became a decidedly secular, scientific investment in China, PUMC. Neither JDR Jr. nor his father nor his son was overly interested in the details of the medical science that his early-twentieth-century philanthropies promoted. This was left to the scientific and medical experts who surrounded them. But they did, without question, fully support the Rockefeller Foundation's China mission—the promotion of elite scientific medicine in China. It was a natural extension of their evolving domestic philanthropic agenda and also reflected a continuing desire to influence the intellectual directions of China's future. By creating an institution designed to be comparable to those in Europe or the United States, the Rockefeller Foundation and the Rockefeller family, perhaps inadvertently, signaled a new American commitment: an investment in world-class science and medicine in China.

At a time when Chinese were excluded from immigrating to the United States, the Rockefeller project looked forward to welcoming PUMC's graduates as medical citizens of the world. As Franklin McLean, the first director of PUMC, predicted when PUMC's cornerstone was laid in 1917: "Given the opportunity for study and research, this country should develop a medical profession to be proud of, and one that may easily take its place among the leaders of the world."[108]

CHAPTER 2

AGENDA

"Missionaries of Science"

The Rockefellers were, of course, not the first foreigners to promote Western science and medicine in China.[1] From the West, Jesuits in the sixteenth century and Protestant missionaries in the nineteenth century had preceded them. Relics of the Jesuit era are found today on one of the last remaining sections of Peking's wall, surrounded by skyscrapers and expressways. Bronze copies of the Jesuit scientific instruments take their place alongside historical Chinese astronomical and seismological devices atop what remains of the imperial observatory. In Guangzhou, beside the Pearl River, a memorial stele commemorates the site where Peter Parker, the first Protestant medical missionary, established his ophthalmology clinic in 1835. Western medicine has been practiced on these grounds continuously ever since, today by Sun Yat-sen Medical University's Zhuhai Hospital.

From the East, Chinese translations of Japanese translations of Dutch scientific and medical treatises were circulated among the nineteenth-century literati. By the end of the century, information about the core concepts of Western science and medicine was widely available. Young Chinese students were being dispatched to Japan, Europe, and the United States to study science, medicine, and engineering. With the demise of the Confucian examination system in 1905 and the collapse of the Qing Dynasty, both Chinese intellectuals and political leaders quickly sought new solutions for the country's weakened state. Recognizing that their hundreds of traditional academies and study societies no longer sufficed, China's elites began to create an almost entirely new knowledge infrastructure.

Thus the timing of the Rockefeller arrival was highly fortuitous. In contrast to the Jesuits, who had arrived prematurely, China was ready for Rockefeller science and medicine. And, although the Rockefeller Foundation (RF) built upon Protestant missionary institutions, its secular elite strategy—not unlike the Jesuits—was a much better match for twentieth-century China's culture and ambitions. By the onset of the Sino-Japanese War in 1937, the foundations of China's modern science and medicine had been firmly established. The RF had been the most significant international influence.[2]

It is hard to imagine a more dynamic period in Chinese intellectual history. The key actors were officials and intellectuals who themselves navigated the transition from Confucian to modern China. Many crossed the Sea of Japan, the Pacific Ocean, and the long sea route to Europe, returning to create China's first institutions of modern science and higher education. They accomplished this during a time when China was politically fragmented, weakened by the continuing unequal treaty system with a semicolonial presence in coastal cities and key regions. The major foreign powers—Great Britain, France, Germany, Russia, Japan, and the United States—and their constituencies all sought cultural as well as political and economic spheres of influence. However, unlike India or the continent of Africa, the newly formed Republic of China remained an independent nation engaged in modern state building. Fueled by growing Chinese nationalism, the creation of China's first modern scientific, technological, and educational infrastructure became a national priority.

Chinese intellectuals were exposed to a wide variety of Western intellectual traditions, both through study abroad and the Japanese, American, and European presence in China. Eclectic borrowing and national adaptation resulted in an explosion of institutes, colleges, and universities. When the Republican era began in 1911, China had three barely functioning national universities, thirteen small American missionary colleges, several European colleges, and no modern scientific research institutions. By 1937, it had fifty-six colleges or universities, sixteen of them sponsored by American missionaries; twenty-three professional schools; scores of modern scientific research institutes and professional societies; and a flourishing academy of science, the Academia Sinica, a Chinese institution with elements adapted from the British Royal Society, the French Academy, and the American National Research Council.[3]

In this yeasty and often highly politicized intellectual milieu, the RF was the single largest source of private foreign funding for China's science and medicine, and its funding probably exceeded international government programs and the League of Nations (the League's Health Organization received 40 percent of its funding from the Rockefellers). Strictly speaking, the American Boxer Indemnity Fund, managed first by Qinghua College and later by the China Foundation for the Promotion of Education and Culture, was larger, supporting both Qinghua and more than 1,200 Chinese students for study in the United States. The Boxer Indemnity Fund was not really American; it was composed of Chinese reparation monies being returned to China by the U.S. government for educational purposes. But the intellectual influences were primarily American.

Together, the RF and Boxer Indemnity programs, including both Peking Union Medical College and Qinghua College, represent the high tide of secular American intellectual engagement with Republican China.[4]

As American "missionaries of science," to borrow the Latin American historian Marcus Cueto's very apt term, what difference did the Rockefeller presence make? How did the intellectual conditions of early-twentieth-century China, including the significant missionary role, shape the nature of the Rockefeller endeavor? How did the Rockefeller priorities, shaped by the American intellectual frontiers of the first third of the twentieth century, change the nature of the American cultural presence in China and influence the development of China's medical and scientific community? Why did the RF shift away from medicine? To answer these questions, we need to look more closely at their major programs—beginning, as did the Rockefellers, with missionary medicine.

MISSIONARY, CHINESE, AND ROCKEFELLER MEDICINE

In much of nineteenth century Asia, Western biomedicine was introduced as colonial medicine, directly linked to improving the health conditions of civilian and military expatriates in order to extend colonial power. Missionary medicine was often supplementary, introducing small-scale clinics for the "natives" in the hinterland. Colonial medicine was not absent in China, and it was especially evident in major urban areas such as Hong Kong, Guangzhou, Shanghai, and Tianjin.[5] Still, the primary introduction to Western medicine came through Japanese texts and Protestant missionaries. By 1914, the year in which the RF commenced work in China, the missionary medical presence included 330 missionary hospitals, 223 dispensaries, 500 Western missionary physicians, and 12 medical colleges.[6] At the very most, there were several hundred Western-trained Chinese doctors— including missionary apprentices, medical school graduates, and those trained in Japan, Europe, or the United States. The health care of the vast majority of the 400 million Chinese people was provided by time-honored Chinese medicine, with its rich pharmacopoeia and physiological and nutritional theories and practice. These traditions were passed on primarily through apprenticeships.

In writing about the RF and medical work in Asia, Soma Hewa and Philo Hove equate "American missionary zeal" and evangelism as characteristic of the Rockefeller presence in Asia, especially China.[7] In reality, however, the story is more complex. How the RF differentiated itself from, while simultaneously supporting, missionary medicine is one of the most important themes of the early decades of its work in China. Three survey commissions (the Oriental Education Commission, 1909; and the first and second Medical Commissions to China,

1914 and 1915) counseled against close identification between the new Rockefeller project and missionary medicine. The commission participants, especially Simon Flexner and William Welch, argued that missionary medicine did not meet current scientific standards. Following their meetings with Chinese officials and educators, Flexner and Welch came to believe that the identification of Western medicine with Christianity was detrimental to the widespread acceptance of Western medicine. Western medical theory was being studied in some late-nineteenth-century Chinese intellectual circles, but this interest was stimulated not by missionaries but by translations of Japanese and Western texts.[8]

Religion was not the only barrier to spreading Western medicine in China. During much of the nineteenth century, Western medicine did not appear especially efficacious compared with traditional Chinese medicine, with the exception of surgery. Advances in understanding the human anatomy coupled with the discovery of anesthesia in the early nineteenth century had laid the foundations for modern surgery in Europe and the United States. Both Chinese and Western clinical systems, however, had changed little since ancient times. European medical practice was still largely based on the works of Hippocrates and Galen, whereas Chinese medicine dated back to the mythical Yellow Emperor. Both traditional medical systems looked at the body as an integrated whole: Illness was something that affected the balance within the organs of the body. Western medicine emphasized the humors, whereas the Chinese believed in a life energy force, the *qi*. Both cultures used a variety of treatments that today seem barbaric; for example, bloodletting continued in the United States well into the twentieth century.

This comparison began to change with the technological breakthroughs of the nineteenth century in Europe and the United States: the stethoscope, the ophthalmoscope, the microscope, and the X-ray. Medicine became more scientific but, without an understanding of disease causation, healing did not necessarily improve. Not until the 1880s was the germ theory of disease confirmed by Louis Pasteur and Robert Koch, and only in the early twentieth century were new vaccines and antibiotics, "miracle drugs," discovered. The Rockefeller mission to China was fortunate to coincide with the advent of this "golden age" in Western clinical practice.

With their lifetime commitment to China and the daily pressures of clinical care, missionary doctors were sometimes isolated from these medical advances, even though many of them had graduated from the foremost medical schools of their day. The Rockefellers' medical advisers, who were in the forefront of this medical revolution, feared that missionary medicine had not kept abreast of the innovations that made medicine scientific, thus rendering it less competitive with traditional Chinese medicine. Of all the Rockefeller educators, it was the redoubtable William Welch, who himself had trained with Robert Koch in Germany, who recognized the tenacity of Chinese medicine. While traveling in

China in 1914, he made a point of studying Chinese medicine and often lectured on it when he returned to Johns Hopkins. Welch found promise in the traditional diagnostic methods, especially multiple pulse sites, and he praised the Chinese pharmacopoeia, noting that "the Chinese surpass the world in their *materia medica*." He also concluded that Chinese traditional views of anatomy, physiology, and the causes of disease were "fantastic and absurd." He believed the successful missionary surgical repertoire masked an inattention to disease causation. These conclusions about both Chinese and missionary medicine reinforced Welch's commitment to creating Peking Union Medical College (PUMC) independent of missionary influence.[9]

In planning PUMC, the Rockefeller group was divided about the role of missionary medicine. In contrast to Welch and Flexner, Frederick Gates had originally believed that the focus of the Rockefeller effort should be the enhancement of missionary medicine. His 1905 letter to John D. Rockefeller urging the support of missionary medicine was published in the *Boston Herald*, and his 1914 blueprint, "For the Orderly and Systematic Development of Modern Medicine in China," presented an ambitious scheme whereby four modern medical colleges (in Guangzhou, Shanghai, Peking, and Chengdu) would serve as centers for the continuing education of missionary medical personnel. He saw Rockefeller funding underwriting an expansion of missionary physicians—increasing their presence to at least two in each missionary clinic. In 1917, Gates resigned from the China Medical Board because he felt missionaries were being excluded; the design for PUMC was overly elaborate and emphasized training Chinese, not missionaries. Gates was sometimes described as a lapsed Baptist, but he changed his mind about missionary medicine in the 1920s, writing caustically that "China needs modern medicine but the hospitals and physicians of the missionaries are merely proselytizing agencies. . . . The missionary societies, therefore, offer little hope to one seeking an avenue of ministration to the present medical needs of China."[10] By 1927, Gates had turned against the entire Rockefeller project in China, noting that the Rockefellers could fund five medical schools in the United States for the cost of one school, PUMC, in China.[11]

As its development unfolded, PUMC presented an alternative, secular scientific model, even as the work of the RF's China Medical Board also greatly enhanced missionary medicine. John D. Rockefeller Jr. himself personally affirmed that PUMC would be nonsectarian and, unlike missionary institutions, would not "impose tests of a doctrinal nature."[12] Because the RF was determined that the new Rockefeller institution would model the highest standards of medical science, it decided that three years of premedical science would be required (a higher requirement than that of many U.S. medical schools at the time) and that all teaching would be in English, creating a Chinese medical elite, not physicians to staff missionary hospitals. Chinese graduates of PUMC were expected to use English in order to become part of a global network of modern medicine. Despite much criticism from the missionary community and Chinese educators alike, this linguistic fluency was, for the Rockefeller educators, a sine qua non; "their" PUMC graduates would become full participants in an international scientific community.

Although previous accounts of PUMC, including my own, have criticized the results of these decisions—PUMC's elite nature and tiny student body—recent studies by Chinese scholars underline the importance of PUMC's contribution to modern medicine and science in China *because of* this elitist, nonsectarian, and scientific emphasis.[13] Two years before PUMC opened its doors in 1917, two new Chinese journals, *Science* and *New Youth*, brought modern science and medicine to the attention of China's urban-educated intellectuals. Two years after its opening, the May 4th Movement swept across China's modern consciousness. Many of the leading intellectuals—including Chen Duxiu, one of the founders of the Chinese Communist Party—castigated traditional Chinese medicine and called for the adoption of Western medicine. These early-twentieth-century modernizing Chinese elites had not been drawn to missionary medicine despite its important contributions to the practice of Western medicine. Absent religion, the scientific and secular presentation of Western medicine was far more attractive to the Chinese, complementing the historic movements of the times.

PUMC was always able to attract students from upper-class Chinese gentry and mercantile families. Missionary institutions sought Chinese Christians, who were few in number, to staff their hospitals and schools. In contrast, PUMC easily recruited the first generation of Chinese medical scientists who had studied abroad. Among the outstanding Chinese hired for PUMC's first faculty were a surgeon, Liu Ruiheng (J. Heng Liu), a biochemist, Wu Xian (Wu Hsien), and a pathologist, Hu Zhengxiang (all from Harvard University). Others included a bacteriologist, Lin Zongyang (C. E. Lim, from Johns Hopkins), and a physiologist, Lin Kesheng (Robert K. S. Lim, from the University of Edinburgh). Each became a founder of his disciplinary profession in China.

Leading Chinese intellectuals and scientists were willing to be identified with the RF, and to serve as advisers. Hu Shi (Hu Shih), a Columbia University–educated liberal intellectual credited with introducing the Chinese vernacular into common written usage and later president of Peking University and an ambassador to the United States, became an early informal adviser to both Henry Houghton and Roger Greene.[14] In the early 1920s, Houghton wrote to Greene about his meetings with Hu Shi:

> During the past few months I have taken occasion to have a series of
> conversations with Dr. Hu Shih on the opportunities and influence of the
> College and possible policies for the future. . . . Dr Hu summed that [PUMC's]
> work would be welcomed by the Chinese . . . because of the obvious excellence
> of its teaching and scientific standards, its policy of building up a Chinese staff

without racial discrimination and its broad attitude on religious matters [no religious programs were compulsory].[15]

During those meetings, Hu Shi also urged PUMC to enlarge "its studies in the ancient oriental pharmacopoeia, not only as a research important in itself, but as a means of linking the East and West, science and empiricism, in medicine."[16] His view was typical of many of this era (and today): Adopt Western medicine, but use science to study Chinese medicine. Although PUMC is not usually associated with such research, Bernard Read, a professor of pharmacology, was one of several faculty members who met this challenge. Working with Chinese collaborators, he translated forty volumes of the *Pen T'sao*, the great Ming compendium of the Chinese *materia medica*.[17]

Hu Shi was one of numerous Chinese intellectual advisers to PUMC during the 1920s. In 1929, a group of prominent Chinese scientists and intellectuals was invited to serve on the PUMC's Board of Trustees. In addition to Hu Shi, these included Zhou Yichun (Y. T. Tsur), president of Qinghua University; Weng Wenhao, director of the National Geological Survey; Wu Zhaoshu (C. C. Wu), an ambassador to the United States and the League of Nations; Zhang Boling, president of Nankai University; and Ding Wenjiang, founder of China's Geological Survey and a leading intellectual critic. All were Western educated and represented China's liberal-oriented elite. Even though the RF dragged its heels on delegating real responsibility to these PUMC trustees, no missionary group could have secured their allegiance.

China's elite increasingly sought treatment at PUMC Hospital. The two most famous Chinese leaders to be treated during the 1920s were Sun Yat-sen and Liang Qichao, an internationally renowned journalist and reformer, both unsuccessfully. In 1925, Sun was diagnosed with inoperable cancer of the liver, and he died at home. Liang's case a year later became highly controversial, giving rise to a new debate on the relative efficacy of Chinese and Western medicine. Suffering from haematuria (blood in the urine), he was diagnosed with cancer of the kidney and one kidney was removed. The fact that there was no subsequent improvement in the haematuria became widely known, with newspapers ridiculing Western medicine and blaming the PUMC surgeon's excessive zeal in removing Liang's kidney. Liang was a longtime advocate of Western medicine and scientific thinking who repeatedly came to the defense of PUMC; thus, he wrote:

> We cannot doubt science itself just because modern scientific knowledge is still not well developed. Such is the case of my petty disease. Although the result of the medical examination was not as good as what the doctors had expected, my case may just be an occasional exception. There is nothing comparable between the strict examination and the groundless guess of "Yin and Yang and five elements" in old Chinese medicine.[18]

Further demonstrating his support, Liang served as PUMC's commencement speaker that same year, proclaiming:

> The Peking Union Medical College is making a great contribution to the
> progress of China. If we ask what China needs most the consensus of opinion
> will be that we need most the scientific spirit and method. How is this need to be
> best met? My reply is, through the medical science.[19]

Identifying PUMC and the scientific method with the "progress of China" was exactly the linkage that PUMC's founders had envisioned.

Even as the RF sought to align itself with China's leading liberal modernizers, there was significant residual support for missionary medicine. Rockefeller officials were more familiar with missionary hospitals and medical schools, while Chinese-managed hospitals and medical colleges were still at an early stage. John D. Rockefeller Jr. personally reviewed the various decisions of the China Medical Board regarding support of missionary hospitals. In an impassioned eleven-page letter to New York, Roger Greene argued that the RF should find the means to fund five qualified medical staff members at all missionary hospitals, not two, as Frederick Gates had proposed. Between 1914 and 1928, when the program was redirected for only Chinese medical personnel, the China Medical Board's most significant contribution to missionary medicine was to offer fellowships for advanced medical study in the United States and Europe. During this period, 244 missionary doctors, perhaps as many as *half* of all missionary doctors in China, received these fellowships. Although a few were hired for the PUMC teaching and hospital staff, most returned to their missionary hospitals or medical schools. This represented an extraordinary educational investment in missionary medicine.[20]

Four other Rockefeller programs enhanced the scientific quality of missionary medicine. First, from 1914 to 1933, the China Medical Board continued to provide financial support to twenty-nine missionary hospitals scattered across China. Although the amounts were small, they provided an infusion of funds for both operating expenses and clinical research. Some missionaries were drawn into PUMC's network of research on local parasitic diseases such as kala-azar and schistosomiasis. Second, the China Medical Board provided funding for X-ray equipment, an important new technological innovation, to many missionary hospitals. Paul C. Hodges established PUMC's Radiology Department in 1919, produced inexpensive X-ray machines, trained Chinese radiologists, and widely disseminated both the equipment and the technology to missionary and Chinese hospitals.[21] Third, several hundred missionary physicians regularly attended continuing education programs at PUMC. Fourth, the China Medical Board provided core financial support to five missionary medical schools, the forerunners of key medical universities in China today: Xiangya Medical College in Changsha (today the

Xiangya School of Medicine of Central South University); Saint John's Medical College in Shanghai (today the School of Medicine of Shanghai Jiaotong University); Qilu Medical College in Jinan (today the School of Medicine of Shandong Medical University); West China Medical College (today the West China Medical School of Sichuan University); and Shanghai Union Medical College (today the Medical School of Fudan University). The total funding for these medical colleges was $1,522,826, with the greatest share, nearly $600,000, going to Shandong. (For a comparative sense of scale, the $1.5 million for missionary medical colleges in China is approximately the same—$1.4 million—as all the RF's pre-1950 funds for India.)[22] The RF decided to concentrate resources at Qilu Medical College because the teaching continued to be in Chinese. The other missionary medical colleges adopted English when PUMC did, but Rockefeller educators were not unaware of the need to develop a Chinese medical vocabulary.

As a result of Rockefeller funding, missionary medicine became more up to date and missionary colleges enhanced their teaching and research. By 1934, mission medical schools had trained almost 1,000 Chinese doctors (compared with only 130 at PUMC), approximately 15 percent of the physicians in China, and two-thirds of their hospital and college staff members were Chinese. Rockefeller funding also reinforced PUMC's model. These institutions endeavored to emulate its high academic standards and its curative approach to medical care.[23]

The RF's identification with missionary medicine limited its relationship with medical colleges or hospitals under Chinese sponsorship. It was also slow to support the National Medical Association (NMA) of China, a Chinese-led body that was formed in competition with the China Medical Association, which was primarily made up of missionary doctors. This reluctance was due in part to the RF efforts to withdraw from supporting medical education after the mid-1920s. Nonetheless, several PUMC faculty felt that the opportunity for collaboration was being missed. In the late 1920s, due to the efforts of John Grant and Lin Kesheng, the Seventh Biennial Conference of the NMA was invited to hold several of its sessions at PUMC, and eventually a very modest grant of $4,000 (paid in Mexican silver) was awarded to the NMA. The two associations merged in the early 1930s.[24]

PEKING UNION MEDICAL COLLEGE

During its first two decades, 1917–37, PUMC developed into the most privileged and respected medical school in Asia. The first RF "business plan" estimated capital expenditures of approximately $600,000 and an annual subsidy of no more than $200,000. But the challenge of building and staffing a world-class medical school and hospital in early-twentieth-century China became far more costly than ever anticipated. The capital expenditures for PUMC came to well over $8 million, and its annual budget in 1921 of $500,000 had grown to almost $900,000 by the end of the decade. Frederick Gates was not alone in declaring in 1927 that, with regard to China, "I regret our lavish expenditures there."[25] For a sense of scale and comparison, the total expenditure for *all* American missionary work in China in 1916 was approximately $3 million.[26]

Simon Flexner and William Welch introduced the American Flexnerian model when they designed PUMC's curriculum. Key components included a direct linkage between the medical school and a teaching hospital, a full-time teaching and clinical staff, a four-year residency system, an emphasis on clinical and biomedical research, at least three years of premedical baccalaureate science education, and postgraduate training. The Flexnerian component that PUMC lacked was a university. And the Johns Hopkins component that PUMC lacked was a school of public health. Having been derived from the German system, an important element of the original Johns Hopkins model was the incorporation of a medical school within a university with a parallel school of public health. In the United States, this ensured ongoing intellectual connections to the basic sciences and humanistic inquiry. It also ensured the parallel evolution of a school of medicine and a school of public health. Through its entire history, PUMC (and the many Chinese medical colleges that have modeled themselves after it) have had to make accommodations because of these omissions. From the mid-1920s to today, first Yanjing University and then Peking University (combined with Yanjing in 1951) and now Qinghua University have provided PUMC's premedical training. Not only has PUMC been intellectually crippled because of this omission, but the PUMC model has likewise been less comprehensive than its American parent.

Otherwise, PUMC may be the only medical school/hospital complex in the world that was architecturally designed to reflect the core Flexnerian elements. Although it emulated the courtyard pattern of Prince Yu's palace, the long garden corridor served as a physical link between the hospital complex and the educational and basic research complex. Student and faculty residence facilities were adjacent to the medical school campus, creating a residential scientific community.

PUMC students of this era remembered how radically different their education was from traditional Chinese learning—entailing a Socratic style of teaching and close mentoring relationships with the faculty. In 2007, nearly a hundred years later, the Flexnerian and Johns Hopkins model would be eulogized in Chinese histories of the institution: "Johns Hopkins University emphasized students' own practice rather than lecturing. . . . Young medical students were no longer passive observers, but participants. . . . A real medical school should produce doctors with scientific thinking, instead of those who get lost in trivialities. . . . Welch termed this a 'scientific habit of thinking.'"[27]

PUMC was initially staffed by leading young American and European medical scientists recruited by Welch and Flexner. The foreign faculty commitment was for five years, but the research and clinical environment was so stimulating and the residential accommodations were so satisfactory that many stayed much longer. Welch and Flexner tracked their careers, assisting in finding good positions when their China sojourn had ended. After the mid-1920s, this career intervention was no longer needed; PUMC had become an internationally recognized institution. A few examples suggest the quality of this initial faculty. Edmund Vincent Cowdry and Davidson Black established the Anatomy Department; Cowdry went on to become professor of anatomy at the University of Chicago, and Black, with Chinese collaborators, discovered Peking Man. A. Baird Hastings, a physical chemist, went from the University of Chicago to PUMC and then concluded his distinguished career at Harvard University. Ernest Caroll Faust became the leading American parasitologist as a result of his research at PUMC on schistosomiasis, clonorchiasis, and malaria. Among the best-known distinguished visiting professors at PUMC were Donald Van Slyke from the Rockefeller Institute, the leading biochemist of the era, and David Edsall, dean of the Harvard Medical School.

These Western faculty engaged in extensive research collaboration with Chinese students and faculty, leading to hundreds of coauthored annual publications, many in the leading American and European medical journals. In 1941, Isadore Snapper, chair of the Department of Medicine, published a widely read summary of PUMC's research: *Chinese Lessons to Western Medicine: A Contribution to Geographical Medicine from the Clinics of Peiping Union Medical College*.[28] PUMC's ability to engage distinguished American medical scientists over sustained periods of time conveyed a scientific legitimacy to the Rockefeller medical presence in China.

A goal of PUMC, often repeated by John D. Rockefeller Jr., was that all teaching positions would be held by highly qualified Chinese. In 1917, relatively few Chinese graduates of top-ranked American or European medical schools had returned to China, but that changed rapidly during the 1920s. PUMC offered a higher salary and much better clinical and research facilities than American or European missionary medical colleges or the relatively few Chinese medical schools. PUMC increasingly hired its own graduates after the mid-1920s, usually sending them abroad first for advanced training in Europe or the United States. Until the mid-1930s, the process of replacing senior Western faculty seemed too slow for the young Chinese faculty. The biggest area of contention was the salary differential: Western faculty were paid in U.S. dollars and Chinese faculty in Mexican silver, exacerbating the difference in status. Nonetheless, by 1937 almost the entire faculty and hospital staff were Chinese.

The PUMC Hospital became widely known throughout China. As a tertiary hospital, it opened its doors to patients from all walks of life and all regions. The hospital came to have a national reputation, and it is better known to this day than the medical college. Most PUMC students were required to spend four years of residency, following their eight-year education program, as residents in the hospital, practicing under the supervision of senior faculty. PUMC's patient record system, copied from Johns Hopkins, became a model for all of China. All 100,000 inpatient records and 550,000 outpatient records from 1920 to 1951 were written in English and are still maintained in the PUMC Hospital Archive. A comprehensive study of these records could provide a detailed picture not only of patient treatment at PUMC but also the pattern of disease and illness in China during the Republican era. Although it had a private ward for foreign patients, and Chinese VIPs included Generalissimo Chiang Kai-shek and his wife Song Meiling (Soong Mei-ling), PUMC was also known for the care of the indigent. Isadore Snapper observed that most of the patients in the regular wards were beggars, inmates of poorhouses, and workshop apprentices. PUMC's Department of Social Service, led by Ida Pruitt, trained the first hospital social workers in China and provided both social and economic support to patients and their families.[29]

When PUMC opened, fewer than 300 nurses practiced in all of China, and many were foreign missionaries. Nursing was not viewed as an "honorable" occupation for young women, and thus most Chinese nurses were male. However, the Rockefeller educators approached nursing education the same way they approached medical education, requiring standards equivalent to those in the United States. The goal was twofold: to train nurses who could provide leadership for nursing education throughout China, and to elevate public views about nursing careers for young Chinese women. In many respects, PUMC's nursing education standards were higher than in most American institutions; a full five-year baccalaureate program was required—in English. Like the medical college, the foreign faculty members gradually trained their replacements, if more slowly; by 1935, thirteen of the twenty-seven nursing faculty members were Chinese. PUMC nurses became founding members and leaders of the Chinese Nursing Association. Although the elite nursing program was integral to a curative system of medical care, PUMC's School of Nursing also developed public health nursing, staffing both the Peking Health Demonstration Station and the rural medical program at Dingxian.[30]

In addition to its medical and nursing school and hospital, PUMC became China's first postgraduate institution. The first graduate students were three missionaries, enrolling in 1920. A year later there were thirty-eight students—half missionaries and half Chinese. The numbers grew until they averaged more than a hundred a year, primarily Chinese, but a few from Europe and other Asian countries as well; students were enrolled in a wide variety of both short-term (three-month) programs and research programs lasting for several years. No formal postgraduate degrees were offered, but these advanced training and research opportunities, primarily funded by PUMC, reduced the need to study abroad, elevating the level of medical training offered in China.

PUMC AND PUBLIC HEALTH

PUMC is best known as a center for modern scientific medicine, but it also became the epicenter of the modern public health movement in China. Innovative and locally designed programs in public health and social medicine emerged out of PUMC's faculty and students, becoming national models first during the Guomindang era and later in the People's Republic of China. Unlike the disease eradication programs for which the RF's International Health Board was best known, the PUMC's programs emphasized comprehensive health care, including the integration of curative and preventive services. John Grant, a PUMC professor of health from 1921 to 1937, sought to unite the two distinct streams of the RF's health emphasis—curative medicine and public health—into a unified system of preventive medicine.

The son of China medical missionaries, Grant was trained in medicine at the University of Michigan and in public health at Johns Hopkins, and he had some exposure to the RF's disease prevention programs in North Carolina. Before it became more fashionable, he concluded that much of the RF's public health philosophy was wrong, that disease prevention alone was inadequate: Improved health also required curative services and improved economic conditions. His accomplishments over a fifteen-year tenure in China were many: infusing public health into the medical curriculum, designing an urban experimental health station, and advising on the creation of a national health administration. All PUMC students were required to include a three- to six-week rotation at either an urban or rural health location. Twenty percent of PUMC students graduated with a specialization in public health, perhaps the highest proportion of any medical school ever. PUMC's graduates were a privileged elite, yet many longed to make a contribution to China's health, to become leaders in China's public health programs. Grant also hoped to establish a School of Public Health in association with PUMC. The RF's International Health Board felt that Grant was overextended with his many initiatives and repeatedly discouraged this new venture.[31]

Grant did not work in a vacuum. The relative weakness of the late Qing Dynasty and early Republican governments that was observed by the Rockefeller officials belied the growing Chinese attention to local and provincial sanitary and epidemic control programs. These had a clear anticolonial purpose: to refute the widespread perception of China as "the sick man of Asia," and to wrest control of treaty-port quarantine from the various colonial powers.[32] Some examples include a Department of Health in Guangdong, public health services in Tianjin, and the North Manchurian Plague Prevention Service. Working in this receptive political climate, Grant began to expand the agenda beyond controlling disease to advocating state responsibility for improving people's health.[33]

At the municipal level, Grant worked with the Police Department to organize the Peking Health Demonstration Station in 1924, a model of urban
community medicine, which included vital statistics, epidemic control, preventive health care, midwifery, and basic curative services for a population
unit of 100,000. As a recent study by the historian Liping Bu illustrates,
the local population was initially hostile to the intrusive presence of policemen serving as sanitary inspectors; local residents resisted policemen collecting data about individual and family sanitary habits, births and deaths, and
changes in night soil collection.[34] But as the curative services of PUMC's
public health nurses and traditional midwives were introduced, residents
gradually responded more favorably, although their preference for traditional
Chinese medicine was not abated.

The Health Demonstration Station served as the training ground for many
future leaders of China's state medicine, including PUMC graduates. Their
experimental work was widely published and emulated; more than fifty studies of urban health were undertaken in nineteen cities located in eight provinces. Their survey template, "Tentative Appraisal for Health Work in Cities
in China," was published in 1928 and adopted nationally. Many involved
in this experimental program went on to provincial or national leadership
positions.[35]

A second spin-off was an experimental rural station in Dingxian, Hebei
Province. Grant's students, led first by Yao Xunyuan and then by Chen Zhiqian
(C. C. Chen), adapted the urban health model to Yan Yangchu's rural reconstruction program, beginning in 1927. As it evolved, Chen's design included
a three-tier system of medical care for the rural areas—village, township, and
county—with the most basic level of health care being provided by village
health workers. Chen traveled to Eastern Europe and the USSR in the early
1930s, and he acknowledged his intellectual debt to Andrija Stampar, who pio-
neered rural community medical programs in Yugoslavia. He also maintained
that his design was indigenous; his health stations were not welfare centers like
the *zadrugas* in Yugoslavia, nor were his village health workers second-grade
physicians, as in the Soviet Union. Dingxian was not the only experimental
program in rural health care delivery in China at the time, but it became the
prototype for a national program.[36]

If PUMC's role as an incubator for innovative public health programs was
unplanned and unexpected, so too was the RF's evolving role in science education. When it decided to create a Flexnerian-type institution in China, the
RF did not appreciate the lacuna in China's science education. First to support
PUMC, and then for its own sake, the RF gradually turned its attention away
from medicine to science. This shift was to significantly broaden the nature of
the RF's work in China.

THE ROCKEFELLER FOUNDATION AND THE NATURAL SCIENCES

James Reardon-Anderson, a historian of science in twentieth-century China, concludes that "as important as PUMC was, the Rockefeller Foundation had an even greater impact on the study of science through grants to Chinese colleges and universities."[37] Certainly the natural sciences had not been part of the RF's initial agenda. An unintended consequence of setting PUMC's scientific standards so high was that there were no qualified Chinese students. The Johns Hopkins model required that students be well versed in the modern premedical sciences—biology, chemistry, and physics. These academic disciplines barely existed in the 1910s in China. As China developed its first modern educational system, the natural sciences were especially weak. The first generation of modern Chinese scientists studying abroad had focused on geology and engineering, disciplines more directly related to China's national development. As a result, Peking University, for example, had a good Geology Department but did not introduce biology until 1925.

To jump-start the premedical sciences, the RF began a program of grants for science instruction in missionary colleges in 1914 and created its own premedical school, opening in 1917. In 1922, Paul Monroe, director of Columbia University's Teachers College and chair of the PUMC Board of Trustees, spent several months in China surveying science instruction in middle schools, technical schools, and colleges in ten provinces. He concluded that the previous focus on missionary colleges had been too narrow, and that the time had come to fund the natural science disciplines at key Chinese universities as well: "It is obvious that the Medical School [PUMC] cannot accomplish either of its purposes unless it draws many students from Chinese schools, government or private, or both, and influences both medical and premedical education under Chinese control."[38]

Monroe recommended that PUMC terminate its own premedical school, turning the natural science instruction over to Yanjing University, and that the China Medical Board begin significant funding for Chinese-led National Central University in Nanjing and Nankai University in Tianjin. He also argued for continuing support for science education at such key missionary colleges as Saint John's University, Fujian Christian University, Canton Christian College, Jinling Women's College, Xiangya University, the University of Nanjing, and Soochow University. This funding brought about accelerated science programs in the missionary colleges, and many of the Chinese who went on for advanced scientific study in the 1930s and 1940s were their graduates.[39]

In 1924, PUMC transferred its premedical faculty and students to Yanjing University; only then did Yanjing begin the science instruction for which it became well known. Of the transferred PUMC staff, of particular note was Alice Boring, who remained at Yanjing until 1951 and was well remembered years later by Yanjing and PUMC graduates. She had been a student of Thomas Hunt Morgan early in his career at Bryn Mawr College, and she was perhaps the first to introduce Mendelian genetics to China.[40]

With this transfer, the RF's funding essentially underwrote the sciences at Yanjing, contributing upward of 25 percent of the university's total annual operating budget until the time of the Japanese invasion. The RF's commitment to the sciences at Yanjing included an endowment challenge grant of $500,000 in the early 1930s, an unheard-of sum at that time. Yanjing's Biology Department became the best in China, growing from two foreign teachers in the mid-1920s to an all-Chinese (plus Boring) staff of ten by 1937. Three of twentieth-century China's most famous geneticists trained under Morgan at either Columbia or the California Institute of Technology: Tan Jiazhen (C. C. Tan) had been a graduate student at Yanjing, and Chen Ziying and Li Ruqi were Yanjing faculty. Rockefeller funding not only enticed them to teach at Yanjing; Rockefeller grants in the mid-1930s sent them back to the United States to continue their research at Cal Tech. All three had returned to China by 1951. With considerable difficulty, they survived the onslaught of Soviet-influenced Lysenkoism, which rejected Mendelian genetics, leading the renewal of modern genetics in China in the late twentieth century.[41]

The RF's funding also underwrote the biology programs of National Central University, the flagship institution for China's incipient university system. Its president, Guo Bingwen, a Columbia University graduate and friend of Paul Monroe, had recruited eight science instructors, all trained at leading American universities: three from the Massachusetts Institute of Technology, two from the University of Illinois, and one each from the University of Pennsylvania, Cornell University, and Lehigh University. This young faculty included Hu Xiansu and Bing Zhi, who became founding members of the Academia Sinica in 1928. They already had international linkages, and the beginning of a research agenda focused on developing a taxonomy of Chinese plant species. By emphasizing Chinese flora, they also sought to create a distinctly Chinese botany, independent from Western sources. This was in keeping with what was called "local science," a national emphasis on China's flora, fauna, and geology. As Laurence Schneider puts it, "These scientists were admonished to develop the interests and the tools necessary to study China's indigenous natural world."[42] This was in keeping with the emphasis on scientific nationalism that emerged out of the May 4th era. The China Medical Board provided matching funds of close to $100,000 for a new science building, equipment, faculty salaries, and visiting professors. Annual support for science programs continued until 1937.[43]

The second-most-important premedical discipline was chemistry, and it was here that PUMC itself made the most important contributions to Chinese education and research. With a Boxer Indemnity scholarship, Wu Xian graduated from

MIT in 1917, then received a PhD in biochemistry from Harvard in 1919. His dissertation became the basis for the Folin-Wu method of blood analysis, which became an international standard. After Wu was recruited as an assistant professor of chemistry at PUMC in 1920, he became PUMC's first Chinese professor. From that position, his research on the denaturation of proteins and immunology also received international recognition. He is considered by some to be China's greatest scientist during the first half of the twentieth century.[44]

Wu's presence at PUMC attracted an especially strong group of young Chinese chemists. Two of them were engaged in analyzing the active ingredients of Chinese herbal medicine: Chen Kehui (PhD, Wisconsin, 1923) and Zhao Chenggu (PhD, University of Geneva, 1914). Their work led to the extraction of ephedrine from the Chinese plant *ma-huang*, perhaps the most important discovery from traditional Chinese medicine during the twentieth century. PUMC thus became the undisputed leader in biochemical research during the early Republican period. The work of the department expanded to strengthen chemistry teaching and research throughout China. Wu also was a leader in organizing the Chinese Physiological Society, as well as the journal *The Independent Critic*, where leading intellectuals commented on the political and social issues of the times.[45]

The RF's support for the natural sciences began in 1914 with the purpose of improving the premedical sciences for PUMC. By the mid-1920s, a broader rationale had emerged: support for the professionalization of modern science in China. As hundreds of Western-trained scientists began to return and as new universities were being established, a national system of research and higher education was emerging. Scores of scientific journals, professional societies, and research institutes began to appear.

PUMC's faculty, along with Roger Greene and N. Gist Gee, a missionary biologist hired to manage the RF's science programs, became leaders and active participants in these scientific societies, many of which received Rockefeller support. William Haas's biography of Gee provides a detailed picture of the many seminars, lectures, and organizational meetings in which new ideas for journals and societies and research were discussed. PUMC visiting professors were included in the conversations. Several of the scientific organizations in which Greene and Gee were most involved were the Peking Laboratory of Natural History, the Fan Memorial Institute of Biology, the China Foundation of Education and Culture, and, most important, the Science Society of China.

The Science Society of China was formed in 1914 by young Chinese scientists studying at Cornell University. It was moved to China in 1916 and became the leading Chinese scientific society during the Republican period. Well known throughout China for its publication of the journal *Kexue (Science)*, it also founded a Biological Laboratory in Nanjing and had many regional offices.

Upon learning that the U.S. government was planning to restore excess Boxer Indemnity Fund monies to China, the Science Society lobbied hard for the funding to be targeted toward the sciences. It asked for and received support from Greene, who went all the way to Washington to lobby the State Department. Their overtures were successful. In 1924, a Chinese American board, the China Foundation for the Promotion of Education and Culture, was appointed to manage this second remission of Boxer Indemnity monies. The members were almost all individuals associated with the RF, including the presidents of both Nankai and National Central universities. Greene, Paul Monroe, and John Dewey were appointed the American members, and Greene quickly took charge, appointing Gee as staff. The RF itself became an important contributor to the Science Society's Biological Laboratory, which became a major center for biological research in China. In May 1927, the Science Society's journal, *Science*, devoted the entire issue to biological research in China.[46]

The RF's continued attention to the natural sciences in China paralleled its domestic agenda. The creation of a Division of Natural Sciences in the 1928 reorganization brought a new RF focus on the fundamental sciences in the United States, especially the life sciences and experimental biology. This reinforced the deepening engagement with Chinese scientists and scientific institutions, which was already being advocated by RF field representatives in China. Greene became passionate about the importance of science to China's future and the value of American participation. The RF's officers, who traveled frequently to China, became familiar with China's leading scientists and knew the presidents of Yanjing University, National Central University, and Nankai University. They tracked the fellowship and grant reports, often posing questions about the directions being proposed. They cared about the type of research that was undertaken in China and what happened to their fellowship recipients. A telling example comes from the detail with which Selskar Gunn, the former RF vice president for Europe who inaugurated the RF's new China programs in the 1930s, requested a modest grant of $6,000 from Max Mason, the new RF president: "The important aspect of this is that the Science Society of China, after having devoted its energies for many years to taxonomic and morphological works, has finally decided to get into the field of experimental biology, and some of the returned fellows of the natural sciences are to be identified with this new development."[47] For Gunn this signaled China's growing interest in an international rather than a local agenda, contributing to the growing cosmopolitan nature of science in Republican China.

The RF's support for the natural sciences came at a critical juncture: China's modern scientific infrastructure and professional norms were being formed. After the mid-1930s, RF scientific funding began to decrease, even as China's Nationalist government began to take on the responsibility of funding its national academic institutions. Although there were other international scientific actors during the

1920s and 1930s, there is no question but that the RF—through its patronage of international networks, its fellowship program, and its direct support for Chinese scientific institutions—was dominant. Laurence Schneider's conclusions, reached almost three decades ago, have not been supplanted by more recent scholarship:

> During the 1920s and 1930s, the Chinese established a highly motivated, self-renewing professional scientific community. The educational and research institutions which structured this community were directly influenced by the experience of American science. . . . This was done primarily through two well-endowed institutions: the Rockefeller Foundation's China Medical Board and the China Foundation for the Promotion of Education and Culture.[48]

Schneider's depiction of a "self-renewing professional scientific community" was prescient. Though they were challenged by war, revolution, and isolation, China's first and second generations of modern scientists not only survived but also replicated themselves in the century to come.

THE SOCIAL SCIENCES

Rockefeller interest in the social sciences lagged behind the natural sciences and medicine in both the United States and China. Philanthropic support began with John D. Rockefeller's first wife Cettie's interest in local welfare, especially projects helping women and children. After her death, in 1918 JDR Sr. endowed the Laura Spelman Rockefeller Memorial with $74 million in her honor. This memorial launched Rockefeller funding for the social sciences, which initially was a controversial endeavor. Within ten years, however, the impact of this fund in the United States was so great that its director, Beardsley Ruml, became known as "the father of the social sciences" in the United States. In 1929, the memorial was merged into the RF as the Division of Social Sciences.

World War I provided an impetus for the growth of the empirically oriented social sciences. The Laura Spelman Rockefeller Memorial began a Rockefeller tradition of funding national centers of applied social science research that continues to this day, including the Social Science Research Council, the National Bureau of Economic Research, and the Brookings Institution, as well as key university departments in a core group of universities, including Columbia, Yale, and Chicago. The dominance of Rockefeller funding is illustrated by the Social Science Research Council; 92 percent of its funding came from the memorial and the RF during the period 1924–40. The impact of Rockefeller funding on the development of social sciences in the United States during the first half of the twentieth century was considerable. The focus was threefold: supporting the strongest individuals, encouraging work that was development oriented or applied, and strengthening the empirical or experiential basis for the social sciences.[49] The philosophical orientation was conservative—in the post-Depression era, the RF emphasized social research that would lead to economic stabilization and a better-governed and -organized society.

In addition to the Laura Spelman Rockefeller Memorial and the RF itself, a third organization—the Institute of Pacific Relations (IPR), played an important role in Rockefeller-related China philanthropy in the social sciences. In 1925, JDR Jr. had led the way with a personal grant to help establish the IPR, which exemplified many of his own internationalist values. For example, JDR Jr. approved of his own son John's participation in an IPR Conference in Kyoto at the end of his 1929 Asia trip. By 1945, the IPR had received more money from a variety of Rockefeller institutions than any other source, and projects related to China accounted for more than half its total expenditures.[50]

Western ideas in economics, international relations, and politics had been introduced to China through many translations, but the modern social science disciplines were just being established in the early 1910s. The National Peking University inaugurated the first economics and political science departments in 1913. Sociology, conversely, had its start at the missionary-sponsored Saint John's College in 1905, with Shanghai Baptist establishing the first sociology department in 1913. It is likely that the missionary emphasis on sociology grew out of the social survey work of the YMCA. The new Republican government needed to train lawyers, civil servants, and businessmen; thus the emphasis of Chinese universities on law, politics, and economics. At the missionary colleges, and most of the governmental ones as well, the curriculum was imported from the West, most of the books were in English, and all the societal examples were based on American or European experience. In China, as in the United States during the first two decades of the twentieth century, research was primarily library based, not experiential.[51]

That the infusion of Rockefeller funding to China was primarily designed to make the social sciences more empirical and more applied made a significant difference in two disciplines, sociology and economics. (There is no record of Rockefeller support for political science.) The thrust from the beginning was, as one writer later put it, to "Chinafy" the social sciences.[52]

The first Rockefeller social science initiative came in 1925, when the Institute of Social and Religious Research, privately funded by JDR Jr., sent a Commission of Social Research to China. It recommended that an Institute of Social and Economic Research be established at Yanjing University. For reasons that are not clear, the funding went instead to the China Foundation for the Promotion of Education and Culture. But three years later, the Laura Spelman Rockefeller Memorial provided a seven-year grant of $140,000 to Yanjing for what became a

College of Applied Social Sciences. According to the Yanjing University historian Philip West, from 1928 to 1936, Rockefeller funding "covered more than half the operating costs of Yanjing's social science program."[53]

By this time, Yanjing University had already established its dominance in sociology and had growing strength in economics; one-fourth of all the sociology courses in China in 1924 were taught at Yanjing, while no Chinese government universities taught sociology. John Stewart Burgess and Sidney Gamble led the Yanjing Sociology Department, and John Bernard Tayler led the Economics Department. All three foreigners sought to apply their disciplinary training to China's major societal challenges. The social surveys of Burgess and Gamble still stand as important documentation of urban life in China in the 1920s, and Tayler's focus on rural industries was one of the intellectual strands that led to the Industrial Cooperative Movement.

The most lasting accomplishment of these academics was to hire outstanding young returned-Chinese scholars, who built strong departments and trained successive generations of young social scientists. Xu Shilian (Leonard S. Hsu, PhD, University of Iowa, 1923) was the first Chinese professor in the social sciences, a sociologist and political activist who led the social survey wing of sociology and quickly became dean. With multiyear Rockefeller funding in hand, additional faculty joined the departments, and graduate training and international study expanded.

Wu Wenzao (PhD, Columbia, 1929) was hired in 1930, and he infused the curriculum with European and American sociological theory even as he directed research toward more locally based community studies in North China. The internationally renowned sociologists Robert Park and Alfred Radcliffe-Brown, both from the University of Chicago, were among those invited as visiting professors with funding from a Rockefeller grant. As Wu's students were thus exposed to both local research opportunities and increasingly sophisticated methodology, they were equipped to go on to become China's next generation of leading sociologists, also receiving their PhDs from leading American and British institutions. Most notable was Fei Xiaotong (Yanjing, 1933; PhD, London School of Economics and Political Science, 1938), who always attributed his interest in community field studies, rather than library research, to the influence of Robert Park. His landmark studies of peasant life in China influenced generations of sociologists and policymakers. As a leading public intellectual in the early 1950s, he quickly came under the fire of the Chinese Communist Party, but he reemerged in the 1980s to lead a renaissance in China's sociology and anthropology.[54]

A second center of excellence for the social sciences, in this case economics, was Nankai University in Tianjin. As we have seen earlier in the chapter, Nankai University was the first Chinese institution supported by the RF, initially in the natural sciences. But Nankai's Economics Department was also able to attract funding from the IPR that eventually led to significant funding from the RF itself. This IPR funding enabled Nankai to compete successfully (against Peking institutions) in hiring several well-educated Chinese economists to its faculty in the late 1920s, including He Lian (Franklin Ho, PhD, Yale, 1926) and Fang Xianting (H. D. Fong, PhD, Yale, 1929). Under He's leadership, the Nankai Institute of Economics was created, and appeals to support this larger endeavor were quickly made to the RF. The proposal was tailored to the known interests of the foundation: "to teach economics with special reference to Chinese problems and to vitalize teaching by research."[55] Nankai received a grant of $75,000 over three years and created the first graduate program in economics in China. As a result, the institute grew to a maximum staff of thirty-two, including eleven professors. Several had American PhDs, and others received RF grants for training in the United States. A master's program was created, and the growing research resulted in the creation of several journals. Sixty graduate students were recruited from 1935 to 1948. Throughout the 1930s, the RF provided half the funding for the Nankai Institute of Economics.[56]

This grant to Nankai was the second RF grant in the social sciences to a developing country (the first was to Beirut University). Decades later, the Nankai program was pointed to as a "forerunner of the social-science component of the foundation's University Development Program launched thirty years later." The RF's objective paralleled those in other countries: "to build and maintain a center of excellence to serve all of China."[57] Although He and others at Nankai had begun as macroeconomists interested in national economic indexes, their research agenda shifted as the RF began its focus on rural reconstruction.

Several recent evaluations of the historic role of Nankai's Institute of Economics testify to its dominance in the field of economics in Republican China and the impact of Rockefeller funding. Yung-chen Chiang concludes that "it was the Rockefeller money that propelled Nankai to become the foremost center of economic research in China."[58] In describing the RF-funded economics programs at Yanjing, Nankai, and the University of Nanjing, Paul Trescott concludes that the work was not derivative but rather was focused on China, noting the focus on "research and teaching on matters related to China," and the emphasis on developmental economics at a time when these topics were not receiving much attention in the West.[59]

AGRICULTURAL SCIENCES AND ECONOMICS

Since the 1940s, the RF has been best known for "the green revolution," the improvement of crop yields in Latin America and Asia through plant breeding. Twenty years earlier, John D. Rockefeller Jr.'s International Education

Board (IEB) began the first international Rockefeller program in agricultural sciences—in China, at the University of Nanjing, a missionary college. The IEB was created in 1923 by JDR Jr., and was led by Wickliffe Rose, the former director of the RF's International Health Board. (After expending its capital of approximately $20 million, the work of the IEB was folded into the Natural Science Division of the RF in 1928.) Although oriented toward Europe, Rose brought an international perspective to his work and encouraged Cornell University, a leader in American agricultural economics and science, to expand its horizons. Simultaneously, John Reisner, a Cornell University graduate and head of the University of Nanjing's College of Agriculture and Forestry, approached Cornell with a plea for support in the field of plant breeding. Thus began a six-year program (1925–31) of collaboration between the two institutions funded by the IEB, whereby Cornell sent specialists in plant breeding who worked with the best Chinese species, resulting in improvement in wheat, sorghum, soybeans, and millet.

In his study *The Stubborn Earth: American Agriculturalists on Chinese Soil, 1898–1937*, Randall Stross, who is generally critical of the American agricultural influence in China, is nonetheless positive about this Cornell connection: "The Cornell professors held to their institution's promise to emphasize the training of Chinese experts. Gains were made in plant breeding work, and the Americans were quite unassuming. They simply wanted to provide China with the most improved crops possible, while causing the least possible disruption of traditional practices." Stross saves his criticism for the "timidity" in the IEB's decision not to increase its agricultural funding to the University of Nanjing nor to the leading Chinese government institution, the National Central University, also in Nanjing. The IEB shied away from these funding opportunities, presumably because of the unsettled political situation at the time.[60] In contrast, the RF had decided to increase its support for the natural sciences in China, including funding the National Central University.

In addition to its work in agricultural sciences, the University of Nanjing developed a strong program in agricultural economics under the leadership of J. Lossing Buck. A visit with Buck in 1928 by J. B. Condliffe, research director of the IPR, led first to funding by the IPR and subsequently by the RF. Buck's studies, *Chinese Farm Economy* and *Land Utilization in China*, both of which drew on extensive surveys conducted by Chinese colleagues, became classics in the field of China's agricultural economics. Most important, the University of Nanjing greatly expanded its faculty and educational programs. Rural cooperative programs were established in several locations, most notably in the nearby town of Wujiang. The primary emphasis was very much on research; institutional reports claimed that by 1931, some 30,000 articles had been published in 350 Chinese journals. By 1934, the faculty included 34 instructors, many of whom continued teaching despite the dislocations of World War II. Altogether, 194 students had received bachelor's degrees and 17 had received master's degrees in agricultural economics by 1945.[61]

Stross's assessments of the University of Nanjing's programs in economics and agricultural sciences is decidedly negative, emphasizing their failure to address issues of land tenancy and the effective distribution of new seeds and agricultural techniques. Conversely, the economist Paul Trescott finds Stross too cynical, arguing that the RF and Buck successfully introduced agricultural studies as a "resource for practical instruction and hands-on development" at a time when Chinese universities still cultivated the traditional image of a detached theoretical scholar.[62] Both perspectives will be relevant when we examine the RF's rural reconstruction program in the next chapter.

CHINA STUDIES IN THE UNITED STATES

Even as "missionaries of science" dominated the Rockefeller agenda in China, Rockefeller philanthropists were also encouraging the American study of China and the Chinese language. This humanistic work had its origins in the 1920s, when both the General Education Board and the IEB provided significant funding for the Oriental Institute of the University of Chicago. Although the Oriental Institute emphasized archaeology in Egypt and the Middle East, Asia also received some attention. The humanistic programs of the General Education Board and the IEB were incorporated into the new Humanities Division of the RF in 1928. In that same year, the RF funded the first American conference on promoting the study of Chinese culture, which was convened by the American Council of Learned Societies.

By the early 1930s, Rockefeller Trustees embraced humanistic inquiry as central to international understanding: "Ignorance of the cultural background of another people is at the root of many misunderstandings that are as harmful internationally as political and economic differences. That ignorance can be steadily lessened by an interchange of cultural values, by discovery of common origins for diversified national ideas and ideals and by the interpretation of one cultural group to another."[63] China and Japan emerged as the most important international focus of the new Humanities Division.

One impetus for this priority was the recognition that Asian studies were quite advanced in European universities. Rockefeller surveys noted the absence of comparable American programs and pledged financial support to introduce the serious study of both China and Japan in American universities. Working with the American Council of Learned Societies, the RF funded programs for

Chinese language study and Chinese libraries at ten universities, including Harvard, Columbia, Cornell, the University of Washington, Chicago, and California, throughout the 1930s and early 1940s. Of particular note was the attention to building Asian library collections and encouraging new pedagogy for teaching Chinese. Beginning in 1932 and continuing for almost a decade, the RF funded the East Asian Collection at the Library of Congress, the first premier American resource center on Asia. It was led by the distinguished pioneering Sinologist, Arthur Hummel, whose seminal *Eminent Chinese of the Ch'ing Period* was also funded by the RF. Another basic resource on Chinese history funded by the RF was Karl Wittfogel's massive translation of Chinese dynastic histories. Derk Bodde's translations of more contemporary Chinese authors, notably Hu Shi and Feng Youlan, were also funded.[64]

By the mid-1930s, the RF had decided that Asian language proficiency required long-term residency in China and Japan. As David Stevens, director of the Humanities Division, wrote: "Young scholars willing to devote their lives to the difficult task of language control require the encouragement of financial support throughout a training period devoted almost exclusively to that purpose of 3–5 years."[65] A fellowship program was inaugurated, and the young John King Fairbank was one of its first beneficiaries.[66] These RF language, library, and scholarship programs for Asian studies created what are today called "area study" programs. Stevens's contributions to these endeavors is considered so substantial that he has been termed the "patron saint" of East Asian Studies.[67]

Not until after World War II did the U.S. government and the Ford Foundation begin their substantial contributions to China studies. These later programs responded to America's growing security concerns in Asia and the advent of the Cold War era. The earlier Rockefeller initiatives were more purely humanistic in motivation, stressing the cross-fertilization of ideas and languages, and the importance of international cultural exchange.

CHARACTERISTICS OF THE ROCKEFELLER PRESENCE IN REPUBLICAN CHINA

By the end of the Nanjing decade, Rockefeller philanthropy in China had helped to establish a state-of-the-field American intellectual presence in the natural sciences, sociology, and economics as well as the premier medical college in Asia. In the United States, moreover, it had sponsored the beginnings of serious American study of China. As its programs unfolded during its first two decades in China, they came to embody a geographically sprawling elite intellectual presence. Instead of funding a single university like the University of Chicago, as had once been envisioned, the RF came to provide support for scores of different institutions in China, a multiple-campus American university without walls. By 1937, more than sixty institutions in thirteen provinces had received RF funding. Most were in the major urban centers of eastern China, but the many missionary institutions in China's interior extended the RF's geographic range.

The comprehensive nature of the RF's intellectual presence in China, coupled with its scale, contrasts with its programs in Europe, Latin America, and South Asia during the same era. In no other country, except the United States, did the RF underwrite so many disciplines or expend such largesse. In comparison with the expenditure of $54 million in China by 1950, grants to the United Kingdom, the second-largest recipient overall, were less than $10 million, and those to Japan, the second-largest country in Asia, were only $2 million.

The RF's wider international role is nonetheless important to the China story, both because of programmatic overlap and because China became linked to the emerging new transnational networks in medicine, the natural sciences, and public health. RF officials were key to this process. Richard Pearce and Alan Gregg, the successive directors of the RF Division of Medical Education (renamed the Division of Medical Sciences in 1930) from 1919 to 1951, spent significant time in China. They were continuously involved in transmitting ideas across the foundation's many country programs. In Asia, Latin America, and Europe, the foundation's International Health Division focused on disease eradication programs, created schools of hygiene to train public health workers, and worked closely with foreign governments in developing national and local public health institutions. Through its Division of Medical Education, the RF endeavored to reform medical education in Europe, Latin America, and Asia by introducing Flexnerian "scientific medicine," with its Johns Hopkins model and emphasis on full-time teaching and clinical research. Outside China, the most ambitious such undertaking in Asia was in Thailand, at Siriraj Hospital Medical School, where the emphasis, like PUMC, was on elite medical training. During the 1920s and 1930s, the RF also worked closely with the League of Nations, especially its Health Organization.

The RF's overarching pre–World War II international priorities were epidemic control, public health institutions, medical education, and the natural sciences. Recent studies of many recipient countries reveal a wide variety of philanthropic approaches within this broad agenda. Local cultures and political, economic, and social systems had a significant effect upon the transplanted Rockefeller models, giving rise to differentiated results.[68]

This was especially true in China. The success of the RF's first model, a Johns Hopkins in China, was contingent upon raising the level of the natural sciences in key missionary and Chinese universities. The focus on the natural sciences that followed responded to the rapid growth in China's modern science infrastructure and the passions of Roger Greene and Gist Gee. These country-based philanthropists extended the fairly narrow vision of medical education to encompass strengthening the natural sciences at key missionary and Chinese institutions. Greene and Gee also recognized the growing importance of Chinese professional societies and professional collaboration by enabling the RF to participate in, and financially support, some of the most important groups of that era. Even though the RF had given public health in China short shrift, John Grant's work in both urban and rural health care influenced not only the Nationalist government but also both the RF's and the League of Nations' work in rural health elsewhere in Asia. As we shall see, the rural health care model also influenced the People's Republic of China. Almost accidental programs in the social sciences led to pioneering Chinese economics and sociology research. The University of Nanjing's work in agriculture, Nankai's work in economics, and Yanjing's work in urban sociology and rural industry began to open the eyes of Rockefeller philanthropists to China's social and economic inequities.

Despite the changing intellectual trends in the United States and the evolution of new programs in China, the RF's strategy remained consistent across all its programs: building institutional capacity in selected disciplines *in* China, elite training, and professionalizing the modern disciplines. This strategy became the standard RF strategy for most of the twentieth century and had a great influence on post–World War II American international philanthropy and governmental development assistance programs.

Building institutional capacity involved several different approaches. PUMC illustrates the first paradigm: a model institution. The second was disciplinary development: natural and social science departments within promising Chinese and missionary universities. Given this early stage in China's modern higher education system, the main challenge was identifying qualified Chinese leaders. Unlike the missionary movement, the RF never envisioned relying on more than a small coterie of expatriates. Implementing their vision required patience and a several-decade funding commitment for Chinese graduate study, professional networks, and scientific research.

Graduate training across many disciplines was provided by the RF's fellowship program, which began in 1914. By 1951, this program had provided approximately 350 graduate fellowships for Chinese to study abroad in the fields of medicine, public health, the natural and social sciences, and the humanities (only a few). By supporting only graduate-level training (post-MD, in the case of physicians), the program differed from the larger Boxer Indemnity Fellowship Program, which also provided undergraduate scholarships. Rockefeller grantees received their baccalaureate or medical education in China, and their fellowships were tied to very specific professional positions upon return to China. These individuals, who were both more mature and more vested in China's domestic educational structure, experienced an easier and more productive reentry into China than many other returnees.[69]

The RF kept close track of both its fellowship recipients and its grantees in China. Several patronage networks evolved during this period. The premier medical network was, of course, that of William Welch at Johns Hopkins and Simon Flexner at the Rockefeller Institute: They selected the American faculty for PUMC positions, found them jobs back in the United States, and placed young Chinese graduates in appropriate American medical institutions. Franklin McLean, the first PUMC director, who became head of the University of Chicago Medical School, also encouraged a cadre of Chicago faculty to become active in China medical work.

In the natural sciences, Paul Monroe of Columbia University played a pivotal role. We have seen that the presidents of both Nankai University and National Central University studied with him at Columbia, so it is not surprising that he singled out their institutions for special attention. But his presence at Columbia, where many of the Chinese Boxer Indemnity Scholars trained, also gave him good access to many promising young Chinese intellectuals, and he was able to assist in directing them back to work in China. Additionally, Roger Greene connected both the RF and the China Foundation to the emerging China-based groups of scientists and social scientists. He and Gist Gee kept careful track of the science faculty in China and helped direct them toward research funding or fellowship opportunities.

In his study of the social sciences in China, Yung-chen Chiang is critical of this patronage network, which emerged between returned scholars and these foundation personnel. He notes that John Condliffe of the Institute of Pacific Relations prepared a map of social scientists and institutions in the late 1920s that continued to influence the funding decisions of Selskar Gunn in the mid-1930s. Chiang observes that these United States–China patronage networks became overly exclusive. A traditional Chinese collegial network was disturbed by the competition between members for external grants and foreign associations.

Chiang is right to critique the array of Rockefeller-affiliated and -interlocked organizations, each of which had a presence in China. The Spelman Memorial was the senior Rockefeller's personal tribute to his wife before it was folded into the RF. The Institute of Social and Religious Research and the International Education Board were both personal philanthropies of John D. Rockefeller Jr. Likewise, the IPR was one of Junior's personal philanthropies before its funding was taken over by the RF. The China Foundation for the Promotion of Education and Culture did not receive Rockefeller funding, but Greene directed its programs for a decade, resulting in considerable programmatic overlap with the RF's own support for the sciences in China. Overlapping staffs and interlocking directorates controlled the flow of Rockefeller money to China. No wonder it was hard to determine where Rockefeller influence began or ended.[70] There is no question but that this overlay of Rockefeller patronage networks steered Rockefeller resources toward certain institutions and individuals and away from others.

Despite Chiang's concern about these exclusive networks, he also pointed out that ties to these American foundations gave Chinese intellectuals subtle power as well: "Clients manipulate patrons as much as patrons manipulate clients."[71] No doubt influenced by foundation priorities, returned scholars also sought funding for the research agendas developed as graduate students in the United States or Europe. This reinforced the ties between young Chinese scholars and the Americans who trained them, widening the network of Sino-American intellectual relations. RF funding did not appear to be a political negative, but rather something of a prize. As Laurence Schneider, who has written authoritatively about biology in China, notes: "In my research in and around this area, I never found an intellectual, politician, academic administrator, or scientist who expressed concern about taking money from an RF-funded agency. Indeed, concerns were limited to the question of who got the money and for what project."[72]

In addition to graduate training, the RF emphasized research funding in China, paralleling its many efforts to support scientific research around the world. The lens through which it evaluated promising institutions was whether or not there was a capacity for high-quality research, thus inevitably narrowing the range of qualified institutions. Although the RF repeatedly stated its intention to diversify its funding away from missionary institutions to encompass more Chinese government universities, in fact it was slow to do so, in part because those research facilities and personnel were so underdeveloped (see appendix A). Support for missionary hospitals and medical colleges tapered off in the early 1930s but was not replaced by support for Chinese medical institutions, in part because of the shift in foundation priorities to scientific research. Most Chinese institutions struggled with funding and teaching; few were able to mount significant research programs.

The perception that some Chinese universities were training radical students was also of concern. For example, in 1931 Selskar Gunn reported that Peking National University's president told him of "the immature minds of students," resulting in a "great deal of Communism." Nor was there any significant research.[73] Perhaps Gunn was also influenced by the fact that Peking University's modest science program was primarily influenced by German science.[74] At any rate, only in the waning days of the Republican period did Peking University receive a small grant of $2,000 from the RF.[75] Likewise, Gunn was not inclined to support Qinghua University, even though it was "far less Marxist than Beida." This was in part because it was already well funded (the China Medical Board had contributed to its biology program in the 1920s) and partly because, as he reported, there is "much trouble going on" and there was not much research work in the social sciences. Therefore, "I believe that there is no opportunity at the present time for any serious consideration of RF aid to Tsing Hua [Qinghua] in either Natural or Social Sciences."[76] Several years later, Gunn did bring Qinghua's engineering program into the RF's rural reconstruction program.

Despite his persistent critiques, Selskar Gunn frequently wrote about the Chinese universities he visited and began a plan to expand RF support for two additional universities—Wuhan University and Zhejiang University.[77] The fact that this never materialized, coupled with the lack of significant involvement with either Peking University or Qinghua University, two of China's premier universities, reveals the limitations of Rockefeller influence.

To be sure, the universities that Rockefeller funding did support became the most important centers for medical and natural and social science research during the 1930s, in part because of Rockefeller funding. The bibliographies of articles and books published also makes clear how much of the RF-funded research was relevant to China's own population and resource needs. This research was distinct to China, and highly relevant to its future development—whether it was on the Chinese flora and fauna at National Central, China's rural industry at Yanjing, or the Chinese pharmacopoeia, nutrition, and endemic contagious diseases at PUMC.

This was the era in which modern professionals and their associations came into being in China. With attributes based on expertise, ethics, autonomy, and a degree of self-regulation, they were permitted by the Nationalist government, which also periodically tried to control them.[78] As these first- and second-generation modern intellectuals created their own institutions and professional societies, American intellectual models—whether Flexnerian medicine or the empirical social sciences—coupled with American funding, extended some measure of cultural intellectual influence. Western associational models of professional societies and scientific norms were especially influential and were reinforced by the popularity of study in the United States.[79] American-funded research was attractive because it enabled young Chinese scholars to begin to establish their own intellectual independence, and, through the growing number of Chinese professional journals, their own voice. As their ability to contribute and then shape the Chinese intellectual agenda increased, many advanced to become the intellectual leaders of China's research and university system.

Young Chinese scholars assumed disciplinary leadership at institutions such as Nankai or fairly quickly replaced the Westerners who had hired them at institutions such as Yanjing and PUMC. The Rockefeller programs would not have existed without a Xu Shilian in sociology, a He Lian in economics, a Tan Jiazhen in biology, or a Zhong Huilan (C. H. Chung) in tropical medicine. Nor would the implementation of John Grant's public health vision have been realized without the presence of a Chen Zhiqian or a Liu Ruiheng. What Yung-chen Chiang concludes in his study of the social sciences was even more applicable to the medical and natural sciences: "Thus, while Chinese social scientists had to accept the research agenda and methodology defined for them by American philanthropies, they were by no means passive partners. The more prominent among them even participated in the formulation of the research agenda and the determination of the methodology."[80] Given the onset of the Sino-Japanese War in 1937, China's civil war, and the complete break with the United States by 1951, there was hardly time to become overly dependent on their American mentors.

A further reason not to overstate this American influence is that there were numerous alternative European and Japanese intellectual paradigms, including Marxism. The twenty-year period between the laying of PUMC's cornerstone in 1917 and the outbreak of the Sino-Japanese War in 1937 witnessed an explosion in the development of China's modern educational and research infrastructure. In addition to the RF, other American, British, French, and German institutions sought linkages with, and gave support to, China's burgeoning academic community. Chinese students returning from study in Europe and Japan as well as the United States brought distinctly different experiences in the study of science and medicine. By the early 1930s, the Chinese government itself was annually committing significant resources to build the nation's scientific infrastructure, especially engineering. Within this context, the RF was the largest external funder. Its support linked key Chinese universities and leading scientists with their counterparts in the United States and to some degree in Europe as well.

That a distinctly modern, distinctly Chinese intellectual agenda—coupled with international linkages in medicine, science, and the social sciences—developed during the formative years of China's modern university development was to have lasting effects. Given that Americans controlled the funds and were the more advanced scientific partners, most of these linkages can be characterized as patron-client relations. Even so, as we have seen, the clients or recipients were often innovators as well. The transpacific network of scholars who became an accepted part of the intellectual culture of the United States and the Republic of China illustrates well the cultural internationalism of this era. If religion had dominated this relationship in the nineteenth and early twentieth centuries, American medicine, science, and higher education prevailed during the 1920s and 1930s. The RF did not replace the missionary role, but it nurtured the secular intellectual relationships that have dominated Sino-American cultural relationships ever since.

John D. Rockefeller Sr. lived to see both Standard Oil and the RF dominate American commercial and cultural relations with China. His death did not go unnoticed in China. On May 25, 1937, the *Peiping Chronicle* announced the passing of the "Croesus of the Modern World" at the age of ninety-seven.[81] Commemorative ceremonies were undoubtedly held at the University of Chicago and Rockefeller University, the two largest American institutions created by his wealth. Yet it is doubtful that those events could have matched in ritual and solemnity the memorial held halfway around the world at PUMC, his third-largest institution.[82]

At the PUMC memorial, faculty members, students, and many guests gathered to remember their benefactor in a modern auditorium within an elaborate Chinese-style pavilion with green-tiled roofs and a double-hipped row of colorfully carved eaves *(figure 2.1)*. The Chinese service combined Eastern and Western traditions. A fine life-size portrait by John Singer Sargent (later lost during the Cultural Revolution) was arranged ancestor-style on the stage while Chopin's "Funeral March" pealed from the organ, reminding everyone that this space was often used for Christian worship services. Attending the ceremony was a microcosm of the Sino-American cultural community—American missionaries, educators, scientists, and diplomats, along with American-educated Chinese intellectuals and young Chinese medical students. The platform party included Chinese and American dignitaries who represented the origins and the future challenges of the Rockefeller scientific and medical programs in China.

It was fitting that the only faculty representative in the platform party was Preston Maxwell, formerly of the Scottish Presbyterian Mission hospital in Fujian, one of the original medical missionaries on PUMC's staff. John Leighton Stuart, also a former Presbyterian missionary and later to become U.S. ambassador to China, was there in his capacity as president of Yanjing University, certainly the strongest American university in China at that time. Without RF funding, Yanjing would not have become China's preeminent biology and sociology institution. Henry Houghton (Johns Hopkins, 1905), a professor of medicine at the University of Chicago, had recently returned to China for his second stint as director of PUMC. Not only did he represent Hopkins and Chicago, two key Rockefeller institutions, he was also well trusted by the Rockefeller family; he had personally coordinated the rescue of Lucy Aldrich from Chinese bandits (see chapter 1). In 1941, it was his turn to be captured. Houghton was incarcerated in Peking by the Japanese from 1941 to 1945.

Leading the Chinese mourners was the distinguished philosopher and university educator Hu Shi, a close adviser and occasional critic, who presided in his capacity as the current chair of the PUMC Board of Trustees. After the Communist victory in 1949, Hu alternated between the United States and Taiwan, becoming head of its Academia Sinica during the early 1960s. The PUMC alumni were represented by Hu Chuankui (PUMC, 1927), one of the first Chinese graduates appointed to faculty status. Although he suffered greatly during the Cultural Revolution because of his PUMC identity, Hu served as president of the prestigious Peking Medical University for three decades, from 1948 to 1979.

John D. Rockefeller Jr. received condolence cables from many of China's political leaders. His son JDR 3rd received perhaps the most meaningful one, from the

78

PUMC alumni—a simple, linguistically awkward cable of gratitude: "Through Mr. Rockefeller came our opportunity and we are grateful. PUMC Alumni. June 4, 1937."[83] With the passing of the senior Rockefeller, it was appropriate that the third John D. Rockefeller be acknowledged; as a trustee of the China Medical Board since 1930, he was already navigating the political shoals of Rockefeller Foundation–PUMC politics, Chinese nationalism, and Chinese Communism.

FIGURE 2.1. The Memorial Service for John D. Rockefeller at Peking Union Medical College. The portrait of Rockefeller is by John Singer Sargent. Article from *Peiping Chronicle*, May 25, 1937. *Photograph courtesy of the Rockefeller Archive Center.*

CHAPTER 3

POLITICS

Encountering Nationalism and Communism

John D. Rockefeller 3rd's grand world tour in 1929 took him to Russia, Japan, and China, introducing him to warlords, Nationalists, and Communists—Russian Communists and stories about Chinese Communists.[1] As a serious and articulate young man of twenty-three, he filled his diary with page after page of description and commentary on the political issues and personalities of the day. This early exposure to the intensity of Chinese nationalism, resentment against Japan, and competition between the Nationalists (Guomindang, GMD) and the Chinese Communist Party (CCP) introduced young John to the key East Asian issues of his lifetime. He developed an interest in both China and Japan and a personal aesthetic appreciation of Asian culture that would inform his role as a member of the China Medical Board, as a trustee of the Rockefeller Foundation (RF) and eventually its chairman, and as the founder of the Asia Society and the Asian Cultural Council.

JDR 3rd stayed abreast of Chinese politics during the next two decades, traveling there again in 1947 to judge for himself the status of the conflict between the GMD and the CCP. For if politics had been almost irrelevant in the founding of PUMC and the expansion of the RF's scientific programs in the 1920s, Rockefeller philanthropists and Chinese beneficiaries would find themselves increasingly drawn into the vortex of Republican China.

What is significant about the 1930s and 1940s is that neither multiple wars nor the shifting political fortunes of the Nationalists, including a likely Communist victory, deterred either the Rockefeller family or the RF from its China mission. As the Chinese historian Zi Zhongyun writes, "Rockefeller's main characteristic was its persistence despite China's turbulent conditions."[2] In this persistence, it mirrored a broad spectrum of China's American constituents—missionaries, educators, and businessmen—whose desire to influence China's future out-weighed concerns about war or politics or even Communism.[3]

Implicit in the ongoing Rockefeller China ventures was a desire to influence China, to be sure, but also a fundamental belief in the values of cultural inter-nationalism, defined by Raymond Fosdick as universality—"the conception that civilization and the intellectual life of men represent a co-operative achievement."[4] Akira Iriye describes the many challenges to this idealism during the 1930s, espe-cially the rise of both fascism and communism. He also writes that "one is struck by the efforts of internationalists to try, against all odds, to keep alive the flames of their hope."[5] Thus, despite the twin challenges of nationalism and commu-nism, Rockefeller China programs took advantage of the fact that the Nationalist era offered many opportunities for nongovernmental intellectual collaboration. And Rockefeller support for the Institute of Pacific Relations provided a venue for dialogue between American, Chinese, and Japanese intellectuals on the difficult security and public policy issues of the day.

For the Rockefeller China enterprise the period reveals the many layers of its increasingly mature and complex China engagement. Chinese beneficia-ries of Rockefeller funding came into their own as leaders of the Nationalists' Public Health Administration, university social science departments, and rural reconstruction projects. Some of the graduates of Peking Union Medical College (PUMC) were hired as assistant professors at the college, while others became hospital directors across China. Their voices became differentiated from their American sponsors; some led the growing Chinese critique of PUMC and its elitist medical model. But all too quickly, the Sino-Japanese War dispersed many to China's southwest. And as World War II ended and the civil war between the Nationalists and Communists intensified, these Western-oriented professionals faced the wrenching decision of whether to flee or remain in Mao's China. At the same time and in collaboration with these Chinese colleagues, the RF's China representatives—especially Roger Greene, John Grant, and Selskar Gunn—wrestled with the challenge of Chinese nationalism and a skepticism toward the Nationalist government even as they seized upon opportunities to engage the foundation more deeply in China's economic and social future.

In New York, the retirement in 1929 of RF president George Vincent, long closely associated with the China Medical Board and PUMC, brought first Max Mason (1929–36) and then Raymond Fosdick (1936–48) into the presidency. Each sought to broaden the RF's influence beyond PUMC, to put his own impri-matur upon a new Rockefeller relationship with China. During Mason's presi-dency, the RF for the first time deployed the humanities as part of its China portfolio while also developing an ambitious program in rural reconstruction. During Fosdick's tenure, throughout the Sino-Japanese War and World War II, the RF sought to protect its earlier investments in people and institutions. After

World War II, Fosdick and his staff pursued a new China agenda even as the RF made a huge final financial investment in PUMC's future.

John D. Rockefeller Jr.'s influence on the RF's China policies—indeed, his paternalistic micromanagement—prevailed throughout this entire period. At the same time, his eldest son began to come into his own as the Rockefeller whose philanthropic career is most associated with Asia. Both Rockefellers persistently defended their vision of PUMC, even when they were at odds with PUMC's Chinese trustees or Rockefeller senior staff and trustees. More than his father, JDR 3rd paid close attention to the fortunes of Chiang Kai-shek and the conflicts between the GMD and the CCP, beginning with his first trip to China.

John D. Rockefeller 3rd's China Trip, 1929

Because John had traveled extensively in Europe and also served as a League of Nations intern before graduating from Princeton, his graduation trip as a scion of the Rockefeller family needed to be more exotic. He decided to attend an international conference in The Hague and an Institute of Pacific Relations conference in Kyoto, and to travel for six months in Russia, China, and Japan with James G. MacDonald, chairman of the Foreign Policy Association (figure 3.1). John's father was a member and financial supporter of the association, and MacDonald had become a family friend. The purpose of MacDonald's trip was to gain a firsthand impression of Stalin's Russia, Japan's influence in Manchuria, and Chiang Kai-shek's new Nationalist government in China.

MacDonald and Rockefeller traveled to Moscow and Saint Petersburg, overland to Asia by the trans-Siberian railway, and by ship to Manchuria. Border tension along the China Eastern Railway prevented them from directly transiting between Russia and China; it took five days to travel by two ships and rail from Vladivostok to Japan to Korea to Manchuria. In Shenyang (Mukden), they met Zhang Xueliang (Chang Hsueh-liang), a regional warlord who had retained his power base after Chiang Kai-shek's nominal unification of China in 1927. With an American's romantic view of warlords, John found Zhang too conventional: "One thinks of the ruler of Manchuria as a burly war lord, but Chang Hsueh-liang certainly is far from this. He is slight in build, quiet, almost timid, very nice looking, well dressed, bright and intelligent." They discussed possible U.S. loans to Japan for the Manchurian railroad, vehemently opposed by the Chinese Nationalist government. As he reflected on the growing Japanese dominance in Manchuria, observable all around him, Rockefeller recognized that "of course this makes the Chinese sore for they hate to see so much power in the hands of a foreign country—especially the Japanese."[6]

FIGURE 3.1. John D. Rockefeller 3rd at the Ming Tombs, 1929.
Photograph courtesy of the Rockefeller Archive Center.

When they reached Peking, John tried to visit two additional warlords, Yan Xishan and Feng Yuxiang. The American consul general, John V. A. MacMurray, was concerned for their safety, but he supported inquiries through the mayor of Peking and the governor of the district. Both telegraphed Yan and Feng on behalf of Rockefeller and MacDonald, and an invitation to visit was forthcoming. Unfortunately, MacDonald became ill and was not up to the two-day trip by donkey to reach the warlord's lair. JDR 3rd was deeply disappointed: "I did hate to make the decision not to see these two interesting Generals though, when we had the chance right in our hands. They, with Chang Hsueh-liang in Manchuria, make up the main government opposition in North China. An alliance between the three is rumored now."[7]

These encounters underlined for both Rockefeller and MacDonald the fragility of the Nationalist government, which had only recently been established in Nanjing. In the eight years since JDR Jr. had traveled to China, the political scene had changed considerably. In 1927, Sun Yat-sen's successor, Chiang Kai-shek, led the GMD in a series of military campaigns that defeated some warlords and implemented alliances with others, established his capital in Nanjing, and began an ambitious program of state building, ushering in what has been called the Nanjing decade. Visiting Nanjing in the early years of this era, young Rockefeller learned that not only had Chiang Kai-shek not consolidated his hold over Manchuria and North China, but he also faced continuing opposition from his former allies, the Communists.

In Nanjing, John met a number of GMD officials and heard reports about the ongoing struggle between the GMD and the CCP. He was especially intrigued by the minister of industry, commerce, and labor, Kong Xiangxi (H. H. Kung), "who wore Chinese style suits and was a descendant of Confucius." More to the point, he was Chiang Kai-shek's brother-in-law. Kong explained the common origins of the GMD and CCP and the fact that the GMD remained structurally a Leninist party. As John summarized: "KMT [i.e., GMD] is 'the' party and is a lot like the Communist party in Russia. In fact it was with Communist backing that the party [GMD] was started. It was only when the Communists wanted to go too far and wreck the party that the Communists were forced out of the party."[8]

From Sir Frederick Whyte, a British adviser to the Nationalist government, more was learned about the potential strength of the Communists:

> Sir Frederick compared the Kuomintang to the Communist Party and pointed out how the Chinese leaders lacked the moral fervor and the willingness to make personal sacrifice; in other words the Chinese party lacks the driving force which gives Communism its great power. We already had this idea from other sources. . . . In regard to Chiang Kai Shek personally, he said that he was able to inspire loyalty and an able military politician but that he lacked far-reaching vision and frequently left situations unsettled.[9]

These observations in 1929 were ones that endured, becoming more widespread when JDR 3rd returned to China almost twenty years later.

Rockefeller and MacDonald also sought the political views of young Chinese intellectuals, including Hu Shi, one of the Western-educated liberals with whom Rockefeller officials consulted regularly. Hu was critical of the "dictatorship" of the GMD as well as the favoritism shown in government appointments, although he acknowledged that the new system of laws was hopeful. Nonetheless, "Hu Shih seemed quite discouraged admitting that he hadn't the courage to write at all to his foreign friends."[10]

The future role of the great powers in China was perhaps the most hotly contested issue during John's trip. Chinese opposition to foreign treaties and foreign control of China's manufacturing base had prompted the May 30, 1925, incident in China—a strike against Japanese textile mills, which then spread throughout the country. At PUMC, students had joined in the national protests, justifying their action in a letter to Henry Houghton: "Our plan is in no sense anti-foreign nor radical, but to have a peaceful and satisfactory settlement of the Shanghai incident as soon as possible in order to stop any tendency towards injuring the international friendship and world brotherhood for which our medical profession stands." Roger Greene and Henry Houghton kept RF president George Vincent and the Rockefeller family apprised of these developments.[11]

Tension increased further after the Nanjing Incident in 1927, when Chiang Kai-shek's troops killed a number of foreigners during the GMD's occupation of Nanjing, the last stage of what was called his "northern expedition." The Nanjing Incident was especially fresh on the minds of the Standard Oil managers who accompanied John on his trip. During the battle for the control of Nanjing, foreigners took refuge in the Standard Oil compound, Socony (the acronym for Standard Oil Company of New York) Hill, and Western gunboats were brought in to save the lives and property of the foreign community. John himself was staying on Socony Hill, and when he saw foreign warships in the Yangtze River, he mused:

> The boats are there, of course, to protect the lives and property of their
> nationals on shore. It gives the foreigners living in the towns along the river a
> real sense of security having the boats there, too. During the Nanking trouble
> two years ago it was a barrage from the British and American gunboats that
> saved the lives of the foreigners gathered on "Socony Hill": gathered in the
> very house that we were living in. Often, too, the foreigners go and live on the
> gunboats in uncertain times.[12]

Chinese officials with whom Rockefeller met were, not surprisingly, adamant in their advocacy of China's rights as a sovereign nation and their intent to end all vestiges of foreign privilege. The "rights recovery movement" was an important component of Nationalist foreign policy. The foreign minister, Wang Zhengting, was especially vehement in his opposition to the continuation of extraterritoriality and foreign concessions. As John wrote:

> The question of extra-territoriality made Wang sit up and take notice. He seemed
> to feel that it was very important that these privileges be removed. There were
> only six countries which still had these privileges, he said, and three were ready
> to give them up now if the other three would. The three that wouldn't give them
> up were the U.S., France, and Japan, I think. . . . Wang felt it would be a fine
> gesture for these countries to give the rights up now.[13]

Minister Wang—undoubtedly aware of the special relationship between Standard Oil and the GMD, and perhaps in deference to young Rockefeller—allowed that private ships, such as those managed by Standard Oil, would not be subject to any new regulations.

Standard Oil had certainly benefited for decades from the relative stability provided by extraterritoriality and the profitability of the low ad valorem tariff of 5 percent, expanding by the late 1920s from Guangzhou in the south to Sichuan in the west and Heilongjiang in far northeast China. American and Chinese agents were stationed in all China's major cities, managing the shipping, storage, and sale of kerosene. Although disputes over the location of oil depots, landownership, safety issues (kerosene was highly combustible), and local tax disputes were common, the company's early success continued: Chinese industrialists required a regular supply of kerosene, and the kerosene (and its 5-gallon tins) was cheap and popular among the Chinese people. Nonetheless, even Standard Oil was not immune from the periodic boycotts against foreign products and the growing efforts to curtail foreign monopolies. In 1925, four years before JDR 3rd's visit, the GMD, by then in control of South China, tried to end the foreign kerosene monopoly in Guangdong and to create its own firm, the China Petroleum Company. Song Ziwen (T. V. Soong) offered Standard Oil the right to source most of the kerosene to the Chinese company, but only if it paid a higher tariff than that allowed under the treaty system. Standard was prepared to do so, and it finally persuaded Consul General MacMurray to approve this exception to the U.S. tariff policy. Once Standard agreed to pay the higher tariff, the GMD abolished its company, and Standard became the primary supplier of kerosene, and later oil, to the GMD.

This direct GMD relationship proved beneficial for Standard Oil, even though Standard's taxes were initially higher; when overall tariffs were raised several years later, Standard received a discount. In return, Standard usually paid its taxes as a cash advance, providing much-needed foreign exchange for the GMD. A study of Standard in China concluded that its success "lay along the path of least resistance to the forces of nationalism and anti-imperialism," and that because it was the first U.S. company to support the GMD, it later received protection and benefits from the GMD.[14]

Because John was accompanied by Standard Oil officials, he must have had some awareness of this history, but in his diary he expressed no opinion on the subject of either the role of Standard or extraterritoriality. During his meetings with Roger Greene in Peking, he was certainly exposed to an alternative American view; Greene was ardently opposed to the continuation of extraterritoriality. He regularly kept Rockefeller officials in New York apprised of the political situation in China and the political positions he took as RF vice president in Asia.[15]

Greene was born in Japan and served for a number of years in the U.S. Foreign Service in China before joining the Rockefeller enterprise in 1914. He became well known not only for his stated opposition to extraterritoriality but also for his open devotion to this cause. He testified before the U.S. Congress in 1926, arguing for the demise of not just extraterritoriality but also the low tariff structure imposed by the unequal treaties. He consistently opposed gunboat diplomacy, even after the Nanjing Incident, when foreign intervention had saved lives. He made the RF's policy crystal clear in a letter to Acting Secretary of State Joseph Grew, stating that "the Rockefeller Foundation preferred to withdraw its people from Beijing rather than have the U.S. use armed force during nationalist upheavals."[16]

It is not necessarily surprising that John D. Rockefeller Jr. himself took the opposite view. Although he had no official position in Standard Oil, he still moved in American corporate circles and continued to pay attention to Standard's foreign interests. In 1925, he signed a public letter from the New York Chamber of Commerce to President Calvin Coolidge that "advocated the support of any government in China which could command the allegiance of the provinces and protect the treaty rights of foreigners."[17] There is no record as to whether Greene and JDR Jr. were aware of each other's viewpoints. With regard to American foreign policy on this issue, the RF and the Standard Oil Company appeared to move in separate orbits.

JDR 3rd left China well aware of these crosscutting issues. He spent much of his time with Standard Oil managers—staying in their homes, visiting their facilities, and playing golf. His many discussions with them as well as other Americans in China often focused on growing Chinese nationalism, especially on how the Nanjing government was tightening institutional regulations on both foreign universities and corporations. He also came away with a keen awareness of China's grinding poverty. In describing a rickshaw ride around the "really Chinese parts of Nanjing," he observed that

> the average house of the Chinese in the country is a pretty sad affair made of what would appear to be clay and straw—like the bricks in Bible times. They are low, hut-like, one-story affairs and would seem to have only one room with partitions perhaps. The roofs are thatched or of straw matting. Many families live in shelters of mats backed up against a wall or even out in the open. There is no system of sanitation around the houses.[18]

Rockefeller's diary notes programs that addressed these challenges, finding some hope in Yan Yangchu's Mass Education Movement. Knowing of his father's support of Yan, John was pleased to meet him personally at a reception in Peking. He commented favorably on Yan's concept of a "model farm" and "model community," writing:

> Men are to be trained there to be sent around to start similar farms or communities elsewhere, for the whole is entirely practical. Chinese tools and

methods are made more modern and efficient instead of importing the foreign things and substituting them for the Chinese. This last would not be practical over any considerable area on account of the cost involved.[19]

John also visited the Shanghai YMCA, likewise funded by his father, and learned of its urban social projects. Years later, JDR 3rd attributed his interest in creating the Population Council (1952) and the Institute for Agricultural Development (1953) to his exposure to Asia's population pressures and rural challenges during this China trip.

When he returned to New York, young John began to work in his father's office, and he was given family responsibility for the China Medical Board (CMB), which was incorporated separately during the 1928 overall reorganization of Rockefeller philanthropies. The RF's non-PUMC interests in medicine, science, and the social sciences in China were transferred from the CMB to the RF's Division of Medical Sciences and its new Division of Natural Sciences and Division of Social Sciences. From this time forward, there is a growing separation between the affairs of the CMB, on the one hand, and the emerging RF interests in other disciplines in China, especially in the New York offices, on the other. Until the mid-1930s, however, Greene coordinated the increasingly diverse programmatic array in China.

With the 1928 reorganization, the CMB Inc. was provided with an endowment of $12 million to support PUMC; the avowed intent was to make the CMB Inc. fully independent, and to reduce the amount of time and attention that Rockefeller senior staff had to pay to PUMC. In reality, the CMB's income from the endowment was insufficient to cover PUMC's annual budget; the CMB and PUMC continued to be dependent on additional annual appropriations from the RF until 1947, a source of much institutional friction.[20] Moreover, joining John on the supposedly independent CMB board were RF senior staff members (Raymond Fosdick, Alan Gregg, George Vincent, and Richard Pearce). The CMB's offices also remained with the RF (and Standard Oil) at 26 Broadway. JDR 3rd was made secretary of the CMB in 1931, regularly attending its frequent meetings from 1928 until the RF divested its relationship with the CMB in 1947. He would have many opportunities to draw upon his first China experience.[21]

Two examples illustrate the nature of John's early involvement in CMB policies, both related to the declining value of the endowment and resource constraints in light of the Great Depression. Concerned about the CMB's reduced endowment income, the CMB and the RF asked John to prepare a report on this issue. After a year of inquiry with officials of Chase National Bank, National City Bank, Socony-Vacuum, and the U.S. Department of State, JDR 3rd's report reviewed the pending issues of the times—world policies regarding silver currency, the deteriorating Sino-Japanese relationship, and investment opportunities in China. Concluding that short-term gains in China were possible, the risks were also great. Asking "whether to risk the principal in order to insure the income," John recommended a policy of "watchful waiting."[22] The time never came for such an investment.

A more controversial area of JDR 3rd's involvement in CMB policies occurred in the early 1930s, when he and Greene came into conflict over the thorny issue of nationalism: Just how responsive should the CMB and the RF be to PUMC's Chinese trustees? Faced with reducing PUMC's budget, Greene insisted, for budgetary reasons, on making the PUMC's chaplain a part-time position. He was overruled several times by JDR 3rd in consultation with his father. JDR Jr. maintained that his original agreement with the missionary societies had included a formal Christian presence within PUMC, which was otherwise secular in nature. The PUMC Trustees, a Chinese body now led by Zhou Yichun, the former president of Qinghua University and acting chancellor of Yanjing University, supported Greene in strong and no uncertain terms. In the end, however, the Rockefeller family had its way: Greene was forced to resign in 1935. Although young John viewed the foreign management of the Shanghai International Settlement negatively, he did not see PUMC in the same light. Both he and his father still thought of PUMC as a Rockefeller dependency.

Religion and finances were not the only issues here; Greene's rather stern personality and advocacy on many issues had made him persona non grata with the Rockefeller family and foundation leadership for many years, perhaps beginning as early as 1916, when he insisted that the new medical institution not be named the "Rockefeller" Medical College in Peking. The resulting governance crisis with the PUMC Trustees, a distinguished group of Chinese intellectuals whom the RF did not want to antagonize, was so severe that Raymond Fosdick, on the eve of becoming president of the RF, made a special trip to China to consult with each trustee. The end result was an agreement that gave the PUMC Trustees, at least theoretically, authority for all PUMC leadership appointments.[23]

This episode is just one example of the incomplete transfer of authority from New York to China during the 1930s. The appointment of Henry Houghton, who had served as PUMC director from 1921 to 1928 and was a longtime Rockefeller family friend, as Greene's successor renewed the family's PUMC connections. In 1938 and 1940, JDR Jr. sent Houghton lengthy letters with specific budgetary and personnel recommendations. These reiterated Rockefeller's commitment to the Christian character of the medical college and included suggestions for working with the PUMC Trustees: "They should be made not only to *feel* but to assume the responsibility which is rightly theirs."[24] The detailed management prescriptions in both these letters exemplify Rockefeller's well-known micromanagement of institutions in which he had a long-term interest. Both the Rockefeller family and long-term Rockefeller officials continued to exert an outside influence over PUMC and CMB affairs well into the 1950s.

PUBLIC HEALTH, STATE MEDICINE,
AND THE NATIONALIST GOVERNMENT

Given the course of history, it is probably fortuitous that JDR 3rd was exposed to the weakness of the GMD government as a young adult, but he also encountered groups whose members had pinned their hopes for China's future on this Nationalist government. Because Chiang Kai-shek and his wife were Christians, these included many in the missionary community and numerous others who longed for a stable and unified Chinese government. Although the Revolution of 1911 had overthrown the Qing Dynasty, no subsequent government had united China nor significantly improved its economic situation. Japan's modernization and growing economic and political power stood in great contrast to China's weakness. Chiang Kai-shek's consolidation of political power in Nanjing in 1928 offered new hope for Americans seeking to make a contribution to China's development. James Thomson's *While China Faced West* and John Hersey's novel *The Call* depict the many different reform efforts with which Americans were involved.[25] In varying ways American missionaries, educators, and social reformers attempted to improve the social and economic conditions of China's rural areas, at times working in concert with agencies of the Nationalist government.

Starting in the early 1920s, Rockefeller representatives were well acquainted with Sun Yat-sen and other leading members of the GMD, even as they endeavored to maintain collegial relations with the ever-changing government in Peking. Sun was initially treated for terminal cancer at PUMC but decided to spend his last days at home under the care of traditional doctors. His autopsy, an unusual event in 1925, was conducted at PUMC, and a Christian funeral was held in PUMC's auditorium. PUMC faculty (Davidson Black and Paul Stevenson) were asked to assume responsibility for the embalmment of Sun's body in mineral oil, which preserved it for public viewing until it was transferred to Nanjing in 1929.[26]

The first formal connection between PUMC and the GMD after Sun's death occurred during Chiang Kai-shek's Northern Expedition, when Madame Sun Yat-sen asked Greene to send medical relief to wounded soldiers in Wuhan. Her appeal was on behalf of the CCP-dominated left-wing branch of the GMD, which had just been ousted by Chiang. Greene was worried that this involvement "might injure the College in its relations with the northern government," but he was encouraged by mainstream GMD leaders to send a modest relief team. Greene's superiors in New York, however, were greatly concerned that this was a political, not a medical, decision, and that he had acted without approval.[27]

Relations with the leftist GMD proved to be fleeting; Rockefeller-affiliated public health personnel emerged as key players in Chiang Kai-shek's government once he had consolidated power in Nanjing. Ka-che Yip's thorough study—*Health and National Reconstruction in Nationalist China: The Development of Modern*

Health Services, 1928–1937—details the extensive involvement of John Grant, a PUMC professor of public health, and Liu Ruiheng, the PUMC director (in absentia) and a professor of surgery, in establishing and then staffing the Ministry of Health. Yip noted the "tremendous influence that PUMC and through it the RF, wielded over health developments in the Republican period." RF-related personnel "dominated new agencies and shaped policies."[28]

Early in his PUMC tenure, John Grant and his Chinese colleagues and students advocated the state's taking responsibility for national medical services. Their philosophical views owed a debt to medical reformers in Eastern Europe, but their model was based on their own experience in urban and rural China. In 1922, Grant arranged for Yan Huiqing (W. W. Yen), the minister of foreign affairs, and Shi Zhaoji (Alfred Sao-ke Sze), the Chinese ambassador to the United States, to visit William Welch at the Johns Hopkins School of Public Health. Government leadership in public health had become an axiom in Europe and the United States, but in the mid-1920s Grant's students took the role of the state even further. Chen Zhiqian began popularizing the concepts of scientific medicine and state responsibility for a nation's health in the *Binying Weekly*, which first appeared as a supplement to the *Peking World Herald* in 1926 and later to the *Da Gongbao*. State medicine (*gong yi*) was defined as "rendering available to every member of the community, irrespective of any necessary relationship to the conditions of individual payment of all the potentialities of preventive and curative medicine."[29] Grant himself published an important article on state medicine in the *National Medical Journal of China* in 1928, reiterating Chen's arguments calling for the new Nationalist government to take responsibility for curative as well as public health services.[30] This advocacy earned Grant the epithet "medical Bolshevik" in Rockefeller circles.

From PUMC had already come prototypes for state medicine: the Peking Urban Health Demonstration Station and Chen Zhiqian's Dingxian three-tier system of village, township, and county health care—with the most basic level being provided by local paramedical personnel, forerunners of the CCP's barefoot doctors (see chapter 2).[31] Chiang Kai-shek's consolidation of power in Nanjing in 1928 gave Grant and his Chinese colleagues the opportunity to take these models to scale, to create a national health care program. Chen's village health program became one of the models for the rural health service program, which was initiated under the National Health Administration. By 1936, 181 *xian*, or county health centers (out of a total of more than 1,000 *xian*), had been established in twelve provinces.

Grant's years of cultivating China's emerging political leaders paid off; he personally knew all but two individuals in Chiang's first Cabinet. He and his PUMC colleague, Liu Ruiheng, were sufficiently well connected politically to influence the creation of the Ministry of Health and its operating arm, the Central Field

Health Station. And Liu became the first director. As Greene would write to George Vincent, then in his last year as president of the RF, Grant encouraged "his people" to leave PUMC and go into public health service: "He even loaned his secretary to J. Heng Liu, who was de facto minister of health during most of the Nanking decade."[32] PUMC graduates or other physicians who had held RF public health fellowships dominated the ministry's organization, and the RF's International Health Board lent one of its American sanitary engineers, Brian R. Dyer, to the ministry.

In addition to Liu, of particular significance are the roles played by Yang Chongrui (Marion Yang) in creating the National Midwifery School, and Zhu Zhanggeng (C. K. Chu) in leading the Commission on Medical Education. Yang had developed the midwifery training programs in both the Peking Urban Health Station and in Dingxian. She designed a short-term instruction program for traditional midwives that taught them modern aseptic measures—how to wash their hands, cut the umbilical cord with a sterilized instrument, and clean the baby's eyes. Correctly followed, these simple procedures greatly lowered infant mortality. This was the only Rockefeller-funded program that attempted to integrate practitioners of traditional medicine into a modern medical system.

Grant was well aware of the political pitfalls of excessive American involvement and the many crosscurrents in China's medical community: The Anglo-American school vied for influence with the Japanese school and with the Continental school, and all vied with the increasingly active associations representing traditional Chinese practitioners, such as the Institute for National Medicine. Liu Ruiheng was especially vulnerable because of his long association with both PUMC and the Anglo-American school. To stabilize health policy in the new government, Grant sought a more neutral international ally, and he cabled Ludwig Rajchman, then director of the League of Nations' Health Organization, who was visiting Japan, and invited him to China. Thus began a decade of active League involvement in China's health policies.[33]

China's National Health Administration went through many organizational and personnel permutations, and the RF had a complicated relationship with it. Many of Grant's students assumed leading positions, and Grant himself continued as an active adviser. Liu would be forced out on several occasions, a casualty of the faction-ridden politics that characterized Chiang's Public Health Administration, but he remained the most important medical leader until the mid-1940s.[34] But although the RF provided fully half the funding for the international work of the League's Health Organization, the League initially advised the GMD not to accept RF financial support for state health programs. This was because League health advisers in China decried the excessive PUMC and RF influence on China's modern medicine. In their view, elitist, curative medicine would never solve China's medical challenges.

THE CRITIQUE OF ROCKEFELLER MEDICINE

Even as PUMC faculty and graduates provided the leadership for the GMD's Health Ministry, the PUMC educational model was widely criticized throughout the Nanjing Period. The many intellectual crosscurrents of this era are also evident in the resurgence of traditional Chinese medicine, an indication that Western scientific medicine would not become hegemonic in China.

The emphasis on state medicine focused attention on the need to provide health care for China's 400 million people; this clearly had not been the goal of the Rockefeller educators when they created PUMC. In the eyes of some Chinese and Western advisers, the elite PUMC model was so dominant that it had become a liability. As Yip observed:

> The education and training of health leaders, the tremendous influence and
> power of the Rockefeller Foundation (which was able to provide funds not
> forthcoming from the government), and the belief on the part of Chinese
> planners in the applicability of the advanced medical techniques of the West led
> to the transfer of the model of scientific medicine to China.[35]

The problem, of course, was that PUMC had become the aspiration model and that no other institution had sufficient staff, funding, or laboratory resources to come close to approximating PUMC. China's twenty-three medical schools in the 1930s were quite small; most had less than a hundred students. The PUMC model would not meet China's need for tens of thousands of modern medical practitioners.

Beginning in the 1930s, three League of Nations health advisers—Knud Faber, Andrija Stampar, and Ludwig Rajchman—all became involved in the question of medical training in China. After doing multiple studies, they recommended that China adopt the Soviet model of two-tier training and that PUMC be maintained only as a postgraduate research institution. Thus, with the support of the League of Nations and utilizing many of John Grant's ideas, the National Health Administration advanced a model of state-provided medicine for China that directly challenged the Rockefeller medical model, especially PUMC. Ironically, the most salient critiques came from the Commission on Medical Education, which was fully funded by the RF and led by Zhu Zhanggeng, a 1928 graduate of PUMC. The commission's goal was to establish a China-wide medical education program and to both certify and regulate existing medical institutions. The criticism of PUMC was not limited to its elite status. PUMC was also already known for skirting the GMD's educational policies, which required that all educational institutions be led by a Chinese national. PUMC had tried to meet the requirement by making pro forma Chinese appointments. Two leading Chinese physicians whose primary responsibilities were in Shanghai and Nanjing, Yan Fuqing (F. C. Yen) and Liu Ruiheng, were successively named PUMC director. In reality, however, Roger Greene, and later Henry Houghton, continued as de facto director.

The Commission on Medical Education intensified the scrutiny of PUMC. In 1935, the commission urged PUMC to comply with all government regulations, expand its student body (it still enrolled only thirty students in each class), and use Chinese as the medium of instruction. Not only was English still the only instructional language; but the commission charged that *none* of PUMC's hundreds of research publications had been translated into Chinese. The English version of this official critique caught the attention of the New York–based CMB, including JDR 3rd. Because the critique had been written by one of their own, Zhu Zhanggeng, its language evoked PUMC's origins: "Unfortunately the Founder's object has not been adequately interpreted. . . . P.U.M.C. should play a more significant role in the development of medical education in China."[36] The founder's grandson, JDR 3rd, was supportive of these objectives, writing to Alan Gregg, director of the RF Medical Science division, "I find myself rather generally in sympathy with the recommendations. . . . At least it is something to have them take a real interest in the school since it is our thought to eventually turn the institution over to the Chinese."[37] In 1937, the Chinese government, for the first time, did offer very modest financial support to PUMC if it would become a graduate medical institution, the apex of a multilayered medical education system.

The return to China of Henry Houghton in 1935 did signal a new willingness for change; Houghton called for significant modification of the PUMC model. In 1936, a commission on PUMC's future was appointed directly by the China-based PUMC Trustees, who were beginning to exercise their constitutional leadership. Proposed changes including expanding classes to fifty, offering bilingual instruction in all departments, eliminating de facto tenure for Western faculty, and strengthening graduate programs.

The "old guard," led by Francis Dieuaide, chair of PUMC's Department of Medicine, and notably including Greene, now retired in the United States, opposed these changes. Of particular importance, John D. Rockefeller Jr. and John D. Rockefeller 3rd and a new generation of foundation officials supported an expanded mission for PUMC. The generation of Welch, Flexner, Gates, and Vincent had passed, and their successors sought new medical and social approaches to China, including a tentative embrace of state or socialist medicine. For example, after some debate, the RF decided to fund Yang Chongrui's midwifery programs, the kind of medical training that would have been anathema to an earlier generation of Rockefeller educators. The RF also continued to fund Zhu Zhanggeng and the Commission on Medical Education until 1949.

With the onset of the Sino-Japanese War in 1937 and the Japanese occupation of Peking, the momentum for change lapsed. PUMC did not implement any of the proposed changes.

A more indirect but far-reaching critique of Rockefeller medicine came from practitioners of traditional Chinese medicine. The unstated assumption of the Rockefeller medical project in China was that Western medicine would demonstrate its scientific superiority and gradually replace traditional Chinese medicine. During the first three decades of the twentieth century, the Chinese government and most of its modernizing leaders concurred; the practice of traditional medicine was not officially recognized. During this same period, however, the theory and practice of Chinese medicine were undergoing systemic change. Prompted by Western medicine's claims of scientific superiority and a more professional medical culture, Chinese medical practitioners made substantial changes in the theoretical canon and practice of Chinese medicine. Beginning as early as 1912, traditional practitioners organized associations to improve medical practice and unite traditional physicians. By the early 1920s, just one of these societies, the Shenzhou Medical and Pharmaceutical General Association, comprised forty branches and more than six thousand members. The traditional apprentice system of training gave way to more formal schools of traditional medicine. Most important, Western anatomy and the germ theory of disease were integrated into Chinese medicine. The rapid expansion of Western medical journals was paralleled by a similar expansion of traditional Chinese medical journals: Western journals expanded from 5 to 171 between 1905 and 1935, while traditional journals expanded from 2 to 133 during the same period.[38]

The most contentious issue during the late 1920s and early 1930s was the licensing of physicians. The officials of Chiang Kai-shek's first Health Administration, led by Liu Ruiheng and other Western-trained physicians, adamantly opposed licenses for traditional medical practitioners. Their views did not prevail. A plethora of traditional medical associations appealed to more conservative elements in the GMD, arguing that not only was traditional medicine part of China's national essence, it was also essential to people's health and livelihood. Traditional practitioners continued to vastly outnumber Western-trained physicians, and the Chinese public continued to rely on their medical care.

By 1935, traditional Chinese medicine had scored a number of critical victories: The GMD recognized a National Institute of Traditional Medicine and legally enshrined equal professional treatment of practitioners of Chinese as well as Western medicine. Traditional Chinese medicine survived in part because of a willingness to seek modern scientific validation and the professionalization of a centuries-old tradition.[39] Although Mao Zedong had long opposed Chinese medicine as superstitious, he too came to recognize that China needed to rely on both traditional Chinese medicine and Western medicine.

RURAL RECONSTRUCTION AND THE CHINA PROGRAM

The critique of Western medicine was but one aspect of a conservative, nationalistic rejection of Western influences that characterized some aspects of the Nanjing era. On his first trip to China in 1931, Selskar Gunn, Rockefeller vice president for Europe, wrote to RF president Max Mason in alarmist tones: "Western civilization is under fire in China. . . . The dangers of wholesale importation of Western doctrines is decried in an ever increasing volume. The demand is now to "Chinafy" Western knowledge. Every subject, except the exact sciences, is under fire."[40] Having been sent to China by Mason on a reconnaissance trip, Gunn became convinced that the RF needed to pay more, not less, attention to China. After several subsequent visits (accompanied by John Grant), he decided that if the RF was to have "an indelible presence," it needed to move beyond medicine and the academic disciplines to contribute directly to China's greatest problem: the ongoing poverty and economic deprivation of rural China. As Gunn wrote Mason:

> There is no doubt that one of the major problems in China has to do with
> the raising of the economic level of the rural population. . . . No government,
> certainly no foreign agency, is capable of giving the Chinese people the
> minimum of the public services to which they are entitled unless the general
> economic level is raised. This involves what is broadly called a program of rural
> reconstruction, and it may be that in this field we shall have our real opportunity
> in China.[41]

Gunn's subsequent recommendation that the RF undertake a new program of rural reconstruction built on the capacity building already undertaken in the agricultural sciences, the social sciences, and public health. Quite intentionally, however, this new program was designed to engage the RF more politically in China. In becoming involved in rural reconstruction, the RF joined a group of nongovernmental Chinese and Western reformers seeking politically moderate solutions to China's rural needs.

Certainly the Rockefeller group, in both New York and Peking, was well aware of the ongoing CCP challenge to the GMD, especially in rural areas. By the late 1920s, the CCP had shifted from an unsuccessful effort to mobilize urban workers to embrace Mao Zedong's peasant revolution. Retreating to southeastern China in the late 1920s, the CCP created the Jiangxi Soviet, where experiments in land reform policies were carried out. This first rural revolutionary base area gave the CCP opportunities to carry out agrarian and administrative reforms, and to actually govern a rural region. During the early 1930s, Chiang Kai-shek's multiple encirclement campaigns drove the CCP away from Jiangxi on its "Long

March" to Yanan in northwest China, where once again land reform programs were implemented.

Chiang Kai-shek primarily sought military annihilation of the CCP, but the GMD did initiate its own competing reform movements, some of which were incorporated into the New Life Movement—a social and cultural promotion of traditional Chinese values. Some GMD ministries paid attention to China's rural development. However, the government did not exercise fiscal control over its provinces, whose leadership remained dependent upon the members of China's landlord class, who were unlikely to reduce their own economic and political power. The members of the GMD were not, however, hostile to the various private rural reform efforts during the 1930s, recognizing some parallels with their own New Life Movement and also hoping to blunt the radicalism associated with the CCP's efforts. Madame Chiang Kai-shek, in particular, reached out to encourage and support many of these efforts, including those of the RF.[42]

The RF took several years to act upon Gunn's recommendation, not approving until 1935 an allocation of $1 million for a new, multidisciplinary China program. This fulfilled a long-standing goal of both Mason and RF adviser Raymond Fosdick, to bring various foundation divisions together into a single project that addressed community development. Several promising regions in Mexico, India, and South America were rejected in order to begin this experimental program in China. In the 1910s, the "plasticity" of China had been cited as a reason for Rockefeller medical intervention. The concept was repeatedly used once again in the 1930s. The 1935 RF *Annual Report*, citing Selskar Gunn, explained the reasons for this new venture:

> The Chinese National Government, and, indeed, many provincial and county authorities and private organizations are undertaking measures designed to reconstruct a medieval society in terms of modern knowledge. The plasticity of the situation, together with the availability of proven Chinese leadership, offered an opportunity for the Foundation to develop its program in an attempt to improve community welfare, particularly with reference to the rural problems.[43]

The "availability of proven Chinese leadership" was the key to the new program, for it was based at Yan Yangchu's already-existing model county program in Dingxian—long supported by JDR Jr. personally—and relied almost exclusively on important social science and agricultural programs, which were already receiving Rockefeller support: the Nankai Institute of Economics, Yanjing's Department of Sociology, and Nanjing's College of Agriculture. Only Qinghua's Department of Engineering was new. Awareness of the Rockefeller shift toward rural concerns had an immediate impact on recipients or would-be recipients of Rockefeller funding. Research priorities shifted to rural issues. This was especially notable at the Nankai Institute of Economics, where macroeconomic projects were set aside for a number of years in order to focus on crucial rural issues: agricultural economy, county government, and rural industry. The North China Council for Rural Reconstruction was created as the organizational entity to manage the program. This experimental program was designed to bring Chinese intellectuals— economists, sociologists, and physicians—into direct contact with rural China. Their task was to train intellectuals for rural leadership and to coordinate the many existing rural reconstruction efforts.

Seeking to demonstrate that this was a new program and not related to PUMC, Selskar Gunn set up a new RF office in Shanghai, and John Grant was reassigned from PUMC to work with him. Their relationship with the GMD appears to have fluctuated. Gunn tried to write Mason every two weeks, keeping him regularly informed of his work and political contacts. In 1933, he sought to avoid close contacts with the GMD, not wanting to be labeled either a "Chiang Kai-shek or T. V. Soong adherent." But two years later, he wrote positively of a meeting with T. V. Soong (Song Ziwen), who, as chairman of the National Economic Council, had asked to be updated on the Dingxian program.[44] In 1935, Madame Chiang Kai-shek encouraged Gunn to go to Jiangxi, which had been newly liberated by the GMD from the CCP, to inspect the GMD's own work in rural reconstruction. And in 1937, she favorably compared the New Life Movement and the RF's rural reconstruction efforts: "Your efforts in the field of rural reconstruction are highly commendable and embody the spirit and the aims of the New Life Movement. The National Government is, as rapidly as possible, developing institutions and techniques that will in course of time improve the life of the rural people, and the work of the Rockefeller Foundation, in enlisting the interest of leading universities in a well-chosen training program, will widen and deepen this work through providing leadership."[45]

Despite this praise, Gunn himself grew progressively more skeptical about the GMD and increasingly aware of the potent CCP challenge. About the same time that he received the commendation from Madame Chiang Kai-shek, he described the tenancy crop-sharing system and the rising influence of the CCP:

> This old system, of course, plays into the hands of the Communists, who are the arch-enemies of the landlord, gentry and usurer group. Communism, while only found operating in rural regions and small towns, is directed by industrial workers and intellectuals from the large centers. It represents a great power, and the childish references of the National Government to the "remnant reds" are preposterous when one considers the size of Soviet China, its large, well-equipped army, and the genuine patriotism and self-sacrificing fervor of the people who live under its regime. What will be the ultimate end of Communism in China is impossible to foretell.[46]

Although Gunn, Grant, and their Chinese colleagues were aware that the concentration of land in the hands of a few landlords was one of the primary reasons
for rural poverty, they did not attempt to address this fundamentally political
issue in their new program. Like most Americans involved in the reform process
during the Nanjing era, they were politically opposed to radical economic solutions and continued to hope that the Nationalist government would embrace land
reform as a part of its agenda.[47] The advent of the Sino-Japanese War in 1937 and
the retreat of the GMD to Sichuan dashed those hopes. The work of the North
China Council for Rural Reconstruction continued during the war, but a possible
opportunity for moderate social and economic rural change in China was gone.
The influence of this Rockefeller-integrated community reform program did not
end in China, however. It is often cited as the model for the post–World War II
Sino-American Joint Commission on Rural Reconstruction, which did address
land tenancy issues and was highly successful in Taiwan.

THE CHALLENGE OF WAR

The Marco Polo Bridge Incident in July 1937 resulted in the Japanese seizure
and occupation of Peking. Three weeks later, Raymond Fosdick brought John D.
Rockefeller Jr. up to date on the status of Rockefeller institutions: "I suppose you
have read the distressing news in relation to the situation in China. It appears that
Nankai University in Tientsin, to which the Foundation has made grants over a
period of fifteen years, was destroyed yesterday, and the situation in relation to
Yenching University just outside Peiping is precarious. We have been unable so
far to get through to Houghton or to receive word from him." A day later, Fosdick
wrote again, reassuring Rockefeller that he had learned from the Department of
State that PUMC was functioning normally.[48] The situation deteriorated during
the next few months. In April 1938, Selskar Gunn made a personal appearance
before the RF's Trustees, describing at length the devastation and subsequent
relocation of most RF activities in China and reminding the trustees of their
moral obligation to scores of long-term Chinese colleagues: "It would be a tragedy
if the effective working groups which have been developed should have to disband
and scatter. Furthermore, there is at least something approaching an obligation
to the individuals who have been enlisted in this work on the strength of the
Foundation's interest."[49]

From this point until the end of World War II, the Rockefeller leadership
kept close track of the war's impact on the many Chinese intellectuals and institutions that were affected. In 1938, Gunn and Grant left China for work in
New York and India, but they were replaced by Marshall Balfour of the RF's

International Health Division, who traveled continuously in China, monitoring the residual work of the North China Council for Rural Reconstruction and other Rockefeller initiatives. Edward Lobenstein and Claude Forkner, successive directors of the CMB, also traveled frequently in the late 1930s and early 1940s, meeting with PUMC faculty and graduates working in "Free China." The RF's wartime policy—to seek to preserve those Chinese institutions and individuals with which it had long been associated—was not dissimilar to that for which it is far better known, supporting intellectuals in Europe. But the political situation was, of course, quite different. In Europe, the RF sought to extricate intellectuals from countries occupied by the Nazis; in China, it sought to sustain those working in wartime conditions in Nationalist China.

After the Japanese occupied Shanghai and Nanjing—accomplished by 1938—Chiang Kai-shek's Nationalist government made a series of retreats, finally settling for the war's duration in far western Chongqing. Faculty and students from many Rockefeller-supported institutions likewise left the Japanese-occupied areas of eastern China, reestablishing their work in the far more primitive southwestern provinces of Yunnan, Guangxi, and Sichuan. The staff and students from Nankai joined with those from Qinghua and Peking University to constitute what became the famous amalgamated university, Lianda, in Kunming. The North China Council for Rural Reconstruction's work in Dingxian (Hebei Province) and Qining (Shandong Province) relocated to Guizhou Province in southwest China. Some of its institutional components, namely, the University of Nanjing and National Central's agricultural research, relocated to Sichuan. Having left its original North China base, the organization was renamed simply the China Council for Rural Reconstruction. The Nationalist Ministry of Health and the Commission on Medical Education ultimately moved to Chongqing and continued to be led by those affiliated with PUMC. Under Zhu Zhanggeng, the commission worked assiduously to assist China's medical colleges as they coped with wartime conditions. Directors of wartime medical colleges included PUMC faculty member Li Zongen, and PUMC graduates Li Tingan (1926), Tang Zeguang (1929), and Zhu Xianyi (1930), while Chen Zhiqian became commissioner of public health for Sichuan Province.

As American-affiliated institutions, both PUMC and Yanjing University were tolerated by the Japanese authorities until Pearl Harbor, although some faculty and students from both institutions migrated to southwest China. On December 8, 1941, the Japanese occupied PUMC, closed the medical college but not the hospital, and incarcerated Henry Houghton along with Trevor Bowen, PUMC's business manager, and Leighton Stuart, the president of Yanjing University. John D. Rockefeller Jr.'s multiple personal interventions on their behalf with Undersecretary of State Sumner Welles were to no avail; these three were not included in the several prisoner-of-war exchanges and were held in isolation until the summer of 1945.[50]

JDR Jr. and his son John 3rd were certainly exposed to the RF's staff's concerns about the weakness of the GMD and its leadership. But like many Americans involved with China, these reservations were set aside when the United States entered World War II and Chiang Kai-shek became an important ally against the Japanese. The Rockefeller family members were not as active in promoting Nationalist China as Henry Luce's, but JDR 3rd did join Luce in chairing the United China Relief.[51] (In the 1950s, however, he distanced himself from the Luce family's promotion of Taiwan, politely declining invitations to give funding or serve on the board of Luce's China Institute.[52]) And his father, in an unusual political appearance in 1943, lent his name and prestige in celebrating Madame Chiang Kai-shek at Madison Square Garden. In introducing Madame Chiang, JDR Jr. praised "one of the most distinguished women of all times, whose brilliant mind and gallant spirit are only enhanced by her winsome femininity and charming modesty." Generalissimo Chiang Kai-shek was honored as a "valiant soldier, astute statesman and loyal patriot." Rockefeller also eulogized the Chinese nation: "We honor, likewise, China, our ally. For five and a half, long, bloody years the peace-loving people of that great nation have sought for freedom—their freedom and ours. . . . No Chinese army has ever surrendered. The Chinese nation has never faltered, never turned back; with courage unabated, it is pressing on to victory."[53]

The degree to which Chiang's armies aggressively fought the Japanese has long been debated, but certainly by 1943 the Japanese occupied much of East China and threatened the central reaches of the Yangtze River. A second "united front" merely postponed the day of final reckoning between the GMD and CCP. Conditions in isolated southwest China were becoming ever more destitute. The RF stepped up its efforts to preserve the scientific and medical infrastructure that it had helped to develop in Republican China. With PUMC closed, the RF decided to assist eight Chinese medical colleges and the thirteen missionary colleges coordinated by the United Board for Christian Higher Education in China, all of which had relocated some of their programs to southwest China. In coordination with the U.S. Department of State, the RF also initiated a program of bringing Chinese intellectuals out of wartime China to spend a year in the United States. This later became the first Fulbright program. The Chinese historian Zi Zhongyun writes that these various Rockefeller programs to "rescue" Chinese colleges and intellectuals were among its most important contributions during the Republican era.[54]

Letters from wartime China were regularly circulated to the directors of Rockefeller divisions. Particularly dramatic were reports from PUMC's Nursing School leaders, who had trekked more than 1,000 miles from Peking to Chengdu to continue nursing instruction after the Japanese occupation of PUMC. Many of the stories were more discouraging—accounts of physical, intellectual, and institutional deprivation. One would have thought that the gloomy accounts coming out of China, especially the eventual collapse of its China Program, would have discouraged the RF from any new China ventures. In fact, quite the opposite occurred.

TOWARD A NEW CHINA

Three days after Pearl Harbor, Raymond Fosdick convened a meeting of RF senior staff in which they discussed not wartime relief work but a foundation vision for the post–World War II era. Thus began a series of foundation conversations, including special sessions on China, that continued until war's end. Liu Ruiheng and Chen Zhiqian, now a PUMC trustee, were consulted, and groups of PUMC faculty and graduates sent written recommendations to the New York office. Fosdick himself usually chaired the China meetings.

For the third time since its inception in 1913, the RF assessed the reasons for its involvement in China. In the 1910s, the RF was enamored with scientific medicine, not just for itself but also for its potential to introduce rational thought and the highest level of Western civilization to China. In the 1930s, the RF was less concerned with China's cultural transformation than with its potential economic and social transformation. In both periods, there was a fair amount of confidence that Americans—or Western-trained Chinese intellectuals—could bring the solutions.

In the mid-1940s, the question was asked once again: "What do we exactly want to do in China?"[55] The earlier confidence had dissipated. Some doubted the relevance of Western cultural traditions to China's national predicament. Some argued for a "complete renovation and re-orientation of most, if not all, of our earlier attitudes toward China."[56] Still others pressed for a deeper understanding of Chinese society, one in which China's humanistic traditions were probed more deeply. And for the first time in Rockefeller history, China's strategic international role was given more attention: "China would appear to be the strategically important country in Asia. . . . As goes China, so goes Asia and perhaps the peace of the world."[57] Ambitious plans were made to send a high-level group of leading American businessmen and intellectuals to China before the end of the war to review the situation and to design future Rockefeller China programs. The new plan should not be based on sentiment but grounded in "China's developing needs and conditions, and 'built into' their own lives and institutions." Projects should not be "RF projects" but "left with the Chinese government or institutions, with RF limiting its help to counsel and financial aid at strategic points."[58]

Much of the conversation also revolved around one question: What to do about PUMC? Until the question of PUMC's future was settled, it would be difficult to chart a totally new Rockefeller China agenda. Even though PUMC was closed during most of the war, the critique of it had continued. When JDR Jr. learned of the heroic role some PUMC faculty and graduates were playing in China's hinterland, he mused that perhaps PUMC itself should be reconstituted. Writing to Fosdick in late 1942, he reflected: "This is an interesting side light on the question we have sometimes discussed—namely the possible wisdom of some day moving the PUMC into the interior and reestablishing it on far simpler and less expensive foundations."[59] Marshall Balfour and Claude Forkner reported on numerous instances in which other PUMC staff were "too elitist" and ill prepared to work with institutions of lesser standing. Even more trenchant was a letter from Li Zongen (C. U. Lee), writing from the isolation of Guiyang Medical College, of which he had become director. Remembering the more privileged PUMC, he wrote that "one reluctantly comes to the conclusion that as a whole P.U.M.C. graduates have among them many technical leaders but their social and intellectual levels have not come up to expectation." Li especially regretted that PUMC, a transplanted first-class American medical college, had not "become an integral part of the national program for medical education."[60] Li was soon given the chance to solve these problems: He was named the first Chinese director of PUMC in 1946.

Despite these negatives, by war's end the resumption of such a strong institution became a symbol of China's postwar recovery. Song Ziwen, then president of the Executive Yuan, wrote the RF urging that PUMC be reopened; and Ma Wenzhao, dean of the competing College of Medicine of Peking University, expressed his desire that the CMB would continue to support PUMC as the "radiating center" of modern medicine and public health in China.[61] The PUMC Trustees, primarily a Chinese body, advocated PUMC's immediate resumption and began to consider the appointment of a new Chinese director.

In 1946, the RF—concerned about the rapidity with which the PUMC Trustees were moving—dispatched a commission that included Alan Gregg, director of the Medical Education Division, along with Sidney Burwell, dean of the Harvard Medical School, and Harold Loucks to China to survey the scene on the ground and decide the fate of PUMC. It is important to note that this was an RF commission, not a CMB commission; major decisions for PUMC, especially financial ones, were still made by the RF. Traveling in China for almost three months, theirs was a comprehensive survey, including meeting with CCP leaders General Ye Jianying and Huang Hua in a rare visit to the CCP-occupied area of Kalgan northwest of Peking (figure 3.2). The commission's political observations mirrored Gunn's earlier reports: "In contrast to the reputed corruption and indifference of some members of the National government or the Kuomintang, the Chinese Communists have a reputation for honesty, high morale and relentless activity in behalf of a peasantry bowed down by impossible taxes and land

FIGURE 3.2. The Rockefeller Foundation's China Medical Commission with leaders of the Chinese Communist Party, 1946. Front row, left to right: General Ye Jianying, Harold Loucks, Alan Gregg, Sidney Burwell, George Hatem, General Lo Suichin. Back row, far right: Huang Hua. *Photograph courtesy of the Rockefeller Archive Center.*

rentals." Gregg, Burwell, and Loucks were partially convinced that mediation efforts between the CCP and the GMD would be successful, and that an all-out civil war would not materialize.

Having been persuaded of reasonable prospects for peace and the ongoing importance of PUMC, the RF commission unanimously recommended that it be reopened under Chinese leadership and that its financial future be guaranteed by adding an additional $9 million to the endowment. To forestall any future financial requests and to complete the separation that had begun in 1928, the RF was urged to fully divest itself of responsibility for the CMB. The commission also recommended that at least one Chinese member be added to the CMB and that the CMB broaden its funding beyond PUMC to other medical institutions in China.[62]

These recommendations provoked major debate within RF circles. President Fosdick, who had become increasingly concerned about the economic and political deterioration in China, was opposed to the recommendations of the commission he had appointed. Though not objecting to the reopening of PUMC, he was against any additional financial investment, rebutting the commission's recommendations in a lengthy point-by-point letter written in October 1946.

Caustically observing that the commission had described at some length the unpredictable financial situation in China, he wrote:

> My question is how in view of this complete "unpredictability"—to use your word—the Trustees of the Foundation can be persuaded at this juncture to undertake a permanent and final financial plan? What possible assurance is there that the solution you propose would be a lasting one, guaranteeing the indefinite continuation, with cessation of further Foundation assistance, of a medical school of high scientific and moral integrity?[63]

He went on to question the political future of the Nationalists, citing the struggle for power with the Communists, concluding that "even if the Central Government could suppress the Communists ('It is hard to contain an idea'), it is unlikely that the forces presently controlling the Kuomintang would then make significant concessions or reforms in the political, economic or social field."[64]

Fosdick was not successful in lobbying against the commission's recommendations.[65] At some juncture in late 1946, John D. Rockefeller Jr.—now in his seventies—let it be known that he favored the commission's recommendations, even increasing its endowment request to $10 million to preserve and enhance PUMC. JDR Jr. had not been a member of the RF Trustees since 1939, but on matters related to China, his views prevailed. The future of PUMC was deemed so significant that a special meeting of the RF's Board of Trustees took place on January 7, 1947, and was attended by both JDR Jr. and JDR 3rd. In voting to give the CMB an additional endowment of $10 million, bringing it to a total of $22 million, the RF also voted to separate the CMB from the RF, once and for all. As one indication, JDR 3rd, who was also an RF trustee, resigned his position on the CMB after eighteen years of membership.

This $10 million terminal grant to the CMB was an extraordinary decision. It was almost half the RF's budget for 1947 and required the largest draw on its capital in its history.[66] PUMC's endowment, to be managed henceforth by the China Medical Board Inc., now came to $22 million—exceeding that of many U.S. medical colleges. Fosdick's opposition was revealed when he wrote in his annual report that it was "an odd moment . . . to make a fresh investment in the development of modern medicine in that unhappy country." However, he loyally went on to reaffirm the historic Rockefeller rationale for creating PUMC—not only to advance modern medicine in China but also to help "to establish in the Far East the value of scientific medicine and inductive reasoning, . . . the best gift that America could offer China."[67]

Somewhat surprisingly, Fosdick and the officers of the foundation lost no time in returning to a new agenda for China, meeting the very afternoon of the PUMC decision. With the decades-old PUMC question resolved, China continued to beckon, and one could argue that the political situation was more "plastic" than ever. Each division had drawn up new, competing institutional plans, and although Fosdick feared a fragmented agenda, it was agreed that staff could make exploratory visits to China.[68] It was in this fluid institutional context that JDR 3rd himself embarked on his second trip to China, expressing the need "to keep abreast of what is going on, to help formulate future Foundation policy."[69] Fosdick opposed his trip, fearing it would lead to unrealizable Chinese expectations, but Rockefeller persisted.[70]

During his three-week visit to Shanghai, Peking, Nanjing, and Guangzhou, JDR 3rd met with Chinese and American business leaders, diplomatic personnel, GMD officials (including several that he had met in 1929), and Rockefeller personnel. Once again, Standard Oil employees were his hosts. He made a point of meeting with Li Zongen, PUMC's new director, and visited the newly reopened institution: "Was very much impressed with him as a person and also with his ideas. Made me feel hopeful as to future."[71] He also visited the rural demonstrations in health and social services that were being funded by the RF near Peking, Nanjing, and Guangzhou.

Trying to gauge for himself the degree of support for the Communists, JDR 3rd sought meetings with Chinese intellectuals representing different political viewpoints. At Yanjing University, he met several leaders in the Rockefeller-funded College of Public Affairs, including two sociologists, Zhao Chengxin and Yan Jingyao. Yan reported to him that "the Communists were doing a good job in China and (he) felt confident that they would not disturb Yenching if they took over the Peiping area."[72] Rockefeller noted that Yan definitely believed that Chinese Communists were different from Russian Communists. He was less impressed with Zhang Xiruo, chair of political science at Qinghua University, who was a "leftist, maybe a socialist . . . confident of his answers." He also met Hu Shi again, now president of Peking University and chairman of PUMC's Board of Trustees, and Qian Duansheng, head of the university's Political Science Department. Rockefeller concluded: "Two intellectuals in one afternoon is rather large order we found."[73]

Rockefeller's most symbolic meeting was with Chiang Kai-shek on September 23. Pleasantries were exchanged, and Rockefeller informed Chiang of the recent RF gift to the CMB, telling him "that R.F. grants to China were larger than to any other country except U.S., of confidence in future of China as indicated by continuing R.F. work in country." Advised not to bring up any "problems," Rockefeller concluded: "The meeting was most interesting, pleasant and satisfactory. . . . It would be terribly difficult to form any kind of appraisal of the Generalissimo from the meeting as it was so correct and restrained at the same time he was friendly. . . . He was on the tall side for a Chinese, then, erect, wore a simple uniform, moved slowly, had a nice face, but all the time seemed far away or maybe I should say out of reach."[74]

Although he periodically uses the vernacular "commies," JDR 3rd's 1947 diary is restrained in its political conclusions. His personal letters to his wife, Blanchette, are more colorful and politically explicit. Peking is a "city on edge as it is pretty much surrounded by the Communists" and Yanjing students "are completely fed up with the Nationalist government and are inclined to look favorably towards the Communists as the way out." As his trip ended in Shanghai, he concluded:

> The longer I am here in China the gladder I am that I am not General
> Wedemeyer, General Marshall or President Truman. I do not envy them the
> responsibility of having to determine what U.S. policy towards China should
> be in the months immediately ahead. On the one hand you have the National
> Government which would appear to be pretty much a totalitarian police state led
> by a reactionary group who seem to be well entrenched. What the chances are
> of a government as this shifting over to more liberal policies it is hard to tell but
> they don't look good. . . .
>
> My viewpoint is that . . . the main reason for the spread of Communism is
> because conditions are bad—economic, political, etc.—and that unless something
> is done to give people . . . confidence that the Government will improve the
> situation, Communism will continue to attract more and more people.[75]

Despite this pessimistic outlook on China's political future, JDR 3rd returned in full support of the RF's continued engagement. And his was not the only China visit in 1947; three of the RF's five divisions sent staff members to China—International Health, Social Sciences, and Humanities. Moreover, they began to implement differing and sometimes competing agendas—just as China plunged into the last stages of civil war.

The RF's International Health Division had a head start because it inherited the Shanghai China office of Selskar Gunn and the original interdisciplinary China Program. By 1947, there were three foreign staff members in the office, and a portfolio of old and new programs. Since the early 1940s, the RF had funded the GMD's National Institute of Health, the organizational successor to the Central Field Health Station, as well as continuing its support for the Commission on Medical Education. By 1948, the Division of International Health had provided $430,680 to various organs of the Ministry of Health, third only to PUMC and Yanjing University in Rockefeller institutional contributions.[76] In 1948, these funds supported work on nutrition, schistosomiasis, and public health nursing, among other issues. Several new ventures included work on malaria in both China and Taiwan. And more initiatives were always emerging—the possibility of a nursing school in Taiwan or a public health school in Peking.

The many Rockefeller-affiliated Chinese physicians and public health specialists who had worked with the GMD health programs were especially vulnerable as Chiang Kai-shek began his retreat from the CCP armies. As the government moved south, most ministries went with him, and some began to be relocated in Taiwan. Zhu Zhanggeng's dilemma reveals the personal and political questions faced by those who had been active in the GMD government. Having long been associated with the Nationalist Health Ministry, Zhu had become acting minister of health. RF officials urged him to remain in Nanjing to await the political outcome. But he felt pulled by the GMD and initially moved much of his staff to Taiwan. He regretted that decision almost immediately and began to plan to return to China. Robert Watson, acting RF director of international health for the Far East, described Zhu's predicament:

> CKC [Zhu Zhanggeng] is going to Taiwan, timing his visit so that it will coincide with the evacuation of Canton. . . . He reckons that in time the situation in Shanghai and on the east coast will be stabilized and that the new government will be planning a national health service. . . . He hopes to go back to Nanking to a position not too unlike that he now holds. . . . He will have saved his face with the KMT [GMD] government and will have made face with the new govt."[77]

In fact Zhu Zhanggeng was not able to go back to China until the late 1950s, after serving in Chiang Kai-shek's government in Taiwan and later in a leading position at the World Health Organization in Geneva.

In time, many of the RF-trained personnel who had been active in the Ministry of Health and in China's public health work retreated with the GMD to Taiwan. Their official affiliation with the GMD made it difficult for them to imagine a future role under the CCP. One exception was Chen Zhiqian, who was offered funding if he would move to Taiwan. Having been less directly involved in the GMD Health Administration, he decided to remain in his native Sichuan.

In February 1949, the RF relocated its Asia International Health Division's office from Shanghai to India, still planning for a future health policy role in China. Robert Watson asked to be able to set aside funds for eventual renewed support for a "reorganization of the NIH under a coalition government."[78] Marshall Balfour, the Asia regional director for the International Health Division, concurred: "If we do not make an effort to maintain relations with the new government, whatever it is, our bridges are burnt and personally I believe that it will be a long period before the RF is in China again on any basis."[79] Not unlike Zhu Zhanggeng, the RF hedged its bets, initially deciding to continue malaria work in Taiwan while reserving some funding for reentry into mainland China. As Watson rather naively responded to Balfour:

> I do not regard too seriously the possible repercussions from our continuing work in Formosa while we have more or less abandoned work in mainland

China, at least during the period of the formation of the new government and its recognition. Whatever their ideologies, the Chinese are eminently sensible people and the fact that we will have more than $30,000 available to help with the reorganization of the NIH, together with our reputation in China, will go a long way toward dissipating any criticism that might arise.[80]

It is symptomatic of what historian Frank Ninkovich has called the RF's hubris that Watson believed $30,000 could have bought the American foundation a health policy role in Mao's China.[81] And because few in the RF had confidence in Chiang Kai-shek, Taiwan in 1949 was not a popular alternative; by the end of the year, the International Health Division had withdrawn from Taiwan.[82]

The Social Science Division was also eager to become more involved in China, but it drew back when confronted with the political realities. Roger F. Evans, assistant director of social sciences, reported that "the best present hope of solution lies in a 'government of liberals under Chiang Kai-shek,' as improbable as that appeared." The troubling China situation also caused him to reflect on the appropriate role of Westerners in China: "The West has too often tried to remodel China in its own image and has transplanted its 'bit' of Western trees to China with little regard to Chinese soil, climate and future means of sustenance." Evans, however, had no "Chinese trees" to propose and was reluctant to go beyond the most general of suggestions: "But RF can and should be giving modest help, especially *in kind*, where that can aid in saving or bringing on good men, . . . and above all in conveying to that industrious, patient and heroic people a token of our continuing interest and concern."[83]

The Humanities Division, heretofore the least involved with China, became the most active in China during the waning 1940s. Although most of its earlier China work focused on the American study of China, beginning in 1936 the RF gave grants to fund basic English in China, an experiment in a streamlined version of English that only included 850 words and 18 verbs. This system—which had been advocated by the British linguist I. A. Richard, who had founded the Orthological Institute in Peking—was designed to give Chinese immediate access to English, without the deeper intellectual context normally associated with language learning. In 1937, the institute, designed to prepare text materials and instruction for middle school, was moved to Yunnan, where it was supported by the Yunnan Commission on Education. The RF saw basic English as one of several approaches promoting the wider use of English as a tool for worldwide linguistic communication. This was judged to be increasingly important as concerns grew about the potential worldwide expansion of Soviet communism.[84]

The experience of the Humanities Division in funding both China studies in the United States and the Orthological Institute in China gave director David Stevens contacts with many Chinese humanists and insight into the Chinese scholarly and intellectual world. In the post–World War II era, he articulated a programmatic philosophy that synthesized "Western and Eastern ideas in literature and philosophy," by maintaining ties with Chinese intellectuals, regardless of their political orientation. He sent his associate and soon-to-be successor, Charles B. Fahs, former professor of Asian studies at Pomona College, to China in 1948. When Fahs returned, he urged the RF to connect with Communist-leaning intellectuals:

> China is going through a revolution. . . . In the process most of the old
> intellectual ties between the United States are being dissolved. It is not now
> inevitable that the new China will be exclusively oriented towards Moscow, but if
> we do not forge new intellectual links with the groups now coming to the fore in
> China, such an orientation will become unavoidable.

Fahs initially recommended that these new links come from the medical and natural science divisions, suggesting the contribution of medical books to "Bethune hospitals, which are the Communist centers of training."[85]

This medical aid never materialized, and it turned out that ties with leftist intellectuals would come from the humanities after all. Fahs recommended a series of small grants to assist leading Chinese universities and research centers, including grants to Robert Winter at Qinghua University (Winter had earlier been associated with the Orthological Institute) and the All-China Literary Writer's Association. These grants, which continued for a short time after the Korean War broke out in 1950, were made knowing the leftist orientation of both Winter and the Writer's Association. It is worth quoting Fahs's rationale at length:

> Bob Winter is of course thoroughly out of sympathy with the present
> national regime and in that sense may accurately be considered a Communist
> sympathizer. He is however, thoroughly independent in his point of view. My
> guess is that his independence of mind and his interest in literature and the arts
> will make it impossible for him to swallow a rigid Communist Party line for any
> great length of time. . . .
>
> The Chinese Literary Writers Association has a considerable left-wing element
> and some known Communist members. . . . It is not possible to do anything
> constructive in literature in China and at the same time avoid the left-wing
> element. . . .
>
> I have worked on the theory in China that in the long run independent,
> stubborn and critical search for new ideas is inconsistent with dictatorship of any
> sort. . . . If we can preserve some of this attitude through the present crisis and
> into the new situation which may develop within the next several years, we will
> have done the most that we can to assure that China does not remain indefinitely
> behind an iron curtain.[86]

Given the growing intensity of the civil war between the CCP and the GMD, and the increasing likelihood of a Communist victory, these foundation overtures to China seem remarkable. But they were not unusual; a number of American corporations and missionary groups were also ramping up their China involvement, encouraged by the Harry Truman administration's desire to keep U.S. options in China open. Everyone wanted to be present when the decades-old struggle between the CCP and the GMD ended and a new era would be born.

Meanwhile, PUMC had reopened in the fall of 1947 under Chinese leadership; there were only three Western faculty, including Harold Loucks, professor of surgery, who also served as CMB representative. There was a sense of normalcy as faculty and staff returned to PUMC. But the relative political calm did not last long. In late 1948, as the GMD kept losing territory in North China to the CCP., Loucks cabled the CMB, asking what the institution should do "in the event of Communist occupation of Peiping." The Executive Committee of the CMB, chaired by Joseph C. Hinsey, met in emergency session two days after Christmas, passing a resolution to continue funding PUMC regardless of the political regime: "It is the current intention of this Board to continue to support the P.U.M.C. as long as the P.U.M.C. can continue effectively to perform its mission in medical, hospital and educational work under the unrestricted direction and control of the present Director and staff."[87] This resolution came just in time; in February 1949, the People's Liberation Army occupied Peking.

As the CCP's ultimate victory loomed, Rockefeller officials and family members began to consider a future philanthropic role in a new China. Foundation officials were less concerned that the new government might be Communist than they were that it might be in the Soviet orbit. Watson echoed the views of most when he wrote: "I am one of the people who believe that we can work with the new government. . . . I still cannot conceive of a Communist government of China in the sense of a rigid adherence to Moscow dictation."[88]

JDR 3rd made a number of efforts to become better informed about the changing situation in China. In the summer of 1949, he invited Loucks, then on a quick trip to the United States, to spend the night. The next day, John gave a full report on conditions at PUMC (for once, the budget was holding) in a letter to his father:

> The big question in so many people's minds about China today is, "is China different?" By that it is meant, will the Communists in China be forced to a different handling of the situation than has been true in other countries of the world where they have taken over? Dr. Loucks feels that the answer is yes—that some modified form of Communism will result. In his judgment our Government is pursuing the right policy towards China since the Nationalist Government is so discredited with the people of China that further assistance to them would only be harmful. In the latter I concur at this time, although I felt different when I came back from the Far East in 1947.

Rockefeller went on to say that the fundamental question was whether or not the United States should recognize the Communists, suggesting a "deferral for a bit."[89] Three days later, he received a response from his father: "What he [Loucks] says about the present condition and prospects for Peking Union Medical College is most gratifying. If the institution is being now run on an annual cost basis of $600,000 and its income is $900,000, I greatly hope the balance is being added to the principal. . . . What you go on to say about the present condition of China . . . is quite in line with my own thinking based on what I have read."[90]

Shortly after the exchange of letters between father and son, Raymond Fosdick, in a letter to Ambassador Philip C. Jessup, who was leading a State Department review of Asia policy, argued that the Nationalist government was fully discredited and that the United States should resist any further assistance. Fosdick was positive about some of the CCP's domestic reforms, noting that "CCP teaching in China is passionately nationalistic, and many of its reforms (like mass-education, improvement of agricultural yields, etc.) are long overdue. The United States must not be maneuvered into a position where we appear to oppose the main purpose of the revolution that started more than 40 years ago."[91] However, like the Rockefellers, he urged no immediate political action regarding Communist recognition, but rather a policy of "watchful waiting."

The watershed moment came on October 1, 1949, when Mao Zedong formally proclaimed the establishment of the People's Republic of China. Writing again to Jessup three weeks later, Fosdick argued that the United States should recognize Mao's government according to long-established diplomatic principles, being neither hasty nor engaging in "futile delay." He advocated the continuation of trade as well as cultural, educational, and missionary contacts, stating: "If there is to be an iron curtain drawn between us and the Chinese CCP regime, we ought to have no responsibility for drawing it." And he urged that the United States not intervene to save Taiwan and the GMD from the expected Communist invasion: "Military or economic intervention on our part to save it from the Communists would arouse Chinese nationalism and anti-American sentiment to white heat. . . . Formosa is properly a part of China."[92]

The RF and the now-independent China Medical Board, Inc., certainly intended to continue their work in China. In mid-October, director Li Zongen wrote to Philo Parker, chair of the CMB, telling him that although it was not clear whether PUMC would become part of the Ministry of Health or the Ministry of Education, "We have considerable evidence, however, that the contribution of PUMC in concentrating on quality rather than quantity is recognized."[93] Though it was not yet evident how PUMC would be assimilated into the new China, the CMB stood by its previous decision. In November 1949, the CMB reaffirmed that "since it appears that the U.S. Government is in favor of continued support of educational institutions in China," there was no need to depart from its 1948 policy of continuing to support PUMC.[94]

The possibility of a political accommodation between the United States and the CCP in the late 1940s or even after the establishment of the People's Republic of China remains a topic of scholarly debate. The historical reality is that on June 25, 1950, the North Koreans crossed the 38th Parallel in Korea, and the United States, backed by the United Nations, went to war. As an ally of North Korea, China and the USSR were quickly brought into the picture. The CMB continued to remit funds to PUMC until the U.S. Treasury froze all financial transactions with China in December 1950. Even as efforts were under way to unfreeze PUMC assets in the National City Bank of New York, on January 23, 1951, the CMB received its last cable from Li Zongen: "PUMC nationalized."[95]

When the door to China closed in 1951, the RF had expended more than $55 million in more than seventy-five institutions throughout China (see appendix A). With the exception of the CMB's $22 million endowment, which remained invested in the United States, almost all the funds had trained Chinese intellectuals and supported China's emerging medical, natural, and social sciences education and research infrastructure. Despite many declarations of intent, only a small share (3.6 percent) had actually gone to fund Chinese institutions. Almost 10 percent had gone to missionary colleges and hospitals. The vast majority of the funding had gone to PUMC. As it turned out, all these foreign institutions became Chinese very quickly; they were nationalized in the early 1950s, becoming part of the backbone of new China's scientific and educational infrastructure.

The multidecade Rockefeller engagement yielded multigenerational opportunities. The young Chinese physicians and scientists funded in the early 1920s became institutional leaders in the 1930s and 1940s. The multidisciplinary rural reconstruction program would not have been possible without the RF's earlier investment in training economists and social scientists. In the late 1930s and 1940s, PUMC's own graduates rose to the fore as medical leaders dispersed throughout China.

The maturation of Chinese professional leadership was not replicated in the institutional and fiduciary responsibilities for the RF and CMB China programs, which remained vested in New York. Only in the late 1940s were the PUMC's trustees permitted to make fundamental decisions about the institution's future, and only then were a few Chinese invited to participate in the Rockefeller deliberations about a future China program.

Likewise, the continuity of John D. Rockefeller Jr.'s personal involvement throughout this period is quite striking, especially given his many other projects (the restoration of Williamsburg and the construction of the Rockefeller Center, to name just two). In addition to the RF's China funding, JDR Jr. personally contributed perhaps $10 million to various additional China-related programs, ranging from the Mass Education Movement to the Institute for Pacific Relations.

Throughout these years, he was intimately involved in the RF's major China policies and funding decisions, especially those related to PUMC. JDR Jr. often spoke in familial terms about PUMC. At the dedication in 1921, he spoke of the christening of PUMC as a "baby" or an "an adult infant," with the RF as the grandparent and his father, the benefactor, as the father.[96] Many years later, in giving instructions to Raymond Fosdick on how to handle the Chinese trustees, he wrote: "Those in charge will see at once how deeply interested the Foundation and the China Medical Board both are in their foster child, the P.U.M.C."[97] The somewhat recalcitrant PUMC had become a "foster" child. With this continuing paternalism, JDR Jr. never fully understood either the Chinese Trustees' desire for independent authority or the RF's desire to reduce its PUMC support; PUMC was like family, the Rockefeller family. His eldest son John became even more involved in the myriad financial and administrative issues linking the RF, CMB, Inc., and PUMC.

The correspondence between the three John D. Rockefellers about China and PUMC over nearly half a century illustrates their detailed financial and policy oversight as well as the formality of their interpersonal relations. In the end, it is quite clear that the RF's steadfast support of PUMC cannot be understood without acknowledging the Rockefeller family's advocacy.

New programmatic directions in the 1930s and 1940s emerged from the critique of PUMC and came from the RF's presidents and staff. Given the primitive level of transpacific communication at the time, the extensive flow of long letters between first George Vincent and Roger Greene and then Max Mason and Selskar Gunn revealed New York's strong and continuing interest in China. The RF's top leadership was kept well informed about Chinese political conditions and the status of Rockefeller-funded institutions and personnel. A commitment to China, if not PUMC, came to permeate the New York office. By the end of World War II, there were no RF personnel based in China; the stimulus for renewed engagement came directly from the New York–based Rockefeller staff.

During this first half century, the Rockefeller Foundation acted as almost a free agent in China, unencumbered by either the U.S. or Chinese government. It appears that in only two instances did the Rockefeller family or foundation request intervention by the U.S. government—the capture of Lucy Aldrich and the internment of Henry Houghton. And the foundation largely circumvented the modest efforts of the Chinese government to implement educational restrictions or modify educational programs. The ambitious rural reconstruction program hinted at political reform, but it required no permits or licenses and encountered no opposition. Although the GMD became progressively more restrictive, the era from 1927 to 1949 was relatively open to foreign engagement. The several Chinese governments during the Republican period saw the work of the RF as contributing to China's modern development and permitted it the civil space within which to operate.

Historians today recognize continuities between the state-building efforts of the GMD and the victorious CCP. The scientific and medical infrastructure that was well established by 1949—including most of its personnel—continued under the People's Republic of China. Recently, some scholars have also come to recognize the Republican era as China's "age of openness,"[98] not to be replicated until Deng Xiaoping's "opening and reform." The interregnum, Mao's era, created a great chasm between China and much of the outside world. Mao's China proved to be very difficult for intellectuals, especially those who had been associated with the RF. Yet twenty-five years later, the RF and the CMB, together with their former Chinese grantees in medicine, the social sciences, and the natural sciences, led the way in reconnecting China and the United States in a new age of openness.

CHAPTER 4

SURVIVAL

Peking Union Medical College

Several months after JDR 3rd's visit to Peking Union Medical College (PUMC) in 1947, Li Zongen met him for lunch in New York City.[1] As the first Chinese director of PUMC, Li was touching base with the Rockefeller family as well as members of the China Medical Board. His follow-up thank you note expressed appreciation for the lunch "in which you showed such keen interest in PUMC and its re-establishment" and included a picture of faculty, staff, and students on the opening day. With an uncanny premonition that this might be his last communication with Rockefeller, Li concluded: "As we go forward it is with a deep sense of the responsibility that rests on us to live up to the hopes and aspirations of the founders."[2] A copy of Li's letter to John D. Rockefeller 3rd is preserved in the PUMC Archives in Peking; it was exhibited in the 1950s to prove that Li was an accomplice of the imperialist Rockefellers. The political persecution against Li increased until 1957, when he was branded a "rightist" and banished from Peking.

Mao Zedong's revolution was a rural revolution, a class revolution, and an anti-intellectual revolution. It was also a highly nationalistic revolution. On October 1, 1949, when he proclaimed that China "has stood up," the cheering crowds were genuinely euphoric. China's century of humiliation, which had begun during the Opium Wars, was over. Although many Chinese intellectuals studying in the West decided to remain abroad, significant numbers returned during the late 1940s to cast their fate with the new People's Republic of China (PRC). Some had been disenchanted with the Guomindang; others had faced discrimination in American universities. Theirs was a hopeful generation of Chinese scientific nationalists, deeply committed to the task of building the scientific infrastructure of a new nation.[3] One of the new government's tasks was to integrate this Western-oriented scientific and educational community into a new socialist regime. With the onset of the Korean War and hostilities with the United States, this became an urgent priority.

Meanwhile, several months after the nationalization of PUMC, in January 1951, its American friends were both optimistic and resigned about its future. John D. Rockefeller Jr., now approaching eighty years old, sent the following consoling words to the longtime China Medical Board secretary, Mary Ferguson:

> With you I deeply regret that the Peking Union Medical College should have passed out of the hands of the China Medical Board and been taken over by the Peking Government. . . . We must not feel that this necessarily means a curtailment of the College's usefulness, but rather only a change in its management attended very probably by certain limitations in its ideals and standards. But who are we to say that this may not be the Lord's way of achieving the intent of the founders, although it be a way so wholly different from what has been in our minds. Let us hope, pray and believe that all may be ultimately for the best.[4]

Rockefeller's vision for PUMC had long been contradictory—that it would become fully assimilated by the Chinese, but that it would also maintain its high American standards. His assumption that Communist management would preserve the institution while only bringing about "certain limitations in its ideals and standards" was—in 1951—to put it mildly, highly optimistic.

By mid-1951, the Korean War was at its height. General Douglas MacArthur had pushed American troops to the Yalu River, and Mao Zedong had ordered Chinese troops to intervene in support of North Korea. All talk of U.S. diplomatic recognition of the PRC had ended. With Chinese and American troops at war, the Resist America/Aid Korea campaign in China was at its height. As much as any institution in Peking, PUMC, with its long RF history and American ownership, by the China Medical Board, was a symbol of American imperialism. Thus, the repudiation of their U.S. connections became a political necessity for the PUMC faculty and staff.

Teams of PUMC medical scientists were drafted into the Resist America / Aid Korea campaign, and some were sent to North Korea to test for evidence of American germ warfare. PUMC director Li Zongen was made an example to all when he acquiesced in the campaign, publicly reporting that "the American aggressors with the collaboration of Japanese and Nazi germ war criminals launched bacterial warfare against Korea and Northwest China in flagrant violation of international law."[5] (Decades later, Zhong Huilan, a 1929 PUMC graduate, who was also a member of the investigatory group, revealed that the PUMC team had seen no evidence of germ warfare.)[6]

Not only were the two nations at war; the PRC government proceeded to obliterate all vestiges of American influence in higher education. Peking University was moved to the Yanjing University campus and the two institutions merged, effectively ending Yanjing's identity. Both its Sociology and Economics departments, long supported by the Rockefeller Foundation, were abolished. The leading sociologists Fei Xiaotong and Wu Wenzao—also previously funded by the Rockefeller Foundation—found themselves, along with other sociologists, in the Institute of Minorities. Qinghua University, which had become known for the humanities, was reorganized as an engineering school; its strong Liberal Arts and Sciences departments were eliminated or transferred to Peking University. Robert Winter, who received Rockefeller Foundation grants through 1951, was among those transferred to Peking University. Missionary colleges across the country were absorbed into existing Chinese institutions or radically reorganized. As China turned to relying on technical and educational assistance from the Soviet Union, the Soviet model of narrowly focused research and technical institutes affiliated with industrial ministries began to prevail. The American models of a liberal arts college and comprehensive university that had begun to take root in China during the 1930s and 1940s disappeared almost overnight.[7] Even today, sixty years later, there are only a few experiments with a liberal arts curriculum, and the wholesale merger of institutions into so-called comprehensive universities has been mainly symbolic.

One might have expected the same fate for the "Johns Hopkins" of China. Indeed, PUMC's elitist education was decried by the Nationalists and the League of Nations advisers long before the Communist victory. PUMC's pioneering School of Nursing was downgraded to a department, and many nursing faculty were assigned out of PUMC to hospitals around Beijing. This abrupt end to higher-level nursing education was to have a severe impact on the nursing profession in China; postsecondary nursing education did not resume until 1983.

In 1952, PUMC itself became the site of a vitriolic campaign against American science and medicine. PUMC students, newly arrived from their premedical program at Peking University (previously Yanjing University), were among the revolutionary activists who helped sort through archival material and hospital records to mount the exhibit "Blood and Tears from PUMC," exposing American physicians as charlatans or, worse, as murderers. Displays purporting to demonstrate medical crimes included videos of patients undergoing psychiatric shock treatments and samples of human tissue biopsies; both were used to demonstrate malicious experimentation and human cruelty. One of the young PUMC students who helped organize the exhibit, today a retired PUMC professor, believes that while most of it distorted reality, there was evidence of clinical research trials that would not meet today's standards.[8] This is likely true. Not only were medical ethical standards different from today; patient safeguards were less likely to be applied to a foreign population than to an American one. The exhibit also highlighted PUMC's connections with the U.S. government, which were considered especially treasonous. A letter from Roger Greene to John Grant about United States–China relations was featured, demonstrating that "from the start the hospital and teaching college was seen by the imperialists as an instrument that fitted in with their plans for controlling China and the Rockefeller Foundation with all its tawdry benevolent trimmings was a useful cover for the purpose."[9]

PUMC graduates and professors were singled out for public "confessions" during much of 1951 and 1952. Members of the senior faculty were required to recant PUMC's high standards and to denounce Rockefeller influence. Typical were statements from Wu Jieping (PUMC, 1942) and Li Zongen: The Rockefeller Foundation's motive for creating PUMC was "the greatest bulwark for cultural imperialism," and "the Foundation is a world organ for cultural aggression."[10]

When PUMC's name was changed to the China Union Medical College in 1952, it seemed likely that the institution was destined for either an entirely new future or obliteration. The Chinese government certainly had a number of choices: It could have combined PUMC with Peking Medical College, or it could have dispersed the faculty and students to hospitals and other institutions, as with the School of Nursing. Elsewhere in China, medical colleges were merged and consolidated; for example, three private medical colleges, including the American Saint John's University Medical School and the French Aurora University Medical School, were combined to form the Shanghai Second Medical College.[11]

In fact, PUMC—despite four different names between 1952 and 1985, and two major periods of closure[12]—persisted. Given the political and cultural challenges that still lay ahead—the anti-rightist movement in 1957, and the Cultural Revolution from 1966 to 1976—what is remarkable is that the core identity of PUMC endured. If it had been possible for JDR Jr. or William Welch or Roger Greene to have visited PUMC in the mid-1980s, when it regained its original name, or in 2007, when it celebrated its ninetieth anniversary, they would have felt right at home. Today, a historic display proudly proclaims that the PUMC system "was handed down and perfected continuously." Its proudly touted characteristics would be music to the ears of the founders: "elite medical education, small-scale classes, high standard."[13] Furthermore, a scan of the key medical colleges throughout China would find near-clones in all key dimensions except the size of the student body. At the apex of China's system of medical education, the original Johns Hopkins curative model—for better and for worse—has prevailed. Recent Chinese writings extol this educational model and its influence on PUMC:

> Johns Hopkins University emphasized students' own practice rather than lectures. . . . Young medical students were no longer passive observers, but participants. The way they acquired knowledge had changed from listening to lectures and observing demonstrations to actual operation in labs, bedside teaching and intern's responsibility for patients. . . . The PUMC, which was greatly influenced by Johns Hopkins, . . . emphasized practice and the cultivation of skills.[14]

Thus, the legacy of Rockefeller medicine in the PRC includes the persistence of the Johns Hopkins model of medical education and research. It also includes a professional community of self-perpetuating medical elites whose careers, from beginning to end, were shaped by both American science and Chinese realities. The conceptual design of China's rural health delivery system, even the famous "barefoot doctors," is also part of the Rockefeller legacy. It is, however, the legacy of Rockefeller medical education that accounts for the endurance of the American curative model of medical education and a relatively weak public health education system. The questions that are being asked today about medical care in China remain ones that have been asked for a century, and to which the Rockefeller Foundation and PUMC gave insufficient emphasis: how to train sufficient numbers of physicians for China's rural population, and how to integrate curative and preventive medicine into an effective health care delivery system.

How does a historian explain not expected change but remarkable continuity—especially when one considers the preservation in a Communist system of the original Johns Hopkins elite model of medical training that linked basic research, clinical training, and full-time professional practice? For what is most surprising about PUMC today is the degree to which it has stubbornly adhered, almost anachronistically, to the original Flexnerian approach to medical education. No Chinese educational or scientific institution has been as buffeted by political forces, even having its famous hospital to be renamed "anti-imperialist," and yet has emerged so little changed. What explains its persistent and ultimately successful effort to maintain and even replicate its original identity?

Conclusions drawn earlier concerning the role of American science in Republican China are relevant here. By 1951, when American support was withdrawn, PUMC had become an institutionally coherent, professionally autonomous, and self-perpetuating institution. It was, after all, thirty-four years old, and it had enjoyed continuous financial support from the Rockefeller Foundation and China Medical Board, strong leadership, and Rockefeller patronage. Repeated efforts by the Chinese Communist Party (CCP) challenged its professional autonomy, but efforts to alter its essence ultimately failed. Scores of interviews with graduates coupled with Chinese studies of PUMC, including an institutional history and biographical reminiscences, reveal an extraordinary professional and emotional identification with the original model, a model that was successfully perpetuated by PUMC's Chinese leaders.[15] Writing in the early twenty-first century about what he called "the PUMC phenomenon," Huang Jianshi, PUMC professor of public health, cites four reasons for PUMC's persistence: a clearly stated mission; a worldwide recognized model, Johns Hopkins; a unique culture and tradition; and a continuous spirit of reform and creativity.[16]

Chapters from a 2004 book about the "old" PUMC, *Huashuo Lao Xiehe*, illustrate the detail with which PUMC memories have been enshrined and passed on for half a century. Its most prominent graduates contributed such articles as "Random Memory of the Weekly Resident Conferences of the Department of Medicine," "The System of 24-Hour Shifts for Interns, "and "PUMC: The Starting Point for My Journey of Science." The Class of 1943 contributed a joint article: "Recollecting PUMC with Love and Attachment." Individual professors were eulogized, with special attention to the biologist Wu Xian and the physiologist Lin Kesheng, even though both left China in the late 1940s. Special programs were featured—the nursing school, the first urban health station, the Dingxian rural health programs, and the social service department.[17]

The concept of epistemic communities is helpful in understanding the role of these memories and the efforts to preserve PUMC's distinct culture. An epistemic community is a knowledge community with a shared sense of values and norms, which is often transnational in its professional identity. Such a community is a network of professionals with "recognized expertise and competence in a particular domain, . . . with a shared set of normative and principled beliefs . . . and a set of common practices associated with a set of problems to which their professional competence is directed, presumably out of the conviction that human welfare will be enhanced as a consequence."[18] Even in authoritarian countries, epistemic communities often manage to preserve their shared professional identity.

To understand this better, we will examine the various ways in which the PUMC community perpetuated its identity and the role it has played in the PRC. We will first look at the period 1951–79: the careers of the first cohort of PUMC medical graduates, the fate of Rockefeller-funded public health programs, and the political challenges to PUMC and its leadership group. This era, essentially Mao's China, witnessed the devastating upheavals of the anti-rightist and Cultural Revolution periods. It also includes the steady growth of China's medical institutions—hospitals, research institutes, and medical colleges. It was here that PUMC's graduates made a real difference. We then turn to the post–Cultural Revolution period (1979 to the present), the Reform era, and examine new challenges to PUMC.

PUMC GRADUATES IN THE PEOPLE'S REPUBLIC: THE MEDICAL COHORT

Between 1923 and 1943, PUMC graduated only 313 students, a number so small as to evoke criticism—from the Rockefeller Foundation itself, the League of Nations, and leading educators of the Republican era. Few could imagine that the members of this tiny group would, in time, justify the expenditures and hopes that were lavished upon them; they were selected, trained, and mentored to become the medical leaders of modern China. Yet this is exactly who they became.

In 2004, Han Qide, president of the rival Peking University Health Science Center and a graduate not of PUMC but of Shanghai Medical College, spoke eloquently of the PUMC model and the record of its graduates:

> The significance of PUMC is that it set the model of modern medical education in China. Many of her department heads were the medical discipline founders in modern China. Many of her graduates became academic leaders and the mainstream in other leading medical institutions. PUMC has been the cradle of medical leadership and has prepared the first generation of medical leaders for China.[19]

My personal interviews with about 10 percent of these graduates, primarily during the 1980s, coupled with detailed biographical information, have resulted in a data bank that profiles all but a few of the PUMC students who graduated before 1949 (appendix B lists all the individuals interviewed). This information suggests that it was not just their PUMC experience that created these leadership patterns. Their attitudes and careers were nested in and shaped by the particularity of their own local China experience, beginning with family background and career choice. Several were the progeny of well-known Chinese statesmen—Liang Qichao, Zeng Guofan, and Zhou Yichun. A few in the early years had fathers who were traditional Confucian scholars, while others increasingly came from modern professional families—military, law, business, and education. Most came from relatively wealthy families, but PUMC provided full scholarships to many, including some who became the most prominent—the obstetrician and gynecologist Lin Qiaozhi, the hematologist Deng Jiadong, and the public health specialist Chen Zhiqian. More than 60 percent came from four eastern provinces: Jiangsu, Hebei, Guangdong, and Fujian. The most common element was their preparatory education; graduates between 1924 and 1930 attended PUMC's own premedical school, while after 1930 more than 50 percent attended Yanjing University, and the remainder primarily attended missionary colleges. PUMC administered its own stringent examination, long remembered by graduates. The preponderance of students from missionary-affiliated institutions was due to their relative strength in the natural sciences and instruction in English. Attendance at a missionary institution did not necessarily indicate that the students were Christian, but the PUMC student body and academic community did include a small percentage of Christians, including Lin Qiaozhi and Yang Chongrui.

The choice of a modern medical career requiring a long preparatory period also set these students apart from other Chinese students of this era. Their family and educational backgrounds meant that they were independent modernists before they came to PUMC. Most seem to have been predisposed against traditional medicine before arriving at PUMC. Two-thirds of those interviewed cited a family death, either unexplained or badly treated by traditional medicine, as the primary personal and familial motive for commitment to an eight-year program of the most sophisticated training. Chen Zhiqian's experience before 1920 was typical: "When I was young, besides my father and his younger brother, everyone passed away during my childhood, my aunt and my mother probably died of the same type of tuberculosis, my brother of typhoid fever, but we never found out what took my sister's life."[20] At the age of fourteen, he traveled with his stepmother to visit the French Consulate in Chengdu to look for Western doctors and to find tutors who could instruct him in science and English.

In making their career choice, these PUMC graduates were also seeking a measure of social autonomy. Their second most frequently cited motive was independence. One graduate noted that when he wrote in PUMC's entrance exam that he wanted "to contribute something for humanity, to help suffering. . . . That was in part true, but I also knew that it would help me to become independent."[21] Financial independence was a factor, but freedom from family-determined careers (business and military) was frequently cited. These memories suggest the degree to which norms of scientific thinking and personal autonomy preceded their intense institutional exposure to American science. After graduation, the influence of locality, of specific institutional site, and of history upon career development was also striking.

The leadership career patterns of PUMC graduates first became evident during the 1930s and 1940s.[22] In contrast to graduates from missionary and Chinese medical colleges, very few went into private practice; only 6 percent in 1934. In 1937, forty-two of the fifty-six earliest graduates were in positions of significant leadership—directors of hospitals or provincial and municipal health administrations and professors at medical colleges. Not unexpectedly, fourteen of that early group remained at PUMC, and they became its core faculty in the 1940s and beyond. Also, like other modern medical doctors, the graduates were disproportionately located in three cities: Peking, Shanghai, and Nanjing. In 1937, 63 percent of the graduates before 1934 were in those three cities, with 34 percent in Peking itself.

One characteristic of PUMC's training was the expectation of study abroad, funded by the China Medical Board. All PUMC degrees were licensed in the State of New York, permitting some medical practice in the United States. Fifty-five percent of those who graduated before 1934 had studied abroad by 1937. Every graduate had returned to China by 1937. This was only partly the result of identifying a position to which they would return; U.S. immigration laws remained very exclusionary. A second characteristic was the popularity of public health as a specialty, second only to internal medicine. As we have seen, not only did John Grant create a strong department, but career opportunities also increased as public health programs sponsored by the national and provincial governments began to spread in the 1930s.

When the PRC was established and all ties with Western countries were sev-
ered, the fate of this elite medical cohort was uncertain. How would their skills be
used in this new era? Individual career profiles of 95 percent of PUMC graduates
after 1949 illustrate the geographical and institutional range of the Rockefeller
medical legacy.[23]

About half the total PUMC graduates were in four of China's largest eastern
cities: eighty-two in Peking, thirty-four in Shanghai, thirty in Tianjin, and eleven
in Guangzhou. This concentration represents a slight decrease from 1937, when
63 percent were in three cities and 34 percent were in Beijing alone. About one-
quarter permanently left mainland China for medical careers abroad. Those who
had been most active in the National Health Administration of the Guomindang
migrated to Taiwan. There they founded and became the leaders of Taiwan's
National Defense Medical University. By the early 1970s, some twenty PUMC
graduates, including a few nurses, were active in medical institutions in Taiwan.[24]
Others joined the World Health Organization (WHO) or continued their medical
careers in the United States. The distribution of the remaining quarter becomes
most interesting; they were widely scattered across thirteen provinces in twenty
different cities. Given the propensity of Western-educated Chinese intellectuals
to remain in the most cosmopolitan centers and at their mother institution, the
forces of dispersal must have been strong. In PUMC's case, these forces appear
to have been the most significant: the disruption of the Sino-Japanese War, the
anti-rightist campaign (more than 25 percent were branded rightists, with some
being relocated permanently to distant provinces), the growth of several major
new medical centers, the reverse pull of one's native province and city, and the
general dispersion of major urban centers after 1949.

Between 1950 and 1980, these PUMC graduates dominated medical education and research in China, despite persecution during both the anti-rightist
and Cultural Revolution periods. These were the peak professional years of
those trained at the original PUMC. Their most evident leadership was as
presidents and deans of China's key medical colleges, directors of hospitals,
and founders of medical specializations and journals. Writing in 1981, PUMC
president Huang Jiasi noted that twelve of the major medical colleges in the
1950s were led by either PUMC graduates or former faculty. Of particular
significance was the leadership of Hu Chuankui (PUMC, 1927), the longtime
(1948–79) president of what is today known as Peking University Health Science Center.[25] Profiles of medical communities in Tianjin, Shanghai, Guangzhou, and Peking further illustrate the cohesiveness of the PUMC community
and its national influence.

With the closure of PUMC in World War II, a group of its graduates migrated
to nearby Tianjin. The cluster of institutions for which they provided leadership
was often called the "little PUMC." Zhu Xianyi (PUMC, 1930) served as president

of Tianjin Medical College, and Jin Xianzhai (PUMC, 1931), was founder and director of Tianjin Cancer Hospital. As with many medical facilities in China, this latter institute evolved from, and was on the site of, the missionary-sponsored MacKenzie Medical School, which dated to the early twentieth century. Shi Xien (PUMC, 1929) developed the first urology laboratory in Tianjin, which included one of the first hemodialysis labs in China.[26]

In Shanghai, PUMC graduates clustered around Shanghai First Medical College (previously National Shanghai Medical College and today Shanghai Medical College of Fudan University). The early leaders of Shanghai First included Yan Fuqing, who had served briefly as pro forma director of PUMC, followed by Zhu Hengbi, who had studied pharmacology at PUMC. Before leaving Shanghai for PUMC in the late 1950s, Huang Jiasi (PUMC, 1933) had been the first Chinese surgeon to successfully complete open lung surgery. Others who made important contributions to Shanghai First were Rong Dushan, (PUMC, 1929) in radiology, Lin Feiqing (PUMC, 1932) in microbiology, and Xiong Rucheng (PUMC, 1936) in surgery and as longtime director of Zhongshan Hospital. In 1984, these graduates were proud to have introduced a section of English-only medical instruction—the first one since PUMC before 1951.[27]

Guangzhou had been the earliest site of Western medicine in China, and today Zhongshan Medical College's Second Affiliated Hospital stands on the site of Peter Parker's original eye clinic. A significant number of PUMC students had originally come from Guangdong, and during the 1930s and 1940s these graduates were encouraged to return to South China. Two of their PUMC colleagues had assumed leadership positions in local medical colleges: Li Tingan (PUMC, 1926) became president of Lingnan Medical College, and Tang Zeguang (PUMC, 1929) became president of Hackett Medical College. These institutions combined to form Zhongshan School of Medicine in the early 1950s, and Chen Guozhen (PUMC, 1933) served as vice president and dean of the Medical College for many years.[28]

PUMC influence in these four key cities was augmented by the scores of faculty and researchers who continued to enroll in PUMC's short-term postgraduate training programs. In this sense, PUMC continued the very important postgraduate training that was highly commended during the Republican era. Because these researchers and faculty members rotated back to their home institution, it was perhaps inevitable that PUMC became the standard to which other medical schools continued to aspire.

PUMC's leadership was not just in education; many of its graduates were involved in the nitty-gritty of hospital administration. Upward of 40 percent of PUMC graduates served as hospital administrators, perhaps the most direct link between Rockefeller medicine and Chinese society. None of the PUMC graduates had any formal training in hospital administration, and the hospitals where they worked were far removed from the relatively pristine conditions of PUMC's hospital, even though some also served as teaching hospitals and eventually became major centers of clinical research. Three examples are the Peking Children's Hospital, the Peking Friendship Hospital, and the aforementioned Tianjin Cancer Hospital.

Zhu Futang (PUMC, 1927) and Wu Ruiping (PUMC, 1933) set up a pediatric clinic toward the end of World War II. When the PRC was established, it was the only children's hospital in Peking. Zhu had been trained at PUMC by Ashley Weech (who went on to a distinguished career at Columbia University), and he had also studied at Boston Children's Hospital. Weech would later recall Zhu as "a brilliant student and scientist—one of the few residents in my career whom I knew would lie awake at night worrying that a baby might be in pain."[29] In 1984, Zhu proudly showed me around Peking Children's Hospital and talked openly about the trauma of the Cultural Revolution. Although proud of the medical advances in China under the CCP, he was also passionate about the importance of his American medical training and the lasting influence of PUMC. Memory and his foreign visitor may have enhanced his appreciation of the past:

> You must understand, the motto of our college was Science and Humanity. Most of us alumni tried to live up to this motto—in a country that has grown to 1 billion people. Whether we are socialists or capitalists, this has been our life guide: science and humanity. For myself, it has been the betterment of child health. It has not been easy.[30]

Zhu was more than a hospital director; he published widely and trained the next generation of Chinese pediatricians, earning him the appellation "the father of pediatrics in China."

The title of founder of tropical medicine goes to Zhong Huilan (PUMC, 1929), who founded the Peking Friendship Hospital, within which he also established the Peking Tropical Medical Research Institute. When he was a young parasitologist in the 1930s, Zhong's pathbreaking research linked dogs to the life cycle of kala-azar, leading to the elimination of this debilitating disease in the 1950s. His career continued with clinical and scientific research on malaria, filariasis, leishmaniasis, and hookworm—contributing to the significant reduction of infectious diseases in China. His professional leadership included editing the *Chinese Medical Journal* from 1950 to 1965 and founding and editing *The Journal of Tropical Medicine*. [31]

PUMC graduates also dominated the medical research infrastructure of China right up to the Cultural Revolution. A cursory survey of Chinese medical journals from 1949 to 1965 revealed articles by seventy-five (about a third of the PUMC graduates remaining in China). The topics ranged from kala-azar to cancer, from plastic surgery to neurology. When the Chinese Academy of Medical Sciences (CAMS) was constituted in 1958, six of its eight institutes were led by PUMC graduates. The Chinese Medical Association, a national professional organization, continued to be dominated by PUMC personnel, just as it had in previous decades. The association's vice presidents included Lin Qiaozhi, Zhong Huilan, Hu Chuankui, Fang Shishan, and Yan Fuqing. The association published the *Chinese Medical Journal*, and in 1962 nineteen of its twenty-six editors were former PUMC faculty or graduates. The most prestigious recognition was to be chosen as a member of the Chinese Academy of Science; seven of the nine biomedical members listed in 1955 were former PUMC faculty or graduates.[32] AnElissa Lucas, who emphasizes the continuities between Guomindang and PRC medical policies and personnel, writes: "The role of PUMC as a network linchpin and continuing conduit to powerful professional and administrative positions continued well after the apparent consolidation of Chinese medical personnel and facilities under the auspices of the CCP."[33]

PUMC GRADUATES: THE PUBLIC HEALTH COHORT

In China today, PUMC is best known and remembered for the leading role of its graduates in medical research and medical education. Nonetheless, China's public health programs benefited from the Rockefeller legacy as well. The PRC's Ministry of Health included PUMC graduates and officials from the public health programs of the Nationalist period. Although some moved with Zhu Zhanggeng to Taiwan, others remained in Nanjing and eventually became part of the new ministry in Peking.

Li Dequan, the wife of the warlord Feng Yuxiang, was an especially important transitional figure in this regard. In 1928, John Grant had known of her interest in health and asked her to assure the appointments of qualified professionals to the new Ministry of Health. She remained associated with public health programs, and in 1949 she was named the first minister of health in Mao's government. From this position, she brought in a number of PUMC-related persons to positions of policy influence, most notably Jin Baoshan (P. Z. King), who was widely regarded as one of China's most competent technical experts in the field of public health. Jin, a Japanese-trained physician, had been one of the first directors of Grant's Health Station in Peking. He received Rockefeller Foundation support to study public health in the United States, and, after serving as health commissioner for Hankou and Peking, he became vice director and then director of the Ministry of Health under the Guomindang during the

1940s. Jin also became a WHO official after the war. Upon returning to the PRC in the early 1950s as a senior member of the Ministry of Health, he became an ardent advocate of extending the three-tier *xian* health care system throughout China *(see chapter 2)*. He later became chairman of the Department of Public Health at Peking Medical College. Also serving with Jin in the PRC Ministry of Health was Yang Chongrui, who headed the Maternal Health Division. Yan Jingqing (PUMC, 1932) became Peking's commissioner for public health in the early 1950s and remained in that position until she was purged during the Cultural Revolution.

The PUMC public health influence after 1951 was, however, diminished by the significant exodus of leading individuals who were closely affiliated with the Nationalist government and left for Taiwan or WHO. These included, most notably, Liu Ruiheng, Lin Kesheng, and Zhu Zhanggeng. In addition, a number of relatively young PUMC public health graduates found jobs at WHO.

The two public health concepts most identified with PUMC—the integration of public health training into medical education for all students, and the *xian* health care delivery system—met very different fates. Ironically, the public health education program disappeared from PUMC's medical curriculum in the early 1950s and has never been reinstated at PUMC or any other medical college in China. What was distinct about the PUMC curriculum from the 1920s to the 1940s was the requirement that all medical students complete an internship or rotation in either an urban or rural health care station. In addition, one of the medical specialty choices was public health.

The primary reason that public health disappeared from medical education was the adoption of the Soviet education system in the early 1950s. In the USSR, public health was a technical track, separate and at a lower level than medicine. Public health schools were created with no linkage to medical schools. This was in contrast to the original Johns Hopkins model, which included both a medical school and a public health school within the same university. Although some of the Soviet model institutions eventually became public health schools within medical universities, the curriculum in China—to this day—has remained distinct. In his memoirs, Chen Zhiqian decried the new public health curriculum: "It emphasized classroom and laboratory instruction rather than field training at rural sites. . . . The public health schools . . . ranked lower in prestige because the best students were selected for medicine, not public health.[34] A few Chinese medical colleges have recently reintroduced some population health science into their curriculum, but this remains a general educational weakness.

Interestingly enough, it was PUMC's most radical contribution to health care in China—the three-tier *xian* health care system and "barefoot doctors"—that persisted. Chen Zhiqian, honored today as "the father of China's rural health care delivery system," continued to make contributions to public health until his death at the age of ninety-seven in 2000. After World War II, Chen was based in Sichuan, his native province, serving initially as founder and director of Chongqing Medical College. After 1952, this college moved to join the former West China Medical College, which was renamed Sichuan Medical College. When it was reorganized along Soviet lines with a separate school of public health, Chen became director, serving until he was removed in 1957 as a rightist. Although he and his family faced many difficulties during those years and the subsequent Cultural Revolution, he was able to continue teaching most of the time. After the Cultural Revolution, he was exonerated and once again became active—redeveloping rural research training programs and traveling internationally.[35] In 2004, four years after his death, Sichuan University honored the one-hundredth anniversary of his birth by dedicating a statue and a conference center and publishing a tribute to him.[36]

Although Chen himself was not directly involved at a national level, his Dingxian health care model, which had influenced both the Guomindang's national health plan and the CCP's medical work in Yanan, was quickly adopted by the PRC government in the early 1950s. Multiple studies have confirmed this author's earlier hypothesis that it was indeed the *xian* plan designed during the 1930s that became the organizational model for health care delivery in China.[37] Neither the three-tiered village/township/county levels of medical care nor "barefoot doctors" were the invention of a populist CCP. Their historical antecedents came directly from the work of PUMC graduate Chen Zhiqian. He himself remembered that He Cheng, first vice minister of public health, was familiar with Chen's writings and the Dingxian experience from the 1920s and 1930s. He Cheng invited Chen to the first national conference on health care in 1950, telling him: "We have known of your work for some time, and it is quite compatible with the Communists. We hope you will cooperate with us."[38] As China struggles today with providing equitable health care to its rural population, there is renewed attention to Chen Zhiqian's voluminous writings on equitable and inexpensive health care delivery. Recent publications in the Chinese journal *Modern Preventive Medicine* summarize his theoretical contributions and call for the renaming of the Dingxian Model the "Chen Model."[39]

These profiles illustrate the role of PUMC's graduates during the PRC's first decades. With selective memory, perhaps, and the desire to project careers that had in the main been productive, few openly expressed bitterness in 1984 about the Cultural Revolution. Set aside were memories of the class labels they were assigned during Mao's China: "running dogs of capitalist imperialists" or "stinking ninth class of intellectuals." The prevailing tone was one of pride, a strong nationalist pride in what China had accomplished in medicine since 1949. *Xiehe ren*, "PUMC person," a pejorative appellation for two decades, by the mid-1980s had come to be a term of respect.

PRESERVING PUMC, 1951–79

The leading role played by PUMC graduates in China's key medical centers in the 1950s and 1960s was an important factor in the political preservation of the medical college itself. At a time when it was far better to be "Red" than "expert," the career patterns of PUMC graduates helped to make the case for a specialized elite. When PUMC reopened in 1947 after World War II, all but three faculty members were Chinese, the majority having been trained at PUMC. After years of residency, study abroad, and junior faculty positions, they were ready to assume leadership positions. The departmental chairs included Zhang Xiaoqian (medicine), Lin Qiaozhi (obstetrics and gynecology), Zhu Futang (pediatrics), Hu Zhengxiang (pathology), Zhang Xijun (physiology), and Wu Yingkai (surgery). These were PUMC's "stars," medical leaders whose reputation eventually earned them election to the Chinese Academy of Sciences and places on China's commemorative stamps. The PUMC culture, which had both challenged and nurtured them, was replicated with their students whenever possible, even under the often heavy-handed CCP rule. A half-century later, aging graduates remembered in great detail the Socratic teaching method, tutorials, and rigorous laboratory training provided whenever possible during the 1950s and 1960s. As one student from the 1950s recalled: "They taught us how to learn, how to think, how to imagine."[40]

However, the institution was not the same. On January 1, 1952, PUMC was taken over by the People's Revolutionary Military Commission. China was at war, and there were many wounded who needed treatment. Military medical institutions were almost nonexistent in Peking. As a result, PUMC faculty and students were assigned military rank and wore uniforms. Some key faculty were dispersed immediately to establish Military Hospital #301, which became the military's elite hospital and continues, to this day, to provide most of the medical care for senior political leaders.

Military officers joined some of the PUMC classes. Many of them graduated in 1956, swelling the numbers of PUMC graduates that year to more than one hundred. One purpose of mixing military students with traditional PUMC students, as remembered by one graduate, was to "mix sand into the American imperialist culture." The periodic political campaigns disrupted but did not cancel classes. Ultimately, the military occupation was short-lived; both the college and the hospital continued to be run until 1956—more or less—along previous standards by PUMC graduates. One exception was Western publications; from 1951 until the late 1970s, there was little access to Western scientific and medical publications. In 1956, PUMC was turned over to the Ministry of Health, and some of the previously dispersed faculty were allowed to return to PUMC.

In the long run, PUMC benefited from its affiliation with the military and with Military Hospital #301. More than sixty PUMC graduates between 1952 and 1958 were assigned to military medical institutions, most of them to Military Hospital #301.[41] China's military and political leaders came to appreciate the clinical competence of PUMC physicians and the overall quality of Peking Union Medical College Hospital. Both Mao Zedong and Zhou Enlai periodically recognized the PUMC leadership group *(see figure 4.1)*, and a number of CCP leaders were treated by its physicians. But this did not translate into political support for its lengthy educational program.

FIGURE 4.1. Mao Zedong and the leaders of Peking Union Medical College, circa 1960. From left: Zhong Huilan, Huang Jiasi, Lin Qiaozhi. *Photograph courtesy of Peking Union Medical College.*

What has been most difficult for PUMC, continuing even today, has been training a successor generation, even though this has been the goal of the PUMC leadership: preserving, at all costs, PUMC's high academic standards and its distinctive educational program. Central to the PUMC tradition was an eight-year educational program that included three years of premedical education, followed by five clinical years, including research. The length of medical training does not necessarily equate with greater clinical competence or research productivity, but PUMC advocates enshrined their "eight-year model," which maintained PUMC's premier status, and resisted all efforts to modify it. What they sought to protect was PUMC's strong premedical foundation in the basic sciences and its attention to both clinical supervision and clinical research. All this was possible in an institution with a strong teaching hospital linked to the educational program *and* with a small student body.

This educational curriculum was anathema to Mao's new egalitarian government, which quickly moved to expand the second tier of the three- to five-year medical education programs started during the 1930s. Political opposition to the PUMC model is fully understandable. In the early 1950s, China had approximately 41,000 college-level physicians and 140,000 intermediate-level Western medical personnel, including nurses, laboratory technicians, midwives, and lower-level physicians[42]—for a population of more than 500 million, 80 percent of them in the countryside. With such an enormous need, PUMC's thirty annual graduates seemed totally irrelevant. Criticism of "eight-year medical programs" became a surrogate critique of PUMC. Nevertheless, the government's repeated efforts to dramatically enlarge the institution and to reduce its standards were rebuffed by PUMC's leaders. For two and a half decades, PUMC refused to enroll large classes or institute a three- to five-year curriculum. The PUMC leaders endured the periodic closure of the educational program rather than lower standards. But the educational and political cost was enormous:

- No new classes were enrolled between 1954 and 1959.
- No new classes were enrolled between 1966 and 1979.
- There were no graduates between 1968 and 1987.

PUMC was not completely closed, because enrolled students were allowed to continue in the 1950s. Those who graduated before 1957 received, in large measure, the same kind of education as their predecessors: three years of premedical science at Peking University, and five years at PUMC, followed by systematic residency training. These are considered PUMC's second cohort of graduates, taught by PUMC's prestigious first generation. Although English was no longer the medium of instruction after the early 1950s, most of this second generation had excellent English, having learned it in high school and at Peking University. Very few were sent to the USSR for advanced training; however, most were sent to provincial areas to practice medicine during the Cultural Revolution. These graduates of the 1950s went on to become the backbone of PUMC in the 1980s and 1990s.

PUMC was not alone among institutions of higher education to have its doors closed during the Great Leap Forward and the Cultural Revolution, but the periods of closure appear to have been longest at PUMC. Nonetheless, as China Medical College, PUMC continued as an identifiable and coherent institution with remarkable continuity of faculty and leadership. Li Zongen retained his position until deposed in the anti-rightist campaign of 1957. Shortly thereafter, Huang Jiasi was named director and held this position until he died in 1984. He was then briefly succeeded by Wu Jieping (PUMC, 1942). All three remained advocates of the traditional PUMC standard, despite extraordinary personal and political pressure *(see figure 4.2)*.

FIGURE 4.2. Peking Union Medical College presidents 1947–84. From left: Li Zongen (1947–57), Huang Jiasi (1957–83), and Wu Jieping (1983–84).

As mentioned above, Li was singled out for criticism in the early 1950s. He was a graduate of the Faculty of Medicine at Glasgow in infectious diseases, and he had joined the PUMC department of medicine in 1923, one of the first Chinese faculty. His political independence was well known, and he subsequently spoke out during the 100 Flowers Campaign in 1957. He was openly critical of the government, deploring the efforts to reduce standards at PUMC and the interference of the CCP. Li was not alone in these public criticisms, but he became the PUMC scapegoat when the anti-rightist movement followed. To affirm their own orthodoxy, many of his longtime colleagues spoke out against him and he was dismissed from his position.[43]

Although communication between PUMC and the China Medical Board was very rare, a personal letter from longtime PUMC professor of bacteriology Lin Zongyang to Harold Loucks, former director of the China Medical Board, indirectly alluded to the travails of the anti-rightist period. Lin described himself as studying Russian and raising 800 rose bushes—surely a reference to his role in the 100 Flowers period, and then went on to ask: "Is there any foundation sponsoring public education against wholesale state exploitation and human bondage and slavery under the guise of freedom and liberty?"[44]

Years after Huang Jiasi became PUMC director, he observed that perhaps he had been selected because he had been in Russia with Guo Moruo, president of the Chinese Academy of Sciences, at the time of the 100 Flowers Campaign and was thus unaffected by the anti-rightist movement.[45] Huang was a surgeon trained by Harold Loucks and later under John Alexander at the University of Michigan. He had chaired the Department of Surgery at Shanghai First Medical College and introduced the field of thoracic surgery to China. While serving as PUMC director for almost three decades, he provided the leadership that saw PUMC from the expansion of the late 1950s and early 1960s through the chaos of the Cultural Revolution to the revitalization of the Reform Era. He was also an early member of the CCP, and was a quiet and astute leader who had the confidence of many of China's most important leaders, including Zhou Enlai. He had attended the same high school as Zhou and had sheltered an activist relative who was a fugitive from the Guomindang during the 1940s.[46] Although his political connections often served PUMC well, they did not protect the institution from the vicissitudes of the era, especially the Cultural Revolution. It was under Huang Jiasi's leadership that the new PUMC came into its own as the institutional home of the Chinese Academy of Medical Sciences. A bridge across generations and political systems, Huang was chosen in 1973 to head the first Chinese Medical Delegation from the PRC to visit the United States. It was this delegation that met with John Knowles, president of the Rockefeller Foundation, reconnecting the two institutions. During the last decade of his life, Huang personally led the process that renewed ties between PUMC and the Rockefeller Foundation, and between PUMC and the China Medical Board.

The symbiotic relationship between PUMC and the Chinese Academy of Medical Sciences, overseen initially by Huang, is among the most important elements in the long-term preservation of PUMC as one of China's leading institutions. The Chinese Academy of Medical Sciences is a direct institutional descendant of the Central Field Health Station (*Weisheng shiyan chu*) of the Republican era, which was funded, in part, by the Rockefeller Foundation and based in Nanjing. In 1941, it was merged with the National Public Health Training Institute to create the National Institute of Health (*Zhongyang weisheng shiyanyuan*), which was led by Zhu Zhanggeng and continued to receive Rockefeller support until 1949. Personnel who did not move to Taiwan were consolidated in a move to Peking in 1950. This institute was then merged with the research faculty at PUMC. In 1957, it was reconstituted to form the Chinese Academy of Medical Sciences (CAMS). In effect, CAMS began as the research arm of PUMC, but when the medical college became more attenuated, CAMS became the larger, more visible entity. Huang Jiasi led both; this dual leadership continues today.

The decision to create an academy of medical science came, in part, from the influence of the Soviet Union, which had separate academies of science and medicine, and the Russian emphasis on research. It also reflected China's own growing attention to strengthening research in all fields, including medicine. From the time of the 100 Flowers Movement to the Cultural Revolution, medical research was protected by the Chinese government, and during the early 1960s there was a significant expansion in numbers of medical conferences and publications. Zhou Enlai was an important advocate of scientific and medical research, writing in 1959: "Attention must also be given to developing the most advanced branches of science and technology." In his study of China's medical policies during the Maoist era, David M. Lampton concluded that during the Great Leap Forward (1958–60), "the more prestigious the institution in which the doctor worked, and the more research oriented his position within the profession, the less he was affected by Great Leap Forward mobilization."[47]

The creation of CAMS also provided an opportunity for PUMC to grow, to "expand its platform," as expressed by the current president, Liu Depei. Although other medical colleges were educating hundreds of students in three- and five-year programs, CAMS's emphasis on medical science could be sustained and expanded even as PUMC almost disappeared. These research institutes also partially compensated for PUMC's lack of intellectual affiliation with a comprehensive university. The appointment of Zhang Zhiqiang as vice president of CAMS was especially important. A college-educated military officer, he had oversight for PUMC during the 1950s and returned as CAMS vice president in 1958. (Later Zhang became vice minister of health in 1975.) Fifteen specialized research institutions were created under CAMS before the Cultural Revolution.

In the more relaxed atmosphere of the late 1950s and early 1960s, PUMC once again led medical research and medical education in China. Even Huang's 1958 appeal to the authorities to reinstate the eight-year program was approved. This is considered such an important event that the official documents are displayed at PUMC today. The eight-year degree program resumed, with PUMC students taking their premedical courses at Peking University. Additionally, the medical and research facilities at PUMC expanded.

This resurgence was, however, short-lived. In 1965, Huang Jiasi was sent to the countryside—leading a prestigious group of PUMC faculty—in what was one of the opening salvos of the Cultural Revolution. The specific charges against him were "lingering on an eight-year program" and efforts to restore "old Peking Union Medical College." The reprinting of his book *Surgery* was delayed for eight years.[48] As he remembered these experiences years later, he chose not to dwell on the adversity:

> Even before the Cultural Revolution, Chairman Mao had said "put the stress
> on the rural area," and the year before, 1965, I had taken a mobile medical
> team to the countryside as something like a course, training for junior medical

people. We were involved in starting the program called "part-farmer, part-doctor," which was later called the "barefoot doctor" program. . . . Later, I was kept in what was called a "cowpen" or shed for three months while I was being investigated, and then spent 6 months in the countryside. . . . Later, I went to a May 7th cadres school for 8 or 9 months. Not so bad; you didn't have to think.[49]

Huang was relatively unscathed by the Cultural Revolution, but other PUMC faculty and graduates were less fortunate. Constant harassment by colleagues and families led at least ten graduates to commit suicide, several during the earlier anti-rightist campaign. In reflecting on one such death in 1959, Lin Zongyang lamented in writing to Harold Loucks: "He should have faced the music." But in a subsequent letter years later, reflecting on the PUMC deaths during the Cultural Revolution, Lin was somewhat more empathetic, quoting Dylan Thomas:

> We are all going that way sooner or later, as a poet wrote:
> "Do not go gentle into the good night,
> Old age should burn and rave at close of day;
> Rage, rage against the dying of the light."[50]

The Cultural Revolution closed PUMC as an educational institution, and research was generally discontinued in the institutes of the Chinese Academy of Medical Sciences from 1966 to 1979. It is impossible to overstate the personal and institutional trauma of these years. Roles were reversed; heads of departments cleaned the hospital floors, and students conducted rounds. Families were divided. Large character posters defamed individuals for the slightest "bourgeois" trait. Young faculty members were blamed for the sins of their long-departed professors. The institutional community was rent asunder; at least 500 families, or one-third of the total PUMC-CAMS family, were sent to the Northwest for nine years (1970–79), primarily to Gansu and Xinjiang provinces.

Especially poignant are the memories of PUMC's third cohort, the students who entered PUMC during the brief period of relaxation in 1959–66. *None* were able to complete a regular eight-year curriculum. All are listed, inaccurately, as graduates of 1968, when PUMC had already been closed. Nearly all were sent to remote areas in 1970. Those that had begun their actual medical program at PUMC by the early 1960s were able to complete all their premedical education and some of their clinical work. Those who began their premedical work at Peking University just a few years later, in 1963 or 1964, were almost immediately plunged into the political chaos of the Red Guard movement. One remembered the factions at Peking University, two wasted years, and the decision of his class (which entered in 1964) to leave Peking University and go to PUMC. "Nobody cared," he said, "there was no supervision—at either institution." At PUMC, the library was open four hours a week and students taught themselves. A courageous dean, Zhang Yangfen, did not want them to give up and so organized underground classes that were politically suspect.

Dispatched to Heilongjiang Province in 1970, this medical student worked successively in a rural commune, a health center, and a city hospital. In 1973, he was invited back to PUMC for one year of reeducation but returned to Heilongjiang. Finally, in 1978, two years after Mao's death, Deng Xiaoping announced a postgraduate program designed to bring students back from the countryside. This student taught himself, retook the entrance exams, and returned to PUMC for a three-year MA program. Only then did he really study medicine.

Another student, who had arrived at Peking University in 1963, joined his medical classmates in 1965 and traveled all over China, including walking part of the Long March route. Hearing about demonstrations in Shanghai, they made their way east as a group, and then returned to PUMC in 1967. Again, there were no classes, "only big poster campaigns." He, too, was sent to Heilongjiang. He, too, studied for the graduate exams and was brought back to PUMC in 1979 to continue his education.

These two students returned to PUMC through the combined efforts of Dean Zhang and Huang Jiasi. Zhang made every effort to keep track of the far-flung students, and Huang personally intervened with Zhou Enlai to bring 180 students back to PUMC.[51] Not all were readmitted, but those who returned in 1979 completed a three-year MA program. For many, this was their only sustained medical training. It is this third cohort, the Cultural Revolution generation, that has provided leadership at PUMC and most of China's educational institutions since the 1990s.

Even though the education program was disrupted, during the Cultural Revolution the PUMC Hospital continued to function as a hospital, albeit with no clinical research and a reduced staff. This was perhaps the beginning of the growing institutional separation between PUMC Hospital and the medical college. PUMC physicians, however, still were called upon to provide medical service to the country's leaders. Indeed, throughout the Maoist era, PUMC's clinical strength was both appreciated and called upon by China's political leaders. Wu Jieping was Zhou Enlai's private physician, and he later led the group that handled the preservation of Mao's body following his death. Huang Jiasi was also close to Zhou and was asked by him as early as 1971 to work on a plan to revitalize the Chinese Academy of Medical Sciences. He also joined Deng Xiaoping's brain trust in the mid-1970s, working on plans to revive science and medicine, a key component of the "four modernizations" and reform era that followed the death of Mao Zedong.

The reconstitution of the Chinese Academy of Medical Sciences and PUMC lagged behind other scientific and medical institutions. Not until 1979 was

PUMC once again approved to reinstate its eight-year program. Because some of the CAMS institutes had disappeared or had been taken over by industry, reconstituting these institutes as scientific, academic institutions affiliated with both a medical college and a number of teaching hospitals took until 1981.[52] Not until then was it clear that CAMS and the PUMC educational model had endured. In reflecting on the survival of these elite medical institutions, Huang Jiasi, Wu Jieping, and Deng Jiadong were convinced that their claim upon scientific competence, their strong sense of professional community, and an almost mystic belief in the "old PUMC" saved the elite PUMC model from extinction.[53] The contributions of PUMC alumni to medicine and medical education was evidence enough that an elite cadre could be successful in "people's" China. Once again, *"Xiehe ren"* evoked a sense of professional autonomy and a scientific standard that epitomized the original Rockefeller goal.

PUMC in the Reform Era

Deng Xiaoping's "four modernizations," with their concomitant emphasis upon higher education, science, and technology, assured a resumed role for both PUMC and the Chinese Academy of Medical Sciences. But this did not happen overnight. Huang Jiasi's and Wu Jieping's successors—Gu Fangzhou (1985–92), Ba Denian (1992–2001), and Liu Depei (2001–present)—were not graduates of PUMC (Liu did receive his PhD from PUMC), but each has sought to balance the long-standing traditions of the institution with the physical and scientific needs of a rapidly modernizing medical system *(see figure 4.3)*. The 1980s remained a time of political constraints; periodic campaigns against "bourgeois liberalization" were clearly felt by the faculty and students at PUMC. A graduate institute authorized to grant PhDs was approved in 1986. But not until 1987, on the joint occasion of PUMC's seventieth anniversary and CAMS's thirtieth anniversary, did PUMC regain its name and both institutions regain the political legitimacy that had eluded them for several decades. Then, unexpectedly, the challenge of training a successor generation proved almost impossible.

The seventieth-anniversary celebration coincided with the graduation of PUMC's first post–Cultural Revolution class of MDs, and a lavish ceremony was held at the Capital Theatre near PUMC. More than thirty Chinese officials, many of them important political personages, sat on the stage. These included not only leading academics such as Zhou Peiyuan and leading medical figures such as the minister of public health but also Xi Zhongxun, a member of the Politburo, four members of the Standing Committee of the National People's Congress, and Peking's CCP secretary.

FIGURE 4.3. Peking Union Medical College presidents: Gu Fangzhou (1985–92), Ba Denian (1992–2001), Liu Depei (2001–present).

Minister of Health Chen Minzhang's congratulatory message was typical of those presented:

> The Academy and the College assume the glorious historical mission of being geared to the needs of the whole country and serving for the whole country. In the past decades the Academy and the College have trained a great number of excellent talents in medicine and health circles and some outstanding pioneers of specialties of sciences for our country. They can be found in many places both at home and abroad. Their contributions to developing and prospering the country's medical science cause has made a deep impression on us.[54]

More unexpected was the flowery tribute from the president of the Chinese Academy of Traditional Medicine. After giving several examples of ways in which PUMC's scientists had cooperated with researchers in traditional Chinese medicine, he waxed poetic:

> It may well be recalled that "peaches and plums" are everywhere, as a Chinese proverb goes, meaning that the College has its students everywhere. You have played a very important role in promoting the progress and development of the country's medical science, medical education, and medical and health cause.[55]

The legacy of PUMC's most famous graduates—for example, the gynecologist Lin Qiaozhi and the thoracic surgeon Huang Jiasi—was invoked by nearly every speaker. There was, however, no public mention of PUMC's American origins.

The highlight of the program was, of course, the graduation of PUMC's successor generation; as in the precommunist era, there were still only thirty graduates. E. Grey Dimond, who attended the ceremony, wrote: "No one could overlook the emotion brought forth as this thin line of excellence crossed the stage, carrying on the tradition of an institution celebrating its seventieth anniversary."[56] The class representative pledged the class to serve the health needs of the Chinese people. That night, the new alumni serenaded the aged graduates from the 1920s to the 1950s who had gathered from all over China and abroad to celebrate the occasion. The fact that PUMC's old school song—with its American tune and rhetoric— was still used by this revolutionary generation spoke legions about the persistence of cultural traditions:

> PUMC Forever, the College of our choice.
> 'Tis here we learn such precepts, as make our hearts rejoice,
> We've learned the truths of Science, we've learned to study men. . . .
> It's ours to help the wretched, to guard the public health,
> To serve our dear old China, without a thought of wealth. . . .

The euphoria was short-lived. "To serve our dear old China" became, instead, a transition to study abroad and then permanent residence in the United States and elsewhere. The "thin line of excellence" was thin indeed; twenty-two years later (as of 2009), *not one* of those thirty graduates had returned to China. All are in the United States. Indeed, of the first five post–Cultural Revolution graduating classes (1987–91), *only four* (out of ninety-two) are in China.

What happened? The young Chinese generation that had come of age during the 1970s had a very different worldview than their parents and grandparents. The Deng Xiaoping era ushered in not just a turn to the West but also a glorification of personal rather than national achievement. A cynicism about collectivist ideals pervaded the youth of the 1980s and 1990s. Deng's "To get rich is glorious" replaced the Maoist slogan "Serve the people." More particularly, the new generation of PUMC students had survived a most rigid high school education and had been chosen from the very top ranks. With a strong scientific background in both high school and at Peking University, most tended to choose the medical sciences rather than clinical medicine as their specialty. This rather naturally led to seeking PhDs abroad, which was encouraged initially by the authorities.

The political crisis of 1989 was also a major factor. In 1987, China was entering one of its most open political periods in decades. This was the era of Premier Zhao Ziyang and talk of political as well as economic reform. This optimistic era ended, literally overnight, on June 4, 1989. The Tiananmen Incident not only ushered in a period of renewed political oppression in China but also sent a chill over those who were studying abroad. Very few wanted to return. President

George H. W. Bush provided political asylum and permanent residency to all Chinese students studying in the United States at that time.

PUMC was, of course, not the only institution to find that its graduates tended to stay abroad. This was true of all Chinese institutions of higher education during the 1980s and 1990s. Less than 10 percent of the tens of thousands of Chinese students who had received PhDs in the natural and physical sciences in the United States had returned to China by 2006.[57]

Nonetheless, PUMC's experience was especially problematic, because so few students were enrolled. PUMC administrators and faculty continued to insist that they could enroll only thirty students a class due to space, laboratory, and faculty constraints. The eight-year PUMC curriculum did include a one-to-one tutorial in the eighth year, but the reality was that the research programs of the Chinese Academy of Medical Sciences, including PUMC's Institute of Basic Research, claimed the time and allegiance of many on the faculty. This resistance to growth in the core educational program continued until 1992, when PUMC agreed to admit 100 students.

Changes in Chinese governmental regulations for study abroad as well as PUMC's own policies have meant that since the late 1990s far fewer graduates have been sent abroad directly after receiving their MD. More are completing residency training and some postdoctoral work in China before study abroad, and more are returning to China. Greatly improved economic and scientific conditions in China are the primary reasons that many see more positive career options in China than previously. This includes medical clinicians, who are not allowed to practice medicine in the United States without extensive retraining. Interviews with five 2007 graduating seniors (all women) reveal a very different career perspective than that of students in the late 1980s and 1990s.[58] All were remaining in China, some at PUMC Hospital, some at institutes of the Chinese Academy of Medical Sciences. They were excited about both their social and career prospects in China. Although they eventually planned some study abroad, it was quite clear that they saw their long-term future in China.

With so few of its own recent graduates available, PUMC and the Chinese Academy of Medical Sciences have had to rely upon graduates of the 1950s and 1960s, the second and third cohorts of PUMC graduates, to lead the institution in this new era. (This is also true of all scientific and educational institutions in China.) Although these physicians had a gap in their formal education, many were able to eventually continue their medical training, study abroad, and take leadership positions. As international "visiting scholars," some were disparaged by their foreign host institutions—many of them lacked fluency in English and currency in their disciplines. Nevertheless, the exposure to modern medical facilities and research, and the collaboration with foreign scientists, updated their knowledge. These middle-aged scholars returned because of the difficulty of finding work abroad, the high positions and prestige that awaited them, and a "hostage" system whereby they were required to leave families in China. They became the departmental and institutional leaders who have led PUMC and China's other medical and scientific institutions during the last two decades.

Because PUMC had so few graduates, it relied on graduates from other institutions as early as the 1950s. This was unusual in China, where the tradition continues to be to train one's own. PUMC was given permission to select several of the best medical students from the other leading medical schools in China during the 1950s and to bring them to PUMC, where they were given a final seventh and eighth year of training. In 1959, for example, when PUMC renewed its eight-year curriculum, it was permitted to invite premedical students from both Shanghai First Medical School and Peking Medical University to jump-start its new program. PUMC's extensive postgraduate training programs also provided a mechanism for attracting new talent. As a result, PUMC's current hospital staff and the research staff of the institutes of the Chinese Academy of Medical Sciences have been drawn from many cities and institutions.

A very large percentage of this entire group has studied abroad, and most have returned to China. This has been made possible by government support, grants from American universities, the reinvolvement of the China Medical Board since 1980, and the personal philanthropy of Dr. Clyde Wu and Helen Wu, who have no PUMC background but are Americans with a long-standing interest in China's medical education. They felt that PUMC would be strengthened if promising junior faculty members could spend a year as visiting scholars in an American medical school. The Wus personally interviewed hundreds of PUMC candidates, selecting thirty-two Wu Fellows for study abroad from 1994 to 2003. Many of the Wu Scholars are today directors of leading medical departments at PUMC or in PUMC Hospital; only three decided to remain in the United States.[59]

REFLECTIONS ON PUMC

Reflecting on these past decades, one cannot overestimate the "hollowing out" of PUMC and similar institutions in China due to the anti-intellectual policies of Mao's China. In most areas, China's science and medicine still lags behind world levels. Nonetheless, rapid strides have been made during the past two decades. New hospitals and research facilities are everywhere, and China's medical research is flourishing. Physical expansion for PUMC had long been problematic due to its landlocked location in central Peking. In recent years, with political support from both Li Peng and Hu Jintao, PUMC Hospital has been able to expand its footprint, building a large adjacent VIP hospital and a large new surgical building. The medical college itself, however, remains space constrained.

PUMC's most recent accomplishments are in graduate medical education and biomedical research. More than two-thirds of its student body are graduate students who avail themselves of the many MA and PhD graduate fields of study offered by PUMC and the CAMS institutes. The eighteen CAMS institutes are the leading medical research centers in China. These include such prestigious and internationally well-known institutions as the Fuwai Institute of Cardiovascular Diseases, the Institute of Materia Medica, the Institute of Cancer, and the Institute of Biomedical Engineering. CAMS has also been designated as the home for four national laboratories: Molecular Oncology, Medical Molecular Biology, Experimental Hematology, and Molecular Virology/Genetic Engineering. PUMC and CAMS often lead China's medical universities in the number of national science and technology awards received.[60]

Despite this record of accomplishment, PUMC has struggled to secure national support in this new era. The Chinese government is underwriting institutions of excellence through two key measures: by designating one hundred key institutions, and by consolidating medical schools into comprehensive universities. For nearly a decade, PUMC refused to enter into a merger agreement, for two reasons: It did not want to sacrifice its distinct identity, and it has been difficult to align with an appropriate university. PUMC's long-standing premedical arrangement with Peking University might have suggested that option, but Peking Medical University had closer ties with, and has now become, the Health Science Center of Peking University. Considerable pressure was applied to PUMC to merge with Capital University, a middle-level institution with a medical school. Although this would have given PUMC much-needed land in a somewhat central location as well as the opportunity to upgrade that institution, Capital University was considered a lower-status institution. The PUMC "old guard" resisted this merger so strongly that the plan was abandoned. In 2006, when it became evident that future government funding for PUMC depended upon a university affiliation, PUMC and Qinghua University reached agreement on a modified partnership. This collaboration has failed to materialize, and the institutional shape of PUMC's second century is yet to be seen.

The contours of PUMC's first nine decades reveal an American-originated institution buffeted by wars and revolutions that survived with its core identity intact. Its graduates not only proved far more adaptable to Chinese conditions than early critics predicted; some were quite innovative, and many became leaders of China's modern medical institutions. PUMC was almost counted out by its Rockefeller founders, by the Guomindang advocates for state medicine, and certainly by many in the PRC. PUMC's history reminds us that when it comes to the transfer of systems of knowledge, the impact cannot be measured in a short time frame or in a single generation. The transnational flow of ideas, with its varied institutional forms, is a lengthy and complex phenomenon, nowhere more evident than in twentieth-century China.

This history illustrates the durability of the patterns of cultural internationalism that began in the first decades of the twentieth century. PUMC's survival speaks to the widespread appeal of Western scientific medicine during the twentieth century, the coherence and medical competence of the Johns Hopkins–PUMC model, and the quality of its Chinese leadership. Timing was everything. PUMC was fortunate to be founded at the cusp of an international medical movement that encouraged globally shared medical and professional norms. That PUMC provided a China-based model of elite training, clinical expertise, and medical research comparable to many around the world helped China to keep apace and to continue building its modern medical infrastructure, despite the political interruptions and anti-intellectualism of the Maoist era. Thus, Li Zongen's 1947 pledge to John D. Rockefeller 3rd "to live up to the hopes and aspirations of the founders" became a reality.

CHAPTER 5

RENEWAL

Rockefeller Philanthropy in Post-Mao China

Three years before President Nixon's opening to China, John D. Rockefeller 3rd denounced the era of Mao Zedong as "China's agony," but he also called for a new dialogue with the People's Republic of China: "Our thinking about that great country has been dominated by fear, so much so that in the recent past many regarded it as virtually treasonable to even raise the question of rethinking China policy." JDR 3rd went on to affirm that "this sort of rigidity has no place in a democracy. We must not only understand China better, but we must understand our own fears." He concluded that the time had come to establish a "reasonable modus vivendi with the world's most populous nation."[1] The setting for his remarks was the New York Hilton at a 1969 conference convened by the National Committee on United States–China Relations, and JDR 3rd's role was to introduce the keynote speaker, Senator Edward Kennedy.

Two decades had passed since JDR 3rd and his father, who had died in 1960, had tentatively looked toward American recognition of the People's Republic of China, two decades in which U.S. policy toward China had been almost as hostile as China's toward the United States. Advocating a new approach to "Red" China in 1969 was still politically risky business. Thus a Rockefeller Republican on the program did more than just give the occasion the bipartisan cover it needed; it also honored JDR 3rd himself as the National Committee's very first benefactor in 1966. He lent his name, prestige, and mainstream legitimacy in the critical beginning of this fledgling organization dedicated to improving relations with China.[2]

JDR 3rd's speech not only looked forward; he also spoke about the past, romanticizing the era when his family had been involved commercially and philanthropically in China:

We can look back on what now seems like a "golden age" in our relationships with China, from the time our first consul arrived in the 1780s up until the 1930s. Throughout that century and a half, our nations enjoyed a growing sense of friendship and exchange. Yet, the relationship was essentially superficial, despite many significant and genuine humanitarian efforts. As a nation, we did not really come to know China and her people.[3]

Rockefeller did not realize it then, but the United States and China were on the cusp of a new era, one in which American philanthropy was to be given a second chance to engage China and its people. But the context was now very different. This time, China would decide the timing, the pace, and the content of cultural relationships. Unlike the Nationalist era, cultural relations were dependent upon a formal relationship between the two governments. Despite a flurry of "scientific tourism" following President Richard Nixon's visit, the Chinese government waited until the official normalization of diplomatic relations before inviting the Rockefeller Foundation (RF) and the China Medical Board (CMB) back into China.

This time, Americans would encounter a proud and mature, if depleted, Chinese scientific, medical, and educational community. Except for Soviet assistance in the 1950s, Chinese institutions had developed independently for three decades, perhaps fortuitously bypassing an era of dependence, which in other regions often resulted from extensive American technical assistance. When "reform and opening" came under Deng Xiaoping, China emphasized access to Western science and technology. The members of its long-repressed intellectual community had not forgotten the transnational values of international science; they were eager and ready to reconnect to the West, especially the United States. In contrast, however much it sought access to Western science, the Chinese government was, and continues to be, leery of American foundations and nongovernmental organizations, many of which promote a more open and liberal Chinese society. The mission of the RF and the CMB was different. With their primary emphasis on science and medicine, these foundations were well positioned to engage China on its own terms. The values of scientific internationalism that had governed their pre-1951 engagement with China continued to motivate both foundations. The fact that China was "Communist" was less important than that it was a developing country attempting to use advanced science, technology, and medicine to improve the lives of its people.

This is not to say that American philanthropy, including the Rockefeller philanthropies, had not been changed by the Cold War years that preceded the rapprochement between China and the United States. The most important difference was that the U.S. government had become a major actor in international cultural relations.[4] No private foundation would ever again compete with the scale of U.S. government programs. Its international cultural efforts, especially the Fulbright program, made scholarly exchanges possible on a global scale. The Agency for International Development provided technical assistance programs in developing countries throughout the world. Both these initiatives were created and funded as part of the U.S. government's effort to block the growth of world-wide Communism. This Cold War strategy cast a long shadow over American cultural internationalism in the 1950s and 1960s.

JDR 3rd's personal philanthropic role during those two decades reflected these broader trends in American philanthropy, especially assistance to developing countries, but it was unique because of his focus on Asia. His biographers captured the moment in the early 1950s when he turned his attention from China to Japan, and thence to Asia more broadly: "China seemed closed to Americans indefinitely: Japan was wide open."[5]

JDR 3rd was forty-four years old in 1950, and his subsequent charitable initiatives reflect the confidence of a seasoned and mature philanthropist. His years as an active member of the CMB had long exposed him to the economic and political realities of Asia as well as its rich cultural heritage. His two trips to China and Japan, unique among his siblings, had awakened his interest in the population and agricultural challenges of developing countries, especially in Asia. In rapid succession, he turned his attention to reinvigorating the Japan Society (1952–53) and to creating the Population Council (1952), the Agricultural Development Council (1953), the Asia Society (1955), and the JDR 3rd Fund (1963, renamed the Asian Cultural Council, 1978). Several had Asia as their central focus, and all included Asia, and directly or indirectly reflected his earlier China interest. Of particular note is his decision to hire J. Lossing Buck to lead the Agricultural Development Council; JDR 3rd was a longtime admirer of Buck's agricultural programs at the University of Nanjing, which had been supported by the RF in the 1930s.[6]

JDR 3rd's focus on Asia came at a time when the United States was endeavoring to prevent Japan from being drawn into the orbit of Communist China. It also came during the McCarthy era, when the RF's previous work in China was subject to repeated charges of "un-American and subversive activities." In 1951, Georgia Representative H. E. Cox exhorted that "the Rockefeller Foundation . . . must take its share of the blame for the swing of the professors and students in China to Communism during the years preceding the successful Red revolution in China."[7] Two years later, Tennessee Representative B. Carroll Reece charged that the RF's emphasis on the social sciences in China had encouraged socialism. A key target was the Institute of Pacific Relations (IPR), which had long been supported by John D. Rockefeller Jr. and the RF; in 1929, the young JDR 3rd had attended one of the first IPR meetings, held in Japan. Between 1925 and 1952, the IPR had received between $1.5 and $1.8 million from Rockefeller sources, constituting upward of 50 percent of its funding. In time, the McCarthy era waned and the RF was politically exonerated, but the IPR never recovered, closing its doors in 1952.[8] JDR's new Asian philanthropies were designed, in part, to avoid these troubled political waters. His interests in agricultural development, population planning, and culture were long-standing, but they were also compatible with U.S. government priorities. They were thus not likely to arouse much negative political attention.

Japan became JDR 3rd's second home. It all began in 1950, when John Foster Dulles, a longtime RF trustee and chair of its board, was invited by Secretary of State Dean Acheson to lead the team that was negotiating the final World War II peace treaty with Japan. He invited Rockefeller to participate, and assigned him the task of designing a new program of cultural relations between the two former adversaries. This required months of dialogue with Japanese intellectuals and politicians, out of which JDR formalized an international cultural philosophy and a program for cultural exchange as well as making lifetime friendships. A recent review of his role by the Japanese historian Takeshi Matsuda criticized Rockefeller for designing what many concluded became an intellectually dependent relationship between Japan and the United States. However, he also credits Rockefeller with inventing the concept of a "two-way street," an exchange process whereby each country would be exposed to the other's leading intellectual and artistic leaders. Although this seems rather prosaic today, insisting on a two-way flow of ideas between recent military adversaries was a direct expression of the values of cultural internationalism. Such values, though championed by Rockefeller, were hardly common at the time. The program that emerged included the creation of the International House of Japan, the promotion of American studies in Japan, an active exchange program between the two countries, and the revitalization of the long-dormant Japan Society. At a time when anticommunist rhetoric was escalating in the United States, Rockefeller eschewed an explicit Cold War rationale even as he clearly reflected U.S. national values: The purpose of cultural exchange was "to regain a world order in which all nations were free to pursue their own conceptions of common goals, free to pursue their own destinies."[9]

In 1953, JDR 3rd began traveling to Asia annually, sometimes for as long as two months, and his itineraries ranged from India to Indonesia to Cambodia to the Philippines, and always back to Japan. Having decided that Asia should be a major focus of his life,[10] he became convinced that new kinds of institutions were needed to introduce Americans to Asian culture, peoples, and societies. Against the advice of all of his advisers—who worried about residual McCarthyism, possible duplication with the Asia Foundation, and fallout from the debate over the IPR—JDR 3rd founded the Asia Society in 1955. He was convinced that a pan-Asian cultural organization would play an important role in Americans' understanding of Asia, and he was prepared to provide most of the initial funding himself. The charter of the Asia Society emphasized its nonpolitical role, dedicated to social and cultural programs designed to educate Americans and Asians about each other. In time, the Asia Society embraced a broader scope of programs, including those related to foreign policy. Today it remains the nation's premier institution promoting a cultural, social, and political engagement with Asia.[11]

Less than ten years later, in 1963, JDR 3rd established a second Asia-centered cultural philanthropy, the JDR 3rd Fund. This new foundation focused on the cultural exchange of individuals in the visual and performing arts between the United States and Asia. JDR 3rd's philosophy of cultural internationalism is well summarized in a statement he made in 1975 about the JDR 3rd Fund:

> Traditionally, Americans have viewed international relations primarily in political and economic terms, with comparatively little attention given to the cultural dimension. The result is that our world outlook has tended to be bound by our own culture instead of being broadened by a sensitivity to other cultures. Through knowledge and respect for other cultures, we come to respect and appreciate the people themselves. In turn, this provides a more effective setting for carrying out political and economic affairs.[12]

Rockefeller was the sole funder of the JDR 3rd Fund until his death in 1978, after which the organization was renamed the Asian Cultural Council; it continues to be led by Rockefeller family members.

JDR 3rd's individual Asian philanthropy during the 1950s and 1960s reflected the generational shift that was occurring in the Rockefeller family philanthropies: JDR Jr.'s five sons and one daughter were ready to make their own mark on American civic and philanthropic life. This third generation's relationship with their grandfather's original philanthropies, especially the RF, had become attenuated. The RF's powerful senior management and some long-standing trustees opposed many of JDR 3rd's ideas for the foundation's postwar role. They resisted continuing the founding family's prerogatives, and thus unexpectedly did not elect JDR 3rd to succeed his father as chairman in 1939. JDR 3rd, eager to make his own philanthropic mark, joined with his siblings—Nelson, Winthrop, Laurence, David, and Abby—to create their own foundation, the Rockefeller Brothers Fund (RBF), in 1940. The RBF's initial goal was to avoid charitable duplication and to streamline decisionmaking, eliminating the entrenched programmatic divisions and bureaucracy of the now-venerable RF. In time, the work of the RBF would reflect a very different agenda than the older, more established RF, especially with regard to China. But the family's influence within the RF was not quite at an end. In 1952, after a long tutelage (he had been a member of the board since 1931), JDR 3rd was finally named chairman of the RF, and he served actively until 1971. With Dean Rusk and then George Harrar as president, JDR 3rd's influence became more pronounced. The RF's international shift from Europe to developing countries and from the basic sciences to more applied scientific programs in both agriculture and population bear his imprimatur.

As the RF looked beyond China to the rest of Asia and the developing world, its prior experience in China served as a model; all major RF divisions (medicine, agriculture, the natural sciences, humanities, and the social sciences) had undertaken pioneering work in China, the RF's first comprehensive developing-country program. The promotion of agriculture science through linkage to both government agencies and universities was conceptually developed in RF's China program for rural reconstruction. The focus on creating institutions of excellence, whether Peking Union Medical College (PUMC) or the Institute of Economics at Nankai University, had become a well-established Rockefeller strategy. The RF viewed its China experience as an early laboratory or field experiment for the foundation's subsequent shift to programs in developing countries.[13]

THE ROCKEFELLER FOUNDATION AND
THE CHINA MEDICAL BOARD IN ASIA, 1951–1970

The nationalization of PUMC by the People's Republic of China in 1951 left the CMB with an endowment of $22 million—and no program. Likewise, the RF's humanistic and medical forays in postwar China came to an abrupt end. Both institutions needed to reconsider their roles in Asia; as the 1950s unfolded, the relationship between them also changed. Issues included the disposition of the CMB endowment, "China" in the name of the CMB, and the appropriate division of responsibility for medical work in Asia between the RF and the CMB.

With the RF's final endowment grant of $12 million to the CMB in 1947 came the severing of fiduciary relations with its junior partner. To symbolize its full independence, the CMB's staff had even moved out of the RF offices at 30 Rockefeller Plaza. Nevertheless, overlapping programs, board memberships, and even staff perpetuated the long historical ties. Alan Gregg, director of the RF's Division of Medical Sciences from 1930 to 1952 and later vice president of the RF, served on the CMB in the 1930s and again from 1951 to 1955. Oliver McCoy, RF representative to Japan in the 1950s, headed the CMB from 1959 to 1973 (first as director and then, with a title change, as president). Even Standard Oil connections continued; William Herod, president of Standard Oil of New York in the 1940s, served on the CMB for two decades, 1947–68. As in the past, John D. Rockefeller Jr. and John D. Rockefeller 3rd continued their interest and surveillance of the work of the CMB. As a former CMB member, JDR 3rd, in particular, was kept regularly abreast of the work of the foundation, returning handwritten notes on dockets and issues being addressed.[14]

The CMB's charter language was geographically flexible, permitting it to "extend financial support to the Peking Union Medical College and/or other like institutions in the Far East or in the United States of America." Accordingly, in 1952 the CMB began a program of diversified support for medical education throughout Asia. The large CMB endowment (then $22 million) was still guarded by RF staff and family; should it be held for PUMC in the future, returned to the RF, or used for new medical programs in Asia? Both JDR Jr. and JDR 3rd weighed in on behalf of the independence of the CMB and its right to spend the endowment, even the principal, as it saw fit, without regard to PUMC. In a 1954 letter to Harold Loucks, director of the CMB and former PUMC professor of surgery, the senior Rockefeller confirmed that "it was the consensus of the group that the Board [CMB] should for a year continue its activities along the general lines it has been following without any sense of responsibility for PUMC, with freedom to extend its work, both in the Orient and this country, as it may see fit, drawing without hesitation on principal as well as income." But JDR Jr., now eighty years old, was not quite ready to completely let go. His letter concludes: "A year hence the same group will review the situation in the hope that a wise decision as to the Board's future may then be reached."[15] The group reference included himself, his son John (by then chair of the RF), legal counsel, and several members of the RF and CMB boards.

This would be JDR Jr.'s last intervention in the affairs of PUMC and the CMB. His death in 1960 brought to an end more than half a century of intense personal interest in PUMC, his first major international philanthropic project. Most associate him with New York City—Rockefeller Center, the United Nations, the Museum of Modern Art, Riverside Church, and the Cloisters. He is also known for the restoration of Colonial Williamsburg and the Acadia and Grand Tetons national parks. Yet, as chair of the RF, he presided over the most important American international philanthropy during the first half of the twentieth century. He was not a charismatic leader, and he was known by colleagues and family alike for being highly formal, stern, and moralistic (although he did love to dance). These personal characteristics and the fact that he was overshadowed by his infamous father and famous sons may account for the fact that he has not received the attention he deserves in American philanthropic and social history. If John D. Rockefeller Jr.'s attention to China is any indication of his many other international interests, he should be remembered as the first global philanthropist.

Clinging to some hope for renewed relations with the People's Republic of China, the CMB continued to set aside funds for PUMC. In 1954, after some debate, it decided not to take "China" out of the foundation's name. JDR 3rd concurred with the CMB's decision to keep its China identity, because it kept China alive as a philanthropic option. As the CMB policy document read: "Despite

China's present withdrawal from the family of free nations and denunciation of its former friends, the Committee finds it difficult to believe that the Chinese people will forever prove willing to forgo the liberty of thought and action which adherence to Communist philosophy demands. For this reason it would seem wise policy not at this time to eliminate 'China' from the Board's name."[16] For the sake of clarification, however, it added "of New York," for a modified title of China Medical Board, Inc., of New York.

By the mid-1950s, both the RF and the CMB were engaged in often-overlapping new medical and public health programs in Asia. After a lengthy interfoundation review, an informal division of labor was agreed upon, whereby the RF would continue medical activities in India, Pakistan, Ceylon, and Japan, and public health work in Indonesia, Malaya, Thailand, and the Philippines. The CMB's charter stipulated that the "Far East" was its geographical zone; during the first half of the century, this term was interpreted to include Southeast Asia but not South Asia. Historically, the CMB had not been active in public health, and therefore it focused more specifically on medical education in Japan, Korea, Taiwan, Hong Kong, Burma, the Philippines, Indonesia, and Malaya.[17]

The CMB quickly rejected the idea of creating a new PUMC somewhere else in Asia, recognizing that such an American institution would not be welcome in the postcolonial and highly nationalistic Asia of the 1950s. Even Harold Loucks recognized that "the PUMC was established at a time when there was no medical college in China worthy of the name and national pride was a virtue to be cultivated. Now, patriotism has become an Asian uniform with only color and style to identify the wearer. It seems obvious that, henceforth, outside aid must take the form of assistance to local institutions, with particular care exerted to keep the initiative in Asian hands." He and others associated with the CMB had also become reconciled to the reality that "even were the National Government of China to return to the mainland, there is doubt that a resumption of direct control of the PUMC by the Board would ever again prove possible, or desirable."[18]

The CMB did continue the Rockefeller tradition of "making the peaks higher"; only key institutions would be supported. At a time when Asian medical education was struggling to recover from World War II, the CMB gave priority to books, equipment, buildings, fellowships, and visiting professorships. Some of Asia's most prominent medical institutions received CMB support at that time, including Tokyo Medical College, the College of Medicine of Seoul National University, Ewha Medical College (South Korea), National Taiwan University, and Chulalongkorn University Faculty of Medicine (Thailand). Between 1952 and 1970, the CMB expended $23 million in sixteen countries. The largest recipients were Japan, South Korea, and Taiwan, and by 1970 medical education in these East Asian countries had become self-supporting.[19]

Not only was a new PUMC for Asia rejected; the CMB also became less idealistic and more pragmatic. Faint echoes of the grand aspirations of the early Rockefeller philanthropists could still be heard, but there were subtle and not so subtle variations. In the early 1950s, the CMB still reiterated the long-standing Rockefeller emphasis on the contributions of the West to the East, but this appears to be the last hurrah of the civilizing claim of inductive reasoning: "The greatest contribution the West had to offer to Eastern civilizations was an example of the manner in which objective observations and inductive reasoning could be combined to achieve scientific progress, and that medicine offered an ideal field for such a demonstration."[20] The focus was already moving away from systemic cultural change to scientific progress and a demonstration model. The Communist triumph in 1949 had clearly dispelled the notion of China's or Asia's "plasticity."

It had also become expedient for the CMB to align its programs with U.S. political objectives. For the first time, the CMB articulated a development strategy to combat Communism:

It also was suggested that, if the future of the world hinges on the ability of free peoples to assist under-privileged populations to overcome disease, poverty and oppression to the point at which they are no longer highly susceptible to the wiles of Communist propaganda, it would seem that the Board [CMB] faces a challenge and opportunity to align itself with other agencies—governmental and private—which are working for physical, economic and educational health in Asia.[21]

To be sure, the nearly half-century CMB agenda of medical education did not change. This adoption of a Cold War rhetoric was characteristic of most American international development programs during the 1950s.[22]

The RF's worldwide programs during the 1950s and 1960s focused on extending the "green revolution," university development, population planning, and combating neglected diseases. Offices in Thailand, India, Taiwan, and Indonesia provided a base for Asia programs.

Thus by the early 1970s, both the CMB and the RF had established extensive new programs throughout Asia. The Rockefeller family's influence on both foundations, however, had almost completely disappeared. JDR Jr.'s death in 1960 appeared to break the half-century Rockefeller family identification with PUMC, and ties between the RF and the CMB gradually lessened. JDR 3rd stepped down as chair of the RF in 1971 (he remained honorary chair until his death in 1978), and his son, John D. Rockefeller IV, was named a trustee in 1968, but Jay, as he is known, did not seek nor was he offered a leadership role.

THE ROCKEFELLER CHINA OPENING: THE KISSINGER CONNECTION

JDR 3rd was not the only member of the Rockefeller family to advocate a new opening to China. In 1968, his younger brother Nelson, the governor of New York, called for more "increased contacts with Mainland China and [to] develop options in our relations with it" while campaigning against Richard Nixon for the Republican presidential nomination. Nelson Rockefeller, like Nixon, opposed China's admission to the United Nations but argued for more active engagement, reminding an audience in Philadelphia that "I think we sometimes forget that one of the great people that we had in the past as friends were the people of China."[23] In 1970, the youngest brother, David Rockefeller, chairman of Chase Manhattan Bank, supported Nixon's decision to relax trade restrictions. Glimpses of these relatively moderate views of China, and the Rockefeller family's association with Henry Kissinger, had first emerged in the late 1950s in the Rockefeller Brothers Fund's seminal report *America at Mid-Century*. Nelson had hired Kissinger, a Harvard professor, to direct this report as part of the RBF's Special Studies Projects. Although these studies reflected the Cold War environment of the times, the foreign policy study "took a more moderate stance toward China, warning of the danger of pushing mainland China into the arms of the Soviets."[24] Such a position became typical of what was termed the more moderate "Rockefeller" wing of the Republican Party. Kissinger went on to become Nelson's chief foreign policy strategist, both when he was governor of New York and as a candidate for the Republican presidential nomination. When Nixon won in 1968, Kissinger accepted Nixon's offer to become director of the National Security Council. Ironically, Nixon almost selected Nelson Rockefeller instead of Kissinger to be his first envoy to China.[25]

When Nixon returned in 1972 from his triumphant week in China, the Rockefeller brothers were ready and eager to take advantage of their long association with Kissinger. Indeed, each angled to be the first to go to China. During 1972, John, David, and Nelson all made direct personal appeals to Kissinger to be invited to China. In doing so, each made reference to the Rockefeller family's legacy of China involvement. Although their prominence in American life and access to Kissinger allowed these exclusive overtures, their persistence in wanting to be among the first to reengage China was characteristic of the China-mania that began to sweep the United States. Americans, for the first time, were standing in line for China's approving nod.

David was the first and most successful Rockefeller supplicant. In his *Memoirs*, David evoked his grandfather's desire to "tap the potential of the 'China market'" and Standard Oil's marketing slogan, "Oil for the Lamps of China," as he contemplated the China financial market of the late twentieth century. In the 1970s, China needed an American bank, and Chase Manhattan was not a stranger to

FIGURE 5.1. David Rockefeller (third from right) at Peking Union Medical College with President Ba Denian (fourth from right) , circa 1990. *Photograph courtesy of Peking Union Medical College.*

the China market. With branches in Shanghai, Tianjin, and Hong Kong before World War II, Chase had been known as "Datong Yinhang"—the worldwide bank. But all its China branches, including Hong Kong, had been closed in 1950. Only later, in the 1960s, did Chase reestablish a significant banking presence in Asia. David sought Kissinger's help in arranging a China visit to explore opening banking relationships between Chase and China. Multiple efforts to write and meet China's ambassador to the United Nations, Huang Hua, resulted in a personal invitation from the Chinese People's Institute for Foreign Affairs.

David Rockefeller remembers that first trip to China in May 1973 as his most extraordinary travel venture. His late-night meeting with Premier Zhou Enlai ranged widely across the international economic and monetary scene, and David found himself giving an impromptu lecture on twentieth-century economic history. With Zhou's approval, Chase Manhattan became the People's Republic of China's first American bank. At that time, inconclusive bilateral negotiations over frozen assets precluded a full banking relationship, but a limited correspondent relationship was put in place. David found Zhou quite knowledgeable about his family's historic role in China, and he was the first Rockefeller to be invited back to Peking Union Medical College Hospital, then named the Anti-Imperialist Hospital.[26] On subsequent visits to China, he returned to PUMC several times *(see figure 5.1)*. In an editorial for the *New York Times*, David deftly commended the Communist government for its economic and social progress but also asked about individuality and creativity, adaptability to foreign trade and technology, and raised a pertinent question: "Are we and the Chinese prepared to accept our very real differences and still proceed toward the closer mutual understanding that must be the basis of substantive future contact?"[27]

JDR 3rd's overtures through Kissinger were less successful. His advocacy was not overtly on behalf of himself, but of the Population Council. Predictably, China's population policies were far more sensitive than its need for banking relationships. Kissinger first told JDR 3rd that he "[would] try to pave the way," but six months later wrote sympathetically that there had been no response on the population front. Somewhat teasingly, Kissinger observed that JDR 3rd's brothers, David and Nelson, would soon be on their way to China.[28] But JDR 3rd was not deterred, and he wrote multiple letters to the Chinese ambassador to the United Nations about World Population Year, only to be put off by Huang Hua, who finally responded:

> I might as well add that Premier Chou En-lai did mention the question of
> population when he met the American scientists last June. However, as I
> understand it, what he said is that we are interested in urban questions, including
> the question of population, and we don't rule out possible research on them. But,
> for the time being, we are not ready to receive visitors in that field, because we
> have to make some preparations.[29]

An invitation to Sheldon Segal, a scientist at the Population Council, did finally arrive in 1977 via a personal contact, but JDR 3rd was killed in an automobile accident the next year. He never made it back to China and did not live to see the normalization of diplomatic relations in 1979. His death brought to an end the direct Rockefeller lineage that had given so much attention to China in the first three quarters of the twentieth century. Two of his siblings became notable collectors of Chinese art—Nelson and David—and Laurence developed a strong interest in Buddhism. JDR 3rd's daughter Hope lived in Peking for several years, working for the *China Daily*. His son, Jay, attended college in Japan and became proficient in Japanese but was also interested in China. In 1974, when he was president of West Virginia Wesleyan College, he "jumped" at the opportunity to be a member of the first delegation of American university presidents to China, sponsored by the National Committee on United States–China Relations.[30]

Other Rockefeller family groups made a point of visiting PUMC when they traveled to China, including Abby "Babs" Rockefeller's daughter, Abby O'Neill, and her family in 1981 *(see figure 5.2)*. None of the many Rockefeller descendants, however, carried on JDR 3rd's patronage of Asian culture, although the Rockefeller family is represented on the boards of the Asian Cultural Council, the Rockefeller Brothers Fund, the Rockefeller Foundation, and the China Medical Board. Nor did any become as involved in the economic and agricultural development of Asia.

FIGURE 5.2. Abby O'Neill (second from right) and her family at Peking Union Medical College, 1981. *Photograph courtesy of Abby O'Neill.*

Though JDR 3rd was twice offered an ambassadorship to Asia (to Indonesia by Dwight Eisenhower in 1959, and to Japan by Nixon in 1969), he preferred the work of the nongovernmental sector. Lacking the magnetic warmth of either Nelson or David, JDR 3rd had inherited his father's quiet, stern, and moralistic demeanor. Those who worked with him in Asian circles admired his personal discipline and lifelong efforts to understand and promote Asian culture. As Sherman Lee, the China art historian, wrote in a eulogy: "One learned to respect his deeply felt response to the often contemplative ideals of Eastern art and to understand the creative tension existing between these ideals and the more pragmatic and concrete achievements of his other artistic love, American painting. This tension was a true meeting of East and West, and to me it epitomized the character of the man, rooted in the traditional American virtues, but increasingly aware of other transcendental realms."[31]

If JDR 3rd did not live to be personally involved with the People's Republic of China, the two Asia-oriented institutions that he personally founded—the Asia Society and the JDR 3rd Fund—became directly involved in promoting renewed relations with the People's Republic. In 1974, the National Committee on United States–China Relations transferred its university-based field staff to the Asia Society, which created the China Council based on this regional network. The council's main purpose was to engage in public education about China, then still a mostly unknown and controversial Communist country. Conferences, publications, and media programs brought up-to-date information on the People's Republic of China to a broad American audience. The council was led by Robert Oxnam, who later became the Asia Society's president, and the council was discontinued in 1989 when its programs were integrated into the parent organization. The JDR 3rd fund, renamed the Asian Cultural Council, funded some of the first cultural groups from the People's Republic in the mid-1970s. Beginning in 1980, the first Chinese individual artists were invited to the United States. Led by Richard Lanier and Ralph Samuelson, the Asian Cultural Council has sponsored hundreds of individual American and Chinese artists in reciprocal cultural programs since that time.[32]

A third brother, Governor Nelson Rockefeller, also assisted in the renewal of ties with China. Although not involved in the RF directly, he found himself seated next to the RF's relatively new president, John Knowles, at a dinner in early 1973. Knowles told him of the RF's renewed China interests, and Nelson offered to call Kissinger: "I'll talk to Henry—he's going to Peking—so you get me some material and he can give it to [Premier] Chou En-lai." The next day, Knowles gave a packet of material to Doak Barnett, a well-known China scholar, to personally carry to Kissinger's office. When he returned from China, Kissinger called Knowles and said that the material had been delivered, and that they needed "to wait and do nothing further."[33]

The RF's interest in China had been rekindled several months earlier by a luncheon with the first group of Chinese medical scientists to visit the United States since 1949. Led by Peking Union Medical College graduates and current faculty members—Wu Weiran and Lin Qiaozhi—the delegation was sponsored by the Committee on Scholarly Communication with the People's Republic of China. In preparation for that meeting, Knowles led his staff through a planning exercise for a new China program that would encompass population and health, agriculture, and schistosomiasis. Meeting with his Chinese visitors, Knowles promoted the RF's historic China claim, expressing the desire to resume "a mutually rewarding relationship that goes back almost 60 years." He emphasized the importance of learning from China, not just exporting Western knowledge: "I know the U.S. in general and the Rockefeller Foundation in particular could profit enormously from seeing the progress that China has made in delivering health care to rural areas, for example. And perhaps the foundation's work in originating and spreading the Green Revolution might interest China."[34]

The Knowles letter that Kissinger delivered to Zhou Enlai included both a proud summary of Rockefeller history in China and an ambitious plan for the future: "We believe that the Rockefeller Foundation can play a unique role in facilitating non-official cultural and scientific interchange with the People's Republic of China to the mutual benefit of both the American and Chinese people." Knowles expansively pledged that the RF was prepared to "explore the possibilities of cultural and scientific exchange with the appropriate officials of the

People's Republic of China in the areas of agriculture, public health, population, the social sciences, arts and humanities."[35]

Knowles reiterated his sensitivity to perceived Chinese concerns about a return of American programs of Western cultural dominance by emphasizing that the RF staff's experience in developing Asian countries has "demonstrated their respect for and sensitivity to different cultures." Although he evoked the long RF China history, he also affirmed that "the foundation recognizes that exchanges between the United States and China now should be, and will be, on a different basis from those in the past, but we strongly believe that exchanges of people and knowledge can be of mutual benefit."[36] This was perhaps the first time that the concept of mutual benefit had entered the lexicon of Rockefeller philanthropy in China. It may have only been rhetorical language designed to assuage Chinese concerns; nonetheless, this signaled that a new era in Sino-American cultural internationalism had begun.

The Rockefeller Foundation and the People's Republic: A "Modest Enhancement"

John Knowles is the only Rockefeller Foundation president since 1970 who was a strong advocate for China programs, but his untimely death from cancer in 1979 foreshortened his institutional influence. Because he did not receive an immediate answer from the Kissinger overture, Knowles made a point of traveling to China in 1975 as a member of a delegation from the National Committee on United States–China Relations and the World Affairs Council, the first group of American foundation and civic leaders to visit the country in the new climate of openness. He also sent nine senior staff on various trips in the mid-1970s, many of them sponsored by the Committee on Scholarly Communication with the People's Republic of China, which the RF also funded. In 1979 Sheldon Segal, director of the RF's Division of Population Science, was the first Rockefeller staff member to be officially invited to China in his capacity as a senior officer of the foundation. Having been castigated for two decades as an agent of cultural imperialism, the RF was still a controversial institution in China. Segal's invitation to China had required approval by the governing council of the Chinese Academy of Sciences and the State Council.

While in Peking, Segal hosted a reception for the graduates of PUMC, the first reconnection with the RF in three decades *(figure 5.3)*. His diary records the emotional reunion: "On Wednesday afternoon, January 31, I represented the RF in hosting a reception for PUMC graduates and other RF-connected colleagues.... It was a dramatic, and I might say, historic event.... It is the first time that they have

FIGURE 5.3. Sheldon Segal at a Peking Union Medical College reunion, 1979. *Photograph courtesy of Sheldon Segal.*

come together as a group in over 30 years."[37] Many elderly graduates traveled from outside Peking to participate in this event, writing poignant comments in a guest book, which Segal always kept in his desk drawer. The PUMC reunion was a clear sign that China's new "open door" was a reality.

On this same trip, Segal began discussions with leaders of the Chinese Academy of Sciences about collaboration on developmental biology and with the Chinese Academy of Agricultural Sciences about agricultural biotechnology. In a letter to Zhang Jingyue, vice president of the Biological Sciences of the Chinese Academy of Sciences, Segal outlined the potential benefits if the RF were to resume its historic role in supporting Chinese science. He focused on molecular biology:

> The recent era of experimental and molecular biology has been of heroic
> dimensions, in terms of both intellectual advances and the development of new
> methodologies for research. The Rockefeller Foundation is proud of its catalytic
> role in these events and would be equally proud to participate in bringing the
> revolution in biological sciences to China.[38]

The Chinese authorities were ready to respond to this overture. A meeting with Vice Premier Fang Yi, the minister in charge of the State Council's Scientific and Technological Commission, confirmed Chinese willingness to "enter into a grant relationship with the Rockefeller Foundation" on topics ranging from developmental biology to demography.[39]

It was clear to Segal that President Knowles's interest in China had not gone unnoticed at higher political levels in Peking. By all accounts, the Chinese political leadership that emerged after the death of Mao Zedong was well aware of the RF's historic relationship with China and its continuing primacy in the fields of agricultural and population science. Knowles and Segal were officially invited to China in the spring of 1979; the purpose was to explore a broad range of collaborative scientific programs, beginning with developmental biology. But Knowles became ill with terminal pancreatic cancer. Fang Yi, who accompanied Deng Xiaoping on his historic visit to the United States in early February 1979, arranged to call Knowles at Massachusetts General Hospital in Boston, extending his sympathies. He then put Deng Xiaoping on the line. The conversation was brief—neither spoke the other's language—but the gesture was remarkable. Upon hearing this story, James Grant, the son of PUMC's John Grant and a member of the RF Board, said that "it took his breath away." It is hard to imagine a stronger signal that the RF was once again welcome in China.[40]

After Knowles's death and a short interim presidency, Richard Lyman, president of Stanford University, became president of the RF, serving from 1980 to 1988. It was during this period that the RF's philosophy toward grantmaking in China took on the form that continued throughout the rest of the century. Knowles's grand vision for the foundation's work in many disciplines did not materialize, but several board members with a keen interest in China ensured that China remained on the agenda. James Grant, who was head of UNICEF, played an active role as a trustee in encouraging the RF's return to China. And John Evans, chair of the RF Board from 1987 to 1995, had earlier initiated the China health program of the World Bank. In contrast to Knowles, Lyman believed that the RF should not—could not—replicate its historic role. His recognition of the changed philanthropic context, enunciated in 1981, continues to influence the RF's China endeavors and deserves to be quoted at length:

> This is a foundation with more history than most, founded in 1913 and relatively
> big and influential from the start. . . . Its first major enterprise was indicative of
> . . . a determination to entertain no small notions. It aimed at nothing less than
> to bring the benefits of 20th-century biomedical science to what was then, as
> now, the world's largest population, the Chinese—an undertaking at once moral,
> missionary in spirit, and "informed by history." . . . Sustaining such a vision is
> not easy in the conditions of the 1980s. True, in one sense the world has shrunk.
> Beijing is no longer a three- or four-week journey from New York, as it was when
> Frederick T. Gates laid before the Foundation's trustees a plan "for the gradual
> and orderly development of a comprehensive system of medicine in China."

On the other hand, his very words suggest the difference in the magnitude of undertakings that this foundation or any other can plausibly tackle now, as compared with 1914. The Chinese government itself has its hands full today trying to provide "a comprehensive system of medicine" for that vast country. No private foundation in the world could add more than a modest enhancement to such an effort, even were it to devote its entire resources to the matter.[41]

Years later, Lyman remembered the many political problems that plagued United States–China scientific collaboration during the 1980s—the politicization of decisionmaking, the absence of well-established peer review, the arbitrary assignment of scientific personnel, and the "ceremonial occasions . . . [where] Chinese hosts proclaimed 'friendship' in terms that clearly implied expectations of our giving them money in far larger amounts that we were at all likely to be able to manage."[42]

As the RF's programs evolved in China, the term "modest enhancement" may understate its role in two important scientific fields—population science and agricultural biotechnology. This term does, however, aptly describe the foundation's more modest philanthropic goals. It was not just that Chinese medical and scientific institutions had become largely self-sufficient, but also that medicine and science no longer provided the rationale for the grand cultural and institutional visions of an earlier era. Nor did the RF's resources permit philanthropic attention to science for the sake of science. Thus, returning to the earlier concept of using science for the cultural transformation of China was no longer a persuasive concept. Rather, science had become the handmaiden of development, promoted to "serve the cause of international equity by helping to reduce the incidence of poverty, disease, malnutrition, unwanted pregnancies and illiteracy in developing countries, and thereby advance the well-being of their peoples."[43] In recognizing this more functional and pragmatic emphasis of post–World War II philanthropy, the historian Frank Ninkovich observes that it lacks the "universalist ardor" of an earlier era in cultural internationalism and has become one "from which the magic of internationalism is missing."[44] However true, this understates the significance of China's being invited back into the global scientific community, and the significance of scientific internationalism.

The rubric under which the RF would return to China was its International Program to Support Science-Based Development, including the divisions of agricultural sciences, population sciences, and health sciences. Despite the historical legacy, or perhaps in rejection of it, no formal China program was developed. As Kenneth Prewitt, the RF executive vice president, put it in 1991 at a New York program on foundations and China: "We do not have the old China focus, but a developing country focus. In the 1980s there was some talk about whether to design a country program, but instead we focused on our existing programs: reproductive biology strategies, rice biotechnology, clinical epidemiology and more recently environmental science. . . . We don't worry about U.S.-China relations; we do worry about how China relates to global infrastructures within these specific areas."[45]

The Rockefeller focus on science-based development programs was characteristic of its theme-based, rather than country-based, international philanthropic work. In contrast, the Ford Foundation has been organized regionally, with country offices. This has meant that the Ford Foundation has had an active China program, with a China office, since the mid-1980s. With its early emphasis on strengthening the disciplines of economics, international studies, and law, the Ford program's approach to strengthening institutional capacity was similar to the RF's pre–World War II efforts in the natural sciences and economics. Speaking on the same program as Prewitt, Peter Geithner, director of the Ford Foundation's China Office from 1987 to 1992, noted that the overall criteria for Ford's China programs—mainly in the social sciences—was their relationship to bringing about "the success of the reforms in China. . . . We are contributing to China as it is in the hopes of making it like we would like it to be."[46] This resonates with the earlier Rockefeller vision of bringing cultural change to China.

With the door to China open, three Rockefeller philanthropies—the Rockefeller Foundation, the China Medical Board, and the Rockefeller Brothers Fund—initiated new China programs. Their philanthropic style and the priorities of counterpart Chinese institutions owed a significant debt to the past. Despite the long hiatus in professional relationships, both Americans and Chinese assumed that the Nationalist-era types of exchange and collaboration would resume. As nongovernmental organizations primarily promoting science and medicine, these foundations were almost immune from the many ups and downs in United States–China relations during the 1980s and 1990s.

"Bringing the Revolution in Biological Sciences to China"

Although the scale was more modest, there was continuity between pre-1950 and post-1979 Rockefeller programs in China.[47] Just as scientific medicine had been the newest knowledge system of the early twentieth century, the science of life—developmental biology and plant biotechnology—was in the forefront of late-twentieth-century science and technology. The Rockefeller Foundation was well known as an international leader in these fields, which corresponded with two of Deng Xiaoping's national priorities: agricultural science and biotechnology. The priority given by Fang Yi and Deng Xiaoping to collaboration with the RF signaled their awareness of these congruent priorities.

With historic irony (although the RF in the 1970s probably had no institutional memory of the challenges of constructing PUMC), two of the first RF China projects involved the construction of modern scientific buildings. At the request of Fang Yi and with significant additional funding from the United Nations Fund for Population Activities, the RF designed, equipped, and oversaw the construction of the Institute of Developmental Biology—the Chinese Academy of Sciences' first new building in many years. When the RF's Board of Trustees voted to approve this first new China initiative, the first John D. Rockefeller's great-grandson and namesake, John D. Rockefeller IV, was asked to make the motion.

This time, the architects were from Columbia University's Graduate School of Architecture, and an entire scientific laboratory was shipped to China to be duplicated. With double-paned windows and central air-conditioning, it was the most modern science building in Peking.[48] Not to be outdone, the Chinese Academy of Agricultural Sciences also requested assistance with construction—a national plant gene bank. China's relatively primitive germ conservation efforts had been destroyed during the Cultural Revolution, with the loss of many seed collections. The new National Gene Bank was designed by Loyi Chan, a protégé of I. M. Pei, and it is today described as "one of the largest and arguably most beautiful gene banks in the world." It opened in 1990, and it has preserved 180,000 varieties of 294 crop species.[49] But these buildings were just a beginning.

The RF's programs in population science were led by Sheldon Segal. During a twenty-year period (1978–99), Segal's program distributed 63 percent of its funding ($10.5 million) in China (for Rockefeller China expenditures since 1970, see appendix A, table A2). During his early trips to China in the late 1970s, Segal came to the conclusion it was open to wide-ranging initiatives in population research, despite the obvious political sensitivities. He identified infertility, abortion, reproductive behavior, and family planning communication as areas for collaborative research. He noted that China itself had been active in contraceptive research but that the efficacy of its intrauterine devices had not been assessed scientifically. His caution against assuming a superior attitude toward Chinese efforts was characteristic of American efforts in the 1980s to minimize conflict with Chinese colleagues:

> I would like to make one point about contraceptive safety. China has done
> very little with regard to the study of safety issues. . . . This does not indicate,
> however, methods that are under investigation, and we should be careful not to
> impose our own regulations on Chinese colleagues. . . . I doubt seriously that we
> have developed systems that are superior to those of the Chinese.[50]

Fang Yi sought Segal out, meeting with him on several occasions, to discuss China's plans to control population, telling Segal that "China was going to announce its one-child policy, a sacrifice this generation was making for the next generation."[51] According to Fang, the Institute of Developmental Biology was being created in part to assure good science in the field of reproductive health: "He [Fang Yi] said that China is perhaps the only country that is asking its people to have one child per family. If the people are going to believe the government and have trust in it, the government must make every effort to assure that the one child is a healthy child and a child of good quality."[52] Because many international observers at this time were urging China to adopt some form of population growth reduction, Segal took Fang Yi at his word and did not voice opposition to this plan.[53]

In addition to support for the Institute of Developmental Biology, the RF explored a possible new male contraceptive, gossypol, a pigment in unrefined cottonseed oil. Having been discovered by the Chinese as a by-product of traditional Chinese medicine, the contraceptive held great promise, but ultimately it proved too toxic for human use. Research on gossypol by the foundation was international, involving more than thirteen countries and thirty-one institutions. Although it failed as a new contraceptive, the worldwide research project brought Chinese scientists into the international arena of contraceptive research.

Contraceptive technology continued to be a worldwide focus of the RF, and China was included in such initiatives as Contraceptive 21, designed to develop new reproductive technologies. The RF's most important success in developing birth control technology was its role in bringing RU-486, the emergency "day-after" contraceptive, to market. China proved to be a good source for mifepristone, the key ingredient. During the late 1990s, the RF provided more than $2 million to Shanghai Hualian Pharmaceutical Company to help it meet the standards of the U.S. Food and Drug Administration. Today Hualian is one of China's largest state-owned pharmaceutical companies and is the sole supplier to the United States of the abortion pill mifepristone, which continues to be known as RU-486.[54]

By the late 1980s, China's draconian birth control policies—including continued use of obsolete contraceptive technologies, forced abortions, and the absence of reproductive choice—were widely known. Nonetheless, the RF plunged ahead with a potentially controversial project: a new "family planning demonstration project" in collaboration with China's State Family Planning Commission, Peking University, and the University of Pennsylvania. The program was "designed to demonstrate the advantages of an enhanced rural family planning system" introducing reproductive choice with modern contraceptives (TCu380A and Norplant) and training family-planning workers. For the RF, the goal was to introduce the overall concept of reproductive choice; but for the State Family Planning Commission, the goal was to improve family-planning services and thus reduce resistance to the one-child policy. The tension between the two goals was never resolved.

The reproductive health training programs had no impact on China's one-child family policy, although they may have advanced the concept of technological choice. The mix of contraceptives introduced—modern intrauterine devices (including Chinese and international versions of Norplant) along with implantable contraception methods—created imprecise study results and confusion among village participants. Foundation concerns about this project led to an RF Board–led project review in 1993, which reported no obvious human rights violations. Although the RF's concerns were not fully abated, the program continued, spending approximately $1.5 million between 1988 and 1999.[55]

The agricultural sciences, which were less contentious than population sciences, emerged as the RF's largest program in China. Here the story of Tan Jiazhen (C. C. Tan) illustrates the many links between pre-1951 Rockefeller-funded scientists and the new era. Tan had been a recipient of several RF grants during the 1930s and 1940s. He was educated at Suzhou and Yanjing universities (he studied with Alice Boring), and he received RF funding for doctoral work at the California Institute of Technology in the 1930s, where he worked with T. H. Morgan and Theodosius Dobzhansky. He returned to China in 1937 with a special RF grant to fund his research at Zhejiang University, and then spent three years trekking through wartime China—conducting research and publishing papers all the way. Funded again during the late 1940s for research in the United States, he asked the RF to assist him in remaining in America. After meeting with Tan, Warren Weaver, the RF director of natural sciences, mused that "it is somewhat bizarre that he, as a geneticist, has more to fear from the Communists than his scientific colleagues. . . . [Tan] is well known as a Morgan geneticist, and he would certainly fare badly under the Communists." Nonetheless, Weaver encouraged Tan to return to China, where he did, in fact, suffer through two decades of Chinese Lysenkoism. However, by the time the RF was ready to return to China, Tan had been rehabilitated, becoming director of Fudan University's Institute of Genetics, the leading university-based biological institute in China.[56] He revisited the RF in New York in the early 1980s and became a collaborator in the Rice Biotechnology Program, which began in 1983.

Although the RF had created the International Rice Research Institute in 1960, little was known about the molecular biology of cereals, especially rice, when the RF started to fund relevant basic science in the early 1980s. Though it was perceived as a risky scientific venture, the rice program was adopted because 60 percent of the world's population uses rice as a primary food crop; an important goal was to strengthen rice research and develop international collaborative research. As the largest consumers of rice, China and India became major participants. The program provided funding to twenty-two Chinese institutions and trained scores of rice geneticists, significantly enhancing China's national scientific capacity.[57]

Approximately 10 percent of the RF's rice biotechnology funding was spent in China ($10 million), and a total of $14 million, or 37 percent of its China funding, went to the agricultural sciences. The Chinese government also steadily increased its support of agricultural biotechnology. The results of this combined international and domestic support have been impressive. From a minimal base in the early 1980s, China has become "the global leader in rice biotechnology and the world's largest investor in rice crop biotechnology."[58] China was the first country to develop several commercially ready varieties of genetically modified rice designed to reduce the use of both pesticides and fertilizers. Gary Toenniessen, the lead RF scientist on the Rice Biotechnology Program, believes that Chinese strains of genetically modified rice are environmentally and medically safe. He praised the Chinese program because it is primarily funded by the Chinese government and the intellectual property rights have remained in the public domain, not dominated by chemical and fertilizer companies, as in the United States. The same is true in India, as Toenniessen concluded: "China and India are the saviors of this revolution because the biotechnology is in the public sphere."[59] If international controversies over genetically modified rice are resolved, China will likely become the first country to export it.

During the last two decades of the twentieth century, the RF's Advanced Training Fellowship was widely used by both the Population and Agricultural Sciences divisions to train scientists in the United States. From 1979 to 2000, the Population Science division funded fifty-six fellows in the many disciplines of population science, while the Agricultural Science division funded eighty-seven fellows in fields ranging from soil fertility to plant genetics to agricultural economics. The RF worked with the China National Center for Biotechnology to select the recipients, introducing China's first peer review process in 1984. Two of the agricultural economists have gone on to international leadership positions; Lin Yifu (Justin Yifu Lin) is today the chief economist of the World Bank, and Wang Ren is responsible for coordinating all World Bank funding of international agricultural research centers. Chen Zhangliang, until recently president of China Agricultural University and today vice governor of Guangxi Province, is but one example of RF fellows who have become national scientific leaders.

The RF fellowship program experienced the same kind of "brain drain" problems as similar programs in the 1980s and early 1990s; only 10 percent of its PhD fellows returned to China. However, when the program's guidelines were modified to provide domestic research support in home institutions and ongoing international research travel funding, the rate of returnees improved significantly.

The issue of brain drain was also accentuated by the Tiananmen Incident in 1989. After this incident, unlike U.S. government agencies, the National Academy of Sciences, and many universities, the RF did not discontinue its programs in China. President Peter Goldmark cited the RF's long relationship with China when he announced: "We decided not to withdraw from programs we were supporting in China following the events of June. But our first representatives to visit that country after those events conveyed in public settings our deep unhappiness at the events of June and the repression that has followed, and stated our insistence that joint projects could command support and promise success only in an atmosphere of free inquiry."[60] There was no significant reduction in funding for 1990 and 1991.

More concerned with encouraging scientists to return to China than providing asylum, the RF created the China Bridges International Fellowship Program in 1992. The RF provided short-term grants for Chinese scientists resident in the United States to return to China to initiate collaborative research projects. Matching funding was provided by several Chinese ministries. As of 2004, the China Bridges fellowships had funded more than two hundred short and long-term research visits and is today based at the University of Connecticut and fully funded by the Chinese government.[61]

Population science and agricultural science were not the only China programs of the RF, but together they constituted more than 60 percent of its total China expenditures (just over $39 million) between 1972 and 2004. Midway through this period, an external assessment of the RF's role in biotechnology, including the molecular and cellular biology of human reproduction and plant sciences, concluded: "These Rockefeller Foundation programs have had a major impact on Chinese biotechnology. . . . The fellowship program allows investigators to work abroad on a regular basis, providing a key incentive for students to return to China. Furthermore, virtually every high-calibre scientist that was met during the one-month evaluation trip had been helped, one way or another, by the Rockefeller Foundation."[62] Other scientific initiatives included bringing China into two global networks, the International Clinical Epidemiology Network (INCLEN) and the Leadership for Environment and Development (LEAD) network, and improving China's capacity for producing a Chinese-developed vaccine for Japanese encephalitis. The China-based INCLEN projects in Shanghai and Chengdu have now evolved into becoming part of a global evidence-based medicine network. Including China in the LEAD program was an early recognition of the importance of China to the global environment.

The RF's China science programs during the 1980s and 1990s shared certain goals. Common to all programs was the purposeful integration of Chinese scientists and research institutes into extensive international networks. At the beginning of this period, China's science was just beginning to emerge from isolation and the devastating Cultural Revolution. By the end of the twentieth century, China's scientific infrastructure had been reinvigorated and was well on its way to becoming integrated with world science. China had established its own cutting-edge research and educational institutions and was poised for takeoff in the twenty-first century.

China was not a special priority of the RF during this era; its China funding constituted less than 5 percent of overall RF funding, in contrast with 12 percent across the entire pre-1950 period. During 1988, the peak year of RF China funding in the 1980s, it expended $2.5 million in China and $64 million globally; during the 1990s, the peak year was 1997, when China received $2.6 million out of a total of $103 million.

Despite this relatively small program, the RF was the largest U.S. funder of China's science during this period. This may seem surprising, but Rockefeller funding promoted China's science in a way that the U.S. government did not, and, with the exception of the China Medical Board, there were no other private foundations focused on science and medicine in China. Although the National Science Foundation and the National Institutes of Health developed programs with China, they were prohibited from providing direct support to Chinese science; scientific initiatives came from American scientists primarily seeking access to Chinese data, including its distinct flora, fauna, and human experiences. Likewise, though the U.S. Fulbright program supports scientific fellowships with many nations, science and engineering were not included in its China programs. These restrictions stemmed from President Jimmy Carter's 1979 normalization agreements, which stipulated that there would be no technical assistance for China, a Communist country, in the form of either scientific or technological support. This is still primarily true today. American scientists must justify their request for U.S. government funds in terms of direct benefits to U.S. science, and the Fulbright program primarily supports the social sciences and humanities.

Of course, the RF's funding was minuscule compared with the role of the Chinese government and many international organizations. Also, American universities were generous in supporting thousands of visiting Chinese scientists and in providing graduate fellowships for young Chinese scientists, the majority of whom, however, have stayed in the United States, benefiting American science. In lending its enormous international scientific reputation to include Chinese scientists just emerging from the Cultural Revolution, the RF reprised its historic role. Its distinct contribution was to draw China into its global scientific networks, once again giving worldwide visibility and legitimacy to China's scientific aspirations.

THE CHINA MEDICAL BOARD:
BEYOND PEKING UNION MEDICAL COLLEGE

The China Medical Board's encounters with the People's Republic of China in the 1970s were less dramatic and less public than those of the Rockefeller Foundation.[63] The CMB is a relatively small foundation (its assets have ranged from $75 million to more than $250 million in the last three decades), and it is led by a single medical professional serving both as president and chief program officer.

The publication of Mary Ferguson's book *China Medical Board and Peking Union Medical College: A Chronicle of Fruitful Collaboration* in 1970, two years before U.S. President Richard Nixon's historic visit, focused the attention of the CMB's president and trustees on their historic China role. The CMB's president, Patrick Ongley, drew a number of sobering conclusions from that historical record. An internationally recognized pediatrician and a citizen of New Zealand, Ongley had no sentimental attachments to the CMB's previous presence in China. His critique of the PUMC era was cogent: difficulty in controlling an overseas project, financial failures, lack of political foresight, and "the time lag between the stated goal of turning the P.U.M.C. over to Chinese nationals and the subconscious resistance on the part of U.S. personnel to loosening control from themselves."[64] He was initially a little skeptical about resuming the CMB's work in China, but he nonetheless took advantage of an opportunity to travel in China and to meet with visiting Chinese medical leaders during the 1970s.

The key issue for the CMB was what to do about its historic responsibility for PUMC. Well over two decades had passed since the Chinese government had nationalized PUMC, thereby assuming full financial responsibility for the previously American-owned and -operated institution. Like other American philanthropies and corporations, the CMB had filed financial claims against the People's Republic for the confiscated property, requesting $9,368,288. In May 1979, the U.S. government reached a settlement with China, and the CMB was awarded $3,659,952. This settlement paved the way for a Ministry of Health invitation for the CMB to return in a grantmaking capacity, with an official China visit scheduled for 1980. In December 1979, just before those official meetings, the CMB reviewed PUMC's historic claim on the CMB endowment and reached a number of conclusions concerning a new era of supporting medical education in China.

The most important decision was that the CMB should "not try to recreate the PUMC" nor focus solely on China Medical University, as PUMC was then called. With 120 medical schools and an extensive public health system, China's medical education infrastructure had evolved considerably since 1951. CMB trustees recognized that times had changed, concluding that "it is unacceptable to have one country dominate a major educational institute in another country." The wiser course was for the CMB to support several institutions: "The multiplying effect of supporting five major schools in the fields of education, training and research, will have a much greater beneficial effect than participating in the programs of any one school." Not only did the CMB decide not to give special attention to PUMC or a similar institution, but it voted that the monies received from the asset claims would return to the endowment and not be given to PUMC. The CMB also decided not to support building or equipping medical schools and hospitals but rather to focus on fellowships, research, medical education, and studies of the socioeconomics of health and health care delivery.[65]

The Ministry of Health concurred with this new approach and asked the CMB to work with seven key medical schools, later expanded to thirteen. (A number of these medical schools were the descendants of missionary medical colleges supported by the CMB during the 1920s and 1930s.) However, some Chinese medical leaders previously associated with PUMC were clearly disappointed by the CMB decision. Throughout the 1980s, informal protests were made, drawing the CMB's attention to its original charter of support for PUMC. Senior PUMC leaders, trained in the "old PUMC," including Huang Jiasi (a 1933 graduate) and Wu Jieping (1942), did become key consultants to the CMB as it reentered China and, as time went by, a special relationship evolved with PUMC. In a one-time exception to its policy, the CMB provided funds to restore PUMC's beautiful Chinese roofs and also to modernize its plumbing system. In time, PUMC emerged as the institution that provided logistical staff support for the president of the CMB when he was in China, and it also functioned as an administrative coordinator for the CMB's work with other medical institutions. From 1981 to 2008, PUMC was the largest recipient of CMB grants, receiving 17 percent of the CMB's China funding, versus the second largest, Peking University's Health Science Center, which received 14 percent (see appendix A, table A3).

During the 1950s and 1960s, the CMB had worked with thirty medical institutions in sixteen Asian countries. In addition to a fellowship program that supported six hundred fellows during these two decades, the CMB provided equipment and laboratory support for these Asian institutions, serving as the purchasing agent in New York. When Ongley became president in 1973, he narrowed the focus, scaling down to concentrate support for twelve grantees in eight countries. The CMB adopted a philosophy of providing large block grants and endowments, all of which had to be matched by recipient countries. By awarding institutional grants instead of individual fellowships, Asian recipients avoided paying U.S. taxes on the funds. More important, academic deans and faculty were given the responsibility for selecting participants and deciding how to expend the CMB funds. As one trustee remembered: "Pat Ongley gets a lot of credit for having brought [grantees] along to understand they were colleagues; they were not serfs of CMB, they were respected, that we were there to help them, and that we were going to do this as a kind of partnership."[66]

This, then, was the philanthropic strategy that the CMB brought to China in the 1980s: to provide general endowment funding for faculty development, libraries, and research. Early visits to impoverished Chinese medical schools reinforced the conviction that this kind of basic institutional capacity building was needed. As Robert Buchanan, director of Massachusetts General Hospital and a CMB trustee, described his first visit to PUMC:

When we went to our first meeting at PUMC, I was struck by the fact that all the people we were meeting were senior—very senior. There were no young doctors who spoke English. . . . And so the people we saw were in their 60s all the way up to their late 70s. . . . And as we moved around and talked to people, the senior and respected doctors had been through the tortures of the damned during the Cultural Revolution. . . . One had the sense that there was a tremendous need in medicine to rebuild. And the only persons with whom to rebuild were these older people whose knowledge of Western medicine was clearly outdated.[67]

Ongley's grantmaking philosophy emerged from this observation that not only were the ranks of medical faculty depleted, but institutional governance and autonomy also needed to be redeveloped. Three decades of authoritarian rule and political oversight had undermined medical faculty leadership. Extending the matching grant program to China with decisionmaking vested in the medical deans was a way of giving them a "dowry," the resources with which they could begin to rebuild the faculty, libraries, and clinical programs. The CMB was not unmindful that the Chinese Communist Party still had oversight of educational institutions, but it hoped that external funding would begin to privilege scientific over political criteria. The relative independence given to institutions as to how they spent the funds was also based on Ongley's realization that PUMC's history, its record of control from the United States, was a still fresh and controversial memory. The CMB would begin again as a grantmaking foundation, not a managing or operating foundation.[68]

To avoid competition between institutions, each Chinese recipient institution received identical grants. The CMB's contributions were denominated in dollars and invested in the United States; these were matched by Chinese renminbi accounts. Although Ongley spent considerable time visiting each institution in China and reviewing expenditures, the detailed financial decisionmaking was left in Chinese hands. A total of $60 million was invested in Chinese endowments during this period, half from the Chinese government.

Ongley's first two successor presidents, William Sawyer (1987–97) and Roy Schwarz (1997–2006), followed a different grantmaking strategy: Institutions were encouraged to submit proposals for specific projects to be reviewed by the president and approved by the CMB trustees. As China's scientific and educational reforms took root and medical colleges began to expand and take on new educational and research programs, the matching endowment strategy was less attractive; lower interest rates meant that endowment income was too modest for the programs that were needed. Also, recipient institutions expressed mixed views about the matching-grant process. Some had found it difficult to persuade Chinese officials to provide matching funds or to manage the banking process. In retrospect, however, the CMB believed that "matching," or joint financial responsibility for medical programs, had accomplished two goals: Shared responsibility avoided the pattern of dependency associated with the CMB's earlier relationship with PUMC, and Chinese institutions were empowered to make their own personnel and financial decisions.[69]

In addition to shifting away from endowments, Sawyer, a research immunologist who had developed science programs for the RF in Thailand, directed the CMB's grants toward specific research or medical education projects. He believed the CMB's working relationship with its partner institutions was sufficiently solid to permit differential funding. His background complemented a growing Chinese interest in medical research. During his tenure, the CMB provided a number of discreet research grants, including some funds for basic medical research. He also emphasized the importance of national and regional medical networks. Of particular significance was the creation of a President's Council, which brought the presidents of key medical universities together on an annual basis. This type of horizontal leadership program was unusual in China, and it enabled the Chinese presidents to discuss common problems as well as to plan collaborative work. A second regional network was set up for nurses. Ongley had initiated a program of nursing education at Thailand's Chiang Mai School of Nursing. Under Sawyer's leadership, Chiang Mai created the Program of Higher Nursing Education Development, a special effort to train Chinese nurses in Thailand rather than send them to the United States. This regional program proved highly successful and, with the continuing support of the CMB, has today been extended throughout China and Southeast Asia.

In China, Sawyer's tenure is perhaps best remembered for his role in establishing the first modern medical college in Tibet and in beginning the CMB's work with three-year medical colleges, not just the elite urban medical universities. In the late 1980s, at the request of the minister of health, the CMB began to work with Jiujiang Medical College, a three-year institution in Jiangxi Province tasked with developing a model curriculum for doctors who would practice in rural areas. Several years later, after a tourist trip to Tibet, Sawyer met with the minister of health and proposed that the CMB provide assistance to an existing lower-level medical school in order to create the first modern medical college in Tibet. In 1993, a three-year medical college opened with substantial support from the CMB, and Tibet Medical College, along with Jiujiang Medical College, became a member of the CMB's network of thirteen medical institutions.

When Roy Schwarz became president in 1997, the CMB's trustees decided that it should refocus on medical education, unique medical research, and social medicine or public health. As a medical educator with leadership experience in several U.S. medical schools, Schwarz was best known for founding WAMI, a system of medical education that linked the states of Washington, Alaska, Montana, and Idaho. He believed that China had given too much attention to medical research and insufficient attention to education. He continued the institutional grant pattern established by Sawyer, including targeted medical research programs, but he emphasized educational innovations, such as standardized patients (persons trained to simulate medical conditions in order to improve clinical diagnosis); regional centers for medical education; medical ethics; and advanced degree programs, including joint MD-PhD programs and nursing MA and PhD programs.

At a time when China was addressing global economic standards in order to enter the World Trade Organization, Schwarz believed that China could play a role in developing international minimum essential requirements for an MD. With the global mobility of medical personnel, some believed that standardized international accreditation was desirable. The CMB created a separate entity, the Institute for International Medical Education, which included health educators from Europe, Latin America, China, and the United States. And it agreed upon a set of sixty essential standards in seven areas: professional values and ethics, the scientific foundation of medicine, clinical skills, communication skills, population health and health systems, the management of information, and critical thinking and research. The basic concept was that 60 percent of a graduate's medical expertise should be based upon these global standards, and 40 percent should be based on local content. A complex, several-day testing process was created whereby the medical students at six Chinese medical universities took the standardized exams. Institutional results were shared with each institution's leaders and with the minister of health but were not made public. Chinese medical leaders believed the exercise provided a useful evaluation of their current medical education standards, and they hoped that the Global Medical Education Requirements (GMER) would, in time, become an international standard.[70]

Schwarz's emphasis upon standards for medical education evoked the earliest CMB work in China—using the standards of Johns Hopkins and American medical education to create PUMC. Whether or not the GMER project will ever influence global medical education, the project did demonstrate that Chinese medical leaders were hoping to create an international educational model and willing to subject their institutions to a global standardized examination.

Under Schwarz, the CMB's programs became increasingly visible in China. In 2005, the GMER project and a new clinical curriculum at China Medical University in Shenyang received the Ministry of Education's only first-prize awards. In the same year, a CMB research program at Sun Yat-sen University Medical School on the genetics of nasopharyngeal carcinoma and collaborative research between PUMC and the Chinese Academy of Medical Sciences' Institute of Medical Biology on Chinese genomic diversity received two of three Ministry of Science and Technology medical prizes.

Schwarz, like Sawyer before him, developed a close working relationship with the minister of health. And working with provincial-level medical colleges introduced the CMB to medical challenges far beyond the scope of national key institutions. By the end of Schwarz's tenure, in 2006, the CMB had been working in the People's Republic for a quarter of a century. China's medical universities had progressed from the skeletal institutions of the immediate post–Cultural Revolution era to become well-funded leaders of modern medicine in China. The CMB was ready to begin a new era.

The CMB spent approximately three times the amount of the RF in the People's Republic between 1980 and 2008, for a total of $131 million, excluding matching endowment grants. The top four recipients were PUMC ($23 million), Peking University Health Science Center ($18 million), Sun Yat-sen University Medical School ($17 million), and West China Medical School of Sichuan University ($15 million) (see appendix A, table A3).

Taken together, these two Rockefeller philanthropies expended approximately $180 million in China, by far the largest American direct investment in China's science and medicine. The Ford Foundation, with a Beijing-based professional staff in China and a more visible program, was the most active American foundation in China during this period. With its focus primarily on the social sciences, governance, public policy, the environment, and poverty alleviation, Ford's expenditures from 1988 to 2008 totaled $260 million.[71]

THE ROCKEFELLER BROTHERS FUND: GLOBAL INTERDEPENDENCE

When the door to China reopened in the 1970s, the Rockefeller Brothers Fund was the only Rockefeller philanthropy in which members of the family remained deeply involved. After the RBF was created in 1940 by John D. Rockefeller's grandchildren, for several decades it functioned primarily to serve the charitable interests of JDR 3rd, Nelson, Winthrop, Laurence, David, and Abby. Among their special projects were the Museum of Modern Art, Rockefeller University, Memorial Sloan-Kettering Hospital, the Population Council, the Asia Society, and restorations in Sleepy Hollow. In the 1970s, tie-off grants to these and other personal philanthropies, coupled with new foundation tax laws and the deaths of both JDR 3rd and Nelson, led to a more professionally managed RBF with a broader strategic agenda. Family leadership was gradually transferred to the "cousins," John D. Rockefeller's great-grandchildren, the Rockefeller fourth generation. By charter, members of the Rockefeller family constitute half the RBF's board, and the president is expected to vote with the family in case of a close vote. In contrast to the scientific focus of the RF and the CMB, an early international commitment to peace and understanding characterized the RBF's ethos.[72]

China received the RBF's very first international grant—in 1945, for war-relief work. Two decades later, prompted by JDR 3rd, the RBF was an early funder of American organizations seeking to restore cultural relations with the People's Republic. RBF staff advised JDR 3rd to make his initial support to the National Committee on United States–China Relations and edited his 1969 speech. In addition to the National Committee, the RBF was the primary funder for the Center for U.S.-China Arts Exchange based at Columbia University, and the China-related programs of the Asia Society. For the RBF, this support was designed to "increase understanding between the [People's Republic of China] and the United States and harmony with the Pacific Community through projects that facilitate analysis and discussion of issues of common concern, as well as through exchanges of people."[73]

During the 1980s, the National Committee, the U.S.-China Arts Exchange, and the Asia Society's China Council sought to reduce barriers between the United States and China through exchanges in professional and artistic fields and public education. The Arts Exchange, led by Zhou Wenzhong, was of special interest to the RBF; Chinese dance, opera, and art were introduced to American audiences, while American music, cinema, and theater were introduced to China. Of these three United States–based programs, the Arts Exchange received the most funding, including a $300,000 endowment grant (for a chart of RBF spending, see appendix A, table A4).

In 1983, the RBF adopted the foundation-wide theme of "Global Interdependence, One World." In this new context, Russell Phillips, vice president of the RBF, shifted the Asia focus to international relations and strategic studies designed to "enhance mutual American and East Asian understanding through . . . strengthening international relations and strategic studies in East Asia and helping them construct links with one another and with similar American institutions."[74] Funding flowed to "think tanks, transnational advocacy networks, and something like a regional security-policy intelligentsia." Although most grants were relatively small, the RBF recognized the need for sustained training of Chinese scholars in the field of international relations; it provided a total of $655,000 from 1984 to 1990 to the Committee on International Relations Studies in the People's Republic of China. This program, which was also funded by the Ford Foundation, provided graduate fellowships for Chinese to study international relations in the United States. Between 1985 and 1992, 115 Chinese were trained in international relations at American universities, including 61 graduate students and 54 visiting scholars. Of the graduate students, approximately half received MAs and half received PhDs. Some with PhDs remained in the United States, creating a new cohort of China-born international relations specialists, while many also returned to China. Those who returned to China introduced fashionable topics and new theoretical models to the emerging Chinese international relations community. Those remaining in the United States brought China as an important case study into highly theoretical political science departments.

Ongoing transpacific discourse today characterizes this field, an important contribution to strengthening bilateral understanding.[75]

As part of its "One World" theme, sustainable resources emerged as the RBF's most important focus in the late 1980s and 1990s. This emphasis on "environmental stewardship" was the result of the growing interest of Rockefeller family board members in environmental issues. China became part of a ten-country Asian Sustainable Resources Program in 1986, with an initial grant to the Guangzhou Institute of Energy Conservation. During the next decade, the program in China became quite complex, covering several provinces (Guangxi, Yunnan, Guangdong), two watersheds (the Mekong and the Pearl rivers), and multiple thematic areas. These included, but were not limited to, sustainable agriculture, integrated pest management, coastal management, food safety, and security, including organic food production and marketing. Types of Chinese institutions ranged from provincial academies of social science (Yunnan Academy of Social Sciences) and universities (South China Agricultural University in Guangzhou) to scientific research institutes (Nanjing Institute of Environmental Science) to nongovernmental social action groups (Civic Exchange Limited in Hong Kong and Participatory Watershed Management Research and Promotion Center, Yunnan). Grants were relatively small and constituted less than 1 percent of the RBF budget, hardly $100,000 a year. The largest recipient between 1997 and 2003 was the Yunnan Academy of Social Sciences, which received $316,000.

The RBF's China strategy meant more attention to, as Peter Riggs, program officer for Asia, put it, "issues of social and political power than is usually the case with most programs focused on the environment."[76] Whether working with local farmer groups or with the Yunnan Academy of Social Sciences, the RBF programs espoused "people's participation." As Riggs advocated in a summary to the RBF trustees, programs concerned with the environment "*must* take on the critical questions of democratic governance, economic transparency, and cultural survival."[77]

The RBF's growing focus on sustainable resources, nongovernmental organizations, grassroots programs, and governance issues reflects a broader trend in American philanthropy and nongovernmental organizations in China since the 1990s. This more activist approach differs from the more socially conservative programs of both the RF and the CMB. Still, the RBF consciously links its new programs to the Rockefeller philanthropic heritage. A docket prepared for the RBF trustees in 1998 compares the RF's twentieth-century historical interest in communicable disease with the RBF's twenty-first-century focus on health challenges from environmental degradation:

> It is hoped that the Trustees will see this program interest as a continuation of the
> Rockefeller legacy in China. During John D. Rockefeller's first forays into Asia,
> some seventy years ago, he became convinced of the overwhelming need to combat
> communicable disease. China still faces grave public health threats, but those threats

no longer stem from cholera, smallpox, and tuberculosis; rather they stem from unsustainable growth and related environmental degradation. . . . The proposed RBF effort to provide support for research and the development of technical "know-how" is consistent with past Rockefeller interests in China's public health and welfare.[78]

Of the three foundations, the RBF has been the most consistent in internal and external acknowledgement of its Rockefeller heritage, continuing to see value in referring to the historic Rockefeller role in China.

These three Rockefeller philanthropies illustrate the role of the nongovernmental sector during the early decades of reengagement with China. As Akira Iriye suggests in his notion of cultural internationalism, cultural institutions bring their own momentum to the course of bilateral relations. Institutional continuity can be a major factor, often providing ballast during periods of rapid geopolitical change. Once political relations between the United States and China were normalized, the Rockefeller philanthropies required no U.S. governmental funding or approval and encountered minimal Chinese government restrictions. The RF and the CMB easily renewed their historic China role and China connections, bringing resources to rebuild China's medical infrastructure, to revitalize its life sciences, and to link China with global scientific networks.

At a time when U.S. governmental technical assistance funds could not be used in China, Rockefeller support demonstrated an American commitment to China's scientific development. Although the RBF attempted to engage a popular Chinese base, all three foundations worked with established Chinese national and local institutions. Although their relationships with counterpart institutions had predictable challenges, they were not particularly susceptible to tensions in the bilateral political relationship. Given the Rockefeller foundations' philanthropic focus in areas vital to China's development—and their role as grantmaking, not operating, foundations—it is not surprising that these three American institutions encountered minimal political obstacles.

After the Tiananmen Incident in 1989, the continuity of their engagement contrasted to the severing of many official U.S. political and military relationships. The presidents of both the RF and the RBF expressed outrage at the Tiananmen massacre, but there was no reduction in financial support for China. Colin Campbell, president of the RBF, explained their decision: "The decision to remain engaged was based on the sure knowledge that there are individuals and institutions, particularly at regional and local levels, that wish to contribute to a process of modernization funded more on reason than on ideology. . . . Should the Fund be unable to conduct free, open and regular dialogue with its grantees in China or determine that those grantees are unable to carry out Fund-supported activities unimpeded, it would be necessary to terminate the relations."[79] The president of the CMB at the time, Bill Sawyer, flew to China during the week after June 4, 1989, pledging the CMB's continuing support to its partner universities.

Despite the many successes of these years, with the dawn of a new century, all three foundations found themselves reassessing their role in China. This was in part because of changes in institutional leadership, but primarily because China itself had changed so dramatically since the early 1980s. In 1997, Peter Goldmark, then the RF's president, suggested that it was time for a new philanthropic approach to China. He reflected on the difficulty of categorizing American philanthropic approaches to China. Does one think about China as a part of a global set of issues or as a unique entity? China is geographically huge—it could easily absorb an entire foundation's program. His call for a new RF approach to China, one that would take into account China's growing national strength, was both ominous and prescient:

> The Foundation should rethink entirely its approach to China. The Rockefeller Foundation's international programs are organized by theme and subject area, not by geography. But the question of China would challenge either organizing principle. . . . The world has entered a period in which China's and the planet's fates are linked, and this period promises to be long and dangerous. . . . The Foundation's long-standing engagement with China needs to be refashioned to take these realities into account.[80]

The first decade of the twenty-first century did bring new Rockefeller philanthropic approaches to a resurgent China—and a surprising Chinese tribute to the senior John D. Rockefeller.

CHAPTER 6

LEGACY

Anniversaries

In Peking on October 14, 2007, Richard Rockefeller, the son of David Rockefeller and chairman of the Rockefeller Brothers Fund, bowed low before a bust of his great-grandfather, John D. Rockefeller Sr., joining the president of Peking Union Medical College (PUMC), Liu Depei, in laying a ceremonial wreath *(figure 6.1)*. The occasion was PUMC's ninetieth anniversary, and members of the fourth and fifth generations of the Rockefeller family gathered as the Oil Prince's honored descendants. The PUMC-commissioned bust is of a young and vigorous Rockefeller and incorporates auspicious Chinese numerology. It is exactly 1.917 meters high— signifying the year that PUMC opened. Representatives of the Rockefeller Foundation, China Medical Board, and Rockefeller Brothers Fund joined in the tribute.[1] The American counterpoint to this Chinese ceremony was the fiftieth-anniversary celebration of the Asia Society in 2004, which highlighted the Rockefeller family's historic and continuing interest in Asia. Even as these sentimental anniversaries eulogized the past, all four Rockefeller-founded institutions were reimagining their China programs, seeking new initiatives for a vastly different century.

FROM VILIFIED CAPITALIST TO MODEL ENTREPRENEUR AND PHILANTHROPIST

It is almost inconceivable that a bust of John D. Rockefeller himself could have been dedicated in Peking at any other moment in China's history. In previous decades, the Rockefeller name—vilified as an icon of American economic and cultural imperialism—evoked memories of Sino-American antagonism and

FIGURE 6.1. The dedication of the John D. Rockefeller Statue, Peking, by Richard Rockefeller and Peking Union Medical College President Liu Depei, 2007. *Photograph courtesy of the Rockefeller Brothers Fund.*

China's semicolonial past. Today, as twenty-first-century China embraces both market capitalism and entrepreneurial philanthropy, there is a more sympathetic interpretation of John D. Rockefeller. He represents the self-made capitalist wealth of the United States as well as large-scale corporate philanthropy. Critics of China's growing culture of wealth express the hope that the country's burgeoning capitalists will emulate his philanthropy. For instance, Zi Zhongyun's book *The Destiny of Wealth: An Analysis of American Philanthropic Foundations from a Chinese Perspective*, written for a Chinese audience, traces the historical evolution of American philanthropy, including Rockefeller's story. Using his life as a parable, Zi describes the rise of a wealthy Chinese business class and the advent of local philanthropy, noting that

> those who became the first *nouveaux riches* often spent their money in excessively
> luxurious or even decadent lifestyles. . . . Of course, there were also some
> charitable donations, but mostly for individual events like natural disasters—
> floods, droughts, earthquakes—or for medical or educational expenses for poor
> children reported by the media. . . . Starting in the mid-1990s, following the
> progress of China's economy, a sense of social responsibility has been growing
> among those who were more fortunate to "get rich first," as Deng Xiaoping put it.[2]

John D. Rockefeller is now a model for some Chinese—from humble origins, he became an extraordinarily successful entrepreneur, a philanthropist, and the world's richest man. In 2007 Guo Xianwei, himself a first-generation entrepreneur, founded the Rockefeller (China) Research Development Institute, which is dedicated to training entrepreneurs and educating businessmen and students to become philanthropists. Guo believes that the Rockefeller model can influence Chinese commerce and philanthropy. His fledgling institute commissions translations of books and articles on the Rockefeller family, businesses, and philanthropies and conducts informal seminars that explore the history of Standard Oil's business practices and Rockefeller philanthropy in China.[3]

There are signs that Standard Oil's economic role in China's history may also be ready for revision. In Jiujiang, an old treaty-port city in Jiangxi Province, one finds the 1911 neoclassical Standard Oil headquarters for the middle reaches of the Yangtze River, the river port boarding house for Standard's American employees, and the original depot, now expanded and modernized.[4] When the last American employees left in 1950, China Petrochemical took over the buildings. Unrestored but still occupying prime real estate, these aging structures are under the protection of Jiujiang's Historic Preservation Office and have recently been declared national historic properties. According to the director of the Preservation Office, this designation means that funds will be available to restore them as a museum about the history of Standard Oil in central China. She hopes this will bring Chinese and American tourists alike to Jiujiang.

Even missionaries are being recognized for their service to China. Not far from the depot is the new Jiujiang University Library, which has wall-size photographic reproductions of missionary medical work, including pictures of Shi Meiyu (Mary Stone), the first Chinese woman to study medicine in the United States and one of the first Chinese recipients of a China Medical Board fellowship in 1914. Her nursing school, founded in 1901, was one of the university's predecessor institutions. And high in the nearby Lushan Mountains, the former foreign summer resort of Guling (Kuling) has already been turned into a museum for Chinese and international tourists. More than five hundred villas of missionaries and businessmen alike have been preserved with realistic dioramas depicting the Western lifestyle of the 1920s and 1930s. A recording of Christian hymns is played continuously in the carefully preserved ivy-covered old church.

These and other remembrances of the American "occupation" are something new in post–Mao Zedong China. The depiction is both fair and accurate. China's rapid growth and increased global confidence have enabled it to move away from the imperialist rhetoric of the past. Because the past is no longer a threat, museums, statues, and photographs depict historical relics (indeed, the English word "relic" is used), which may no longer have political relevance but about which there is much public curiosity. One is reminded of Joseph Levinson's depiction of Communist China's relegation of Confucius to a museum, "preserved, embalmed, deprived of life in a glass case instead of in a cultural holocaust."[5]

PUMC's ninetieth-anniversary celebration in 2007 honored John D. Rockefeller precisely because the era of American domination has become deep history: PUMC's identity has become fully, confidently Chinese. Rockefeller's bust today stands in the old auditorium where both his and Sun Yat-sen's memorial services were held, across the street from PUMC's anatomy building, where Davidson Black's laboratory once housed Peking Man's bones. A large sepia-colored photograph of the 1917 cornerstone-laying ceremony hangs in PUMC's walnut-paneled board room (once dominated by John Singer Sargent's Rockefeller portrait). It depicts Americans in morning coats with several Chinese officials while a Chinese laborer maneuvers the large cornerstone into place, an ever-present reminder of PUMC's distinct American origins. In the background is the Ceremonial Hall of Prince Yu's elegant seventeenth-century palace just before it was demolished to make room for the new modern medical college. History records that the cornerstone ceremony featured the U.S. Marine Band playing on the steps of Prince Yu's palace.[6]

This time, the ceremony began with the Chinese national anthem. And it almost seemed as if PUMC's compound had morphed back into Prince Yu's palace, becoming once again essentially Chinese. The early-twentieth-century medical complex, today designated a national historical site, appears as an island of old Peking surrounded by shining high-rise hospitals, shopping centers, and a massive Grand Hyatt Hotel *(see figure 6.2)*. A ninetieth-anniversary commemorative album blends pictures of Prince Yu's pavilions with near-matching elements of PUMC—marble balustrades, green carved roofs, long garden corridors, traditional doorways, and welcoming Fu dogs. In his preface, PUMC Communist Party secretary Liu Qian evokes the ineffable "long-lasting and distinctive PUMC spirit" embodied in each of the "the buildings, corridors, doors, windows, bricks, and tiles [that] were built with the standards of most beautiful, most splendid, and most high quality." He calls on their ethical and aspirational essence:

> Aren't these buildings the concrete reflection of PUMC's mission to deliver
> education at high standard, high starting point, and high level, and in fine
> craftsmanship? When you walk alongside the green sticks [columns], gray walls,
> and long corridors, don't you feel that you are running through the space-time
> channel with the former pioneers accompanying you?[7]

The power of this place, which enshrines PUMC's history, continues to exert a magnetic pull; groups of PUMC staff and alumni posed for ninetieth-anniversary celebratory portraits in its courtyard. The survival of PUMC and its historic influence on Chinese medical education is surely one of the most important Rockefeller legacies.

The official commemorative ceremony included congratulatory speeches by leading Chinese political, medical, and educational personnel. Yet, unlike previous

FIGURE 6.2. The Peking Union Medical College auditorium and the Grand Hyatt Hotel, 2010. *Photograph by the author.*

PUMC anniversaries, this occasion received scant attention in the Peking press. Perhaps it was because as China confidently enters its second century of modern higher education, centennial anniversaries have become commonplace. Some universities even consciously stretch their founding dates back into the missionary era to have an edge on longevity. Some had urged that PUMC take 1906, the founding year of the Union Medical College, as its year of origin. But with a keen sense of historical accuracy, and in protection of PUMC's unique identity, President Liu Depei preferred to recognize the Rockefeller origin, not its missionary predecessor.

At this ceremony, with the presence of fourth- and fifth-generation Rockefellers, PUMC's faculty and students were exposed, probably for the first time, to the depth of the Rockefeller family's historic involvement in China *(figure 6.3)*. In his dedication remarks, Richard Rockefeller, himself a physician, remarked:

> The warm and close ties which my family feels for PUMC began with my great-grandfather, who developed a strong interest in China as a very young man. Once he became wealthy, his newly formed Rockefeller Foundation began providing support for medical research through the China Medical Board. His son and my grandfather, John D. Rockefeller Jr., stood near this very spot when he spoke at the dedicatory ceremony of PUMC in 1921. . . . I believe my great-grandfather would have been enormously proud to see this great institution

FIGURE 6.3. Fourth- and fifth-generation Rockefellers at the dedication of the Rockefeller Statue on the ninetieth anniversary of Peking Union Medical College, 2007. From left: Steven Rockefeller, Wendy O'Neill, Richard Rockefeller, Anne Bartley, Eliza Messinger. *Photograph courtesy of the Rockefeller Brothers Fund.*

now. . . . I believe my great-grandfather would be proud of what PUMC has become after these 90 years: of its world-class students and faculty, and of its extraordinary achievements in biomedical research, education and clinical care.[8]

The slide-illustrated presentation by Wendy O'Neill, Rockefeller's great-great-granddaughter, however, mesmerized the audience. Her grandmother, Abby, attended PUMC's 1921 dedication with her parents, and family records described her memorable journey. Influenced by this family China history, Wendy herself went from Harvard University to study at Peking University, marry a Chinese citizen, and live for many years in Hong Kong. She has even been an anonymous patient at PUMC Hospital. The young audience gasped as she related her personal experiences:

As for me, this is my 4th time at PUMC. The first was with my family in 1981 when we were on a trip to China as tourists. The second time I came was as a patient. In 1988, while I was working in Beijing for CITIC, I became engaged to be married to a co-worker. So, my *danwei* informed me that as a foreigner I needed to go to PUMC for a pre-marriage medical exam. I quietly came over here, and didn't tell anybody I was a member of the Rockefeller family. The kind PUMC doctor examined me, announced I was healthy and could marry. If it weren't for that PUMC doctor's approval, I wouldn't be married. . . . I don't think that John D. Rockefeller would have ever dreamed that PUMC would one day play a role in his great-great-granddaughter's marriage and great-great-grandson-in-law's health.

Wendy went on to personally convey the philanthropic heritage that has motivated the Rockefeller family:

Like all families, we are bound together by blood and memories, but perhaps what is unique about the Rockefeller family is that we are also bound together by philanthropy. This sense that we have been given much and must find a way to help our fellow mankind is a fundamental belief of the Rockefeller family.[9]

Intergenerational Rockefeller family philanthropy, intrinsic to the Rockefeller family culture, is an indisputable Rockefeller legacy.

PUMC'S FUTURE DEBATED

PUMC's Rockefeller history was only one aspect of the ninetieth-anniversary celebration, which was primarily an opportunity to engage the national and institutional issues of medical education and health care delivery. Not surprisingly, the concerns with which the original Rockefeller educators wrestled are still present. The optimism of the "golden age" in modern medicine has given way to a more somber realization of the challenges that medical discoveries and health care delivery still pose—in both the United States and China. The Flexnerian educational system of curative medicine has proved insufficiently responsive to the need for preventive medicine and equitable health care delivery. No nation has solved the most fundamental challenge of medical education and health care delivery: How do you provide sufficient numbers and incentives for high-quality medical care for all citizens? As PUMC's Chinese leaders looked ahead to their own centennial in 2017, there were still conflicting visions of PUMC's future role, arguments that evoked the 1930s. These still-unresolved debates about medicine and health care are a continuing Rockefeller legacy.

Chen Yuanfang (PUMC, 1957), a professor of medicine, dramatically called for PUMC's leaders to reintroduce the virtues of the "old PUMC," emphasizing the Flexnerian ideals of a broad liberal arts and science premedical curriculum, a hands-on mentoring and residency program, and clinical research in an academic hospital. This produced a "rich, blooming Eden in which one may develop freely." She highlighted the medical accomplishments that resulted from such an educational and research environment, including creating the "world's earliest urban and rural demonstration bases in Peking City and Ding County of Hebei Province"; introducing electrocardiograms, electroencephalography, and gastroscopy; establishing the first departments of nuclear medicine, endocrinology, allergy, and rheumatology; diagnosing the first case of AIDS in China; and developing the only standard virus line for developing vaccines for severe acute respiratory syndrome.

Chen also sought to demonstrate that PUMC graduates since 1951 were equal in leadership to the highly vaunted first cohort. Taking her own class, 1957, as an example, she noted that there were eleven physician generals (reflecting PUMC's close ties to the People's Liberation Army in the early 1950s), nine presidents of national medical societies, nine editors and vice editors of core medical journals, and multiple winners of the top National Science Prize and Ministry of Health Science Prize. She also noted that today fifty-seven PUMC professors are in positions of leadership in national professional medical associations and are chief editors of seventy-six journals.

Chen then asked the key question: "Are PUMC's traditions outdated? Should PUMC be sent to the museum?" The new challenges include the explosion of knowledge, the need for curriculum reform, the globalization of public health issues, and the need to emphasize medical ethics. Chen herself published one of the first books in China on medical ethics. She blames the new market economy for distorting China's traditional service-oriented medical practice: "Doctors' incomes are closely linked to medical expenses of their patients; as a result, some hospitals raise the charge for their own interest, thus creating a tension between doctors and patients and resulting in erosion of trust." Seeing these challenges as common to all medical practice and education in China, she called for PUMC to revive its traditional service-oriented and courageous leadership in medical education.

Chen's talk is almost a eulogy for the old PUMC. For her, the "PUMC spirit" is the result of a long-vested institutional culture, where "the PUMC Man . . . works conscientiously, meticulously and dedicatedly, who loves science and pursues excellence, who sticks to the truth, dares to speak out and despises drifting with the tide."[10]

President Liu, a graduate of Shanghai Medical University with a PhD from PUMC and an elected member of China's Academy of Engineering, affirmed the continuing relevance of PUMC, but he also presented a vision for a somewhat alternative future.[11] He is not ready to "send PUMC to a museum," but he emphasized the importance of medical science and research, not undergraduate medical education. For him, PUMC is one component of a group of medical institutions—the eighteen research institutes of the Chinese Academy of Medical Sciences (CAMS), their hospitals, and the PUMC Hospital. His outline of PUMC's educational values was similar to that of Chen, but he saw PUMC moving from a parallel position with CAMS to a lesser level, an affiliated technical unit under CAMS. In the future, CAMS would grow "stronger and larger," while PUMC would become "consolidated." But it is hard to imagine a more consolidated PUMC; the tiny size of PUMC's undergraduate medical education program that had so bedeviled its earlier history continues—there were only 614 MDs graduated between 1988 and 2007, approximately 30 a year, while the master's and doctoral programs are significantly larger; in 2010, there were 84 undergraduate MD students, 571 master's candidates, and 500 PhD candidates. Despite the continuing appeal of PUMC traditionalists such as Chen, it is possible that PUMC's identity as a center for elite undergraduate medical education may atrophy in the future. If it becomes primarily a graduate institution for the medical sciences, it will become the model long discussed since the 1930s.

The medical challenges and opportunities that President Liu outlined for Peking Union Medical College and the Chinese Academy of Medical Sciences evidenced a sophisticated, technologically advanced medical complex, approaching comparability with the most advanced medical centers in the world. One is reminded of Franklin McLean's prediction at PUMC's opening in 1917: "Given the opportunity for study and research, this country should develop a medical profession to be proud of, and one that may easily take its place among the leaders of the world."[12]

REENVISIONING ROCKEFELLER PHILANTHROPY WITHIN THE NEW SINO-AMERICAN RELATIONSHIP

The near fulfillment of McLean's prophecy contains a challenge for American philanthropy today. If China's scientific and medical institutions are approaching world standards, what comes next? In his toast to PUMC's future, Richard Rockefeller saluted a China that is taking "its place among the leading nations of the world." China's transformation from the early-twentieth-century "sick man of Asia" to its current status as a global economic and technological power is changing the calculus of not only Rockefeller philanthropy but Sino-American cultural relations in general.

Rockefeller philanthropy still functions as an American bellwether. The institutional continuity, impressive achievements, capital preservation, and decades of charitable giving from the several original early-twentieth-century Rockefeller gifts belie their earliest critics. But even with significant investment appreciation, the scale of these foundations pales beside the newer Bill & Melinda Gates Foundation or the level of U.S. government and international financing in such traditional foundation fields as health, agriculture, science, and education. In China, the wholesale investment of a rapidly modernizing giant economy in its own knowledge and health infrastructure dwarfs any potential contribution from an American foundation or nongovernmental organization. Clearly this new era will require strategically reenvisioning the Sino-American cultural relationship, especially for Rockefeller philanthropy, which was so heavily engaged in science and medicine.

This has been the challenge faced by the new executive leadership of the three foundations represented at PUMC's anniversary—Judith Rodin at the Rockefeller Foundation (RF), Lincoln Chen at the China Medical Board, and Stephen Heintz at the Rockefeller Brothers Fund. Each undertook a review of past programs and initiated, in the prevailing parlance of the times, a fresh strategic plan. The approach to China, which is still evolving in all three, marked a significant change for each foundation.

The change for the venerable RF is the most dramatic, reflected by the surprising absence of a senior RF leader at PUMC's anniversary. China no longer receives much attention or funding from the RF. This change began when the RF decided to discontinue several programs that had included China, especially the population science program that ended in 2000. The ebbing trajectory of China-related programs intensified when Judith Rodin became president in 2004. Under her leadership, the RF terminated most of its previous program areas, nationally and internationally, and embarked on a new global mission to have an "impact on poor and vulnerable people." Internationally, the RF redoubled its long-standing commitment to Africa, shifting all its agricultural programs to Africa and joining with the Gates Foundation to create the Alliance for a Green Revolution in Africa.

In the process of reviewing both the RF's history of its China programs and its renewed attention to Africa, China's growing economic and technical role in Africa attracted special attention: "Can China's engagement with Africa benefit poor people?" The RF explored such policy-oriented questions as whether it could shape the Chinese technical assistance plan for Africa or assist Africa to negotiate more advantageous trade policies. The goal was to strengthen Africa's capacity for managing its transition into a new era dominated by Chinese economic power and to assist China in strengthening its intellectual, economic, and cultural understanding of Africa.[13] Among the grants have been several to South Africa's University of Stellenbosch to support research on China's economic impact in Africa and to support the African Economic Research Consortium Inc.'s efforts to "harmonize the approach to policy related to China's impact on Africa." Between 2006 and 2010, the RF expended approximately $1 million on funding to both Chinese and African institutions exploring "how China and Africa might both maximize the benefits of this growing relationship."[14]

The RF's current strategic approach to Asia is based on the assessment that much of the region has made dramatic strides in providing better health, better education, and a better livelihood for its people. With the RF's overall focus on poverty, it recognizes that Asia still has underprivileged groups: "But there is also another Asia. Hundreds of millions of people have been left out of the positive picture."[15] With a regional office in Bangkok that began in the 1960s (the office closed but was then reestablished in the 1990s), Southeast Asia is the primary focus of newer RF Asia-based programs that often, as in the past, are transnational in scope. These include strengthening global disease surveillance networks, assessing climate change in Asian cities, transforming health systems, and advancing innovations that address social problems. As of 2010, China was involved only marginally in some of the RF's continuing projects in the Mekong River Delta, which has now evolved into the global disease surveillance networks program.[16] Because the Mekong originates in China, some of China's border facilities and Yunnan research institutions were included in the project. Initial RF grants addressed issues ranging from disease surveillance to the livelihood of ethnic minorities to agricultural practices in this impoverished multiethnic, multinational region. China's economic growth relative to the poorer Southeast Asian countries to its south is seen as a challenge. For example, a major grant to Cambodia of $350,000 focused on "the consequences of China's rise as an economic power on poverty reduction in the region."[17] Today the RF prefers to focus on how China's economic growth and resource expansion is affecting both Southeast Asia and Africa, rather than direct philanthropic contributions to China.

The RF celebrates its one-hundredth anniversary in 2013. China was once its most important foreign beneficiary. The arrival of China's twenty-first century of wealth and power has brought to an end the RF's historic mission of strengthening China's science and medicine. China's transition to great power status has also modified the work of the China Medical Board (CMB) and the Rockefeller Brothers Fund. Yet, in many ways, both are more engaged than ever before, each with a more visible physical presence in China and greater engagement with the policy issues of the times.

The new strategic plan for the CMB predictably called for less radical change toward China than that of the RF. But it is worth noting that one option considered by the CMB in 2007 was withdrawal from China in order to focus on the poorer countries of Southeast Asia—the option chosen by the RF. The reasons are relevant to all Americans involved in educational and scientific relations with China: The Chinese government has now become a huge investor in its own scientific, technological, and educational infrastructure. What difference can a relatively small amount of American funding make? This is the question both the CMB and the Rockefeller Brothers Fund have attempted to address.

In choosing Lincoln Chen as its new president in 2006, the CMB deliberately selected an internationally known public health specialist whose foundation experience included serving as executive vice president of the RF and a former program officer for the Ford Foundation in India and Bangladesh. The choice of Chen signaled that the CMB would move away from traditional medical education programs and toward more strategically targeted population health challenges. Chen prepared an analysis of China's major twenty-first-century health challenges, which include the collapse of the Mao-era rural commune health system, the rise of profit-driven hospitals, and new threats of infectious, behavioral, and environmental illness. With this analysis as background, the CMB decided to shift its China focus from a general strengthening of the educational, clinical, and research capacity of key medical universities (now well provided for by the Chinese government) to a tighter focus on education and research for equitable access to basic curative and preventive health services. These are congruent with China's own newly stated policy of addressing health inequity. The CMB's new mission statement reads:

> In 2008, CMB will seek to strengthen modern scientific capacity to address the premier challenge of equitable access to basic services in China for the 21st century. From a global perspective, China is an emerging power with growing health inequities as it grapples with an onslaught of chronic diseases and new threats. . . . CMB will attempt to strategically position itself as an international catalyst of people and ideas on health in China. To achieve its mission, CMB will seek to craft strategic alliances with co-investors—both Chinese as well as international—thereby expanding resources for advancing mutually-shared program goals while retaining institutional autonomy.[18]

The CMB continues to work with its thirteen core and newly joining key Chinese medical university partners, but to strengthen their capacity in new ways: for leading China's ongoing health policy debate, for providing innovative programs related to the extension of rural health care services, and for training a new generation of China's population health science leaders. Three new CMB fellowship programs are designed explicitly for these long-term institutional partners. Distinguished professors are supported for a five-year term, selected by an international committee on the basis of their research, educational achievement, and social leadership. Young faculty development awards are concentrated in the fields of health policy, health systems, and population-based sciences. Next-generation fellowships are offered for emerging young professionals. Nursing education, a CMB priority since the founding of PUMC, is funded through a network of both China-wide and regional nursing schools with a focus on policy research, community nursing, and PhD programs in order to elevate the quality and status of nursing within

China's medical universities. Harking back to the ideals of Chen Zhiqian as well as more recent programs in Tibet and Jiangxi, the CMB is also reaching beyond elite medical universities to develop a new network of provincial medical institutions that promote innovative medical training programs for rural China. The CMB is also partnering with the Gates Foundation to spark tobacco-related research and education in China's premier medical institutions. Although targeting specific diseases was long the emphasis of the RF's International Health Board, this is the CMB's first program that focuses attention on one serious public health issue.[19]

In 2009, for the first time since 1949, the CMB opened an office in China. Entirely staffed by young Chinese professionals, this presence in China means that the CMB has become more operational than in the 1980s and 1990s, directly facilitating new programs and a wider array of institutional grantees. As it looks toward its centennial in 2014, the CMB will, once again, be reassessing its role. From a division of the RF managing Peking Union Medical College to an independent foundation working first throughout Asia and then returning to primarily focus on China, the CMB has been engaged in China's medical modernization for nearly one hundred years. Its endowment is based on the original Rockefeller grants of 1928 and 1947, and (with the decline from the 2008–9 recession) in 2010 is just over $200 million. Expenditures in China have averaged about $8 million a year since 2007, with an additional $1 to $2 million continuing to fund programs in Southeast Asia.

Although not insignificant, this is a modest level of funding in comparison with the hundreds of millions being spent by the Chinese government for medical education. The CMB will continue to face the question of how its limited resources, especially relative to China's growing largesse, can make a difference. However, with a century's accumulation of what one Southeast Asian health policy specialist termed "CMB human capital," and the presence of an office in China, there will be opportunities for new modes of collaboration in the years to come.

One such possibility may emerge from the CMB's increasing emphasis on expanding the global awareness of China and Southeast Asia's health care accomplishments and challenges. The CMB has worked with *The Lancet*, one of the world's leading medical journals, to sponsor two special issues devoted to China.[20] The first issue, in 2008, focused on health system reform in China. The articles resulted from the collaboration of sixty-three scientists, two-thirds from China and the rest from ten other countries, evaluating the progress of China's health reforms. The second special issue, in 2010, continued to track the progress of China's health reforms during the economic recession. As noted by the *The Lancet* editors, the purpose of these studies is not only to introduce China's health system—its achievements and challenges—to a global medical community but also to recognize that "China can produce and harness knowledge, create innovative approaches, and implement large-scale effective solutions for both its own people as well as the world community."[21] A hundred years after the Rockefellers sought to bring scientific medicine to the "sick man" of Asia, the CMB seeks to bring China's medical contributions to the global health community, to engage China collaboratively in a broader international health mission.

Of the three foundations, the Rockefeller Brothers Fund (RBF) is the only one that has dramatically increased its philanthropic investment in China. The reason that a number of Rockefeller family members were in Peking for PUMC's ninetieth anniversary was also to review RBF's new China programs. Stephen Heintz became president in 1998 and instituted a full-scale review of RBF programs. Viewing the RBF as a "mid-sized foundation with large ambitions," Heintz believed that RBF's giving was divided into "too many bits and pieces," and therefore he sought a way to scale back both geographically and programmatically. After two years of study, the RBF decided to adapt Paul Kennedy's concept of "pivotal states" to "pivotal places," selecting New York City, South Africa, Serbia/Montenegro, and South China as its four geographic areas of concentration.[22]

The choice of China in Asia was not a foregone conclusion; the RBF also seriously looked at Indonesia and the Mekong River Delta, areas of earlier significant investment. China was selected for a number of reasons: its geostrategic importance in the twenty-first century; its rising economic profile; and the global implications of its ecological challenges, rural-to-urban migration, and domestic political evolution. The very reasons that turned the RF away from China provided a compelling rationale for the RBF. South China, including Hong Kong, is not only China's leading economic region; it is also known for its pragmatic politics and for the growing role of its civic and environmentally oriented nongovernmental organizations. It is seen as an area that the "RBF has to itself," and where it can pursue cross-programmatic work in "addressing the links between the environment and human health; advancing sustainable approaches to meeting the region's energy needs; and strengthening community leadership in support of sustainable development."[23]

The RBF's decision to concentrate on South China was influenced in part by board member Robert Oxnam, a China scholar and former president of the Asia Society, and also by Rockefeller family board members who retained a long-standing family interest in China. But President Heintz's background is also relevant to the RBF's decisions to focus on South China and to intensify its focus on civil society. His first trip to China was in 1979, when his parents moved to Hong Kong. His second was in 1989, leading a trade delegation for the governor of Connecticut. His group was on a train when the death of Chinese premier Hu Yaobang was announced, and they returned to the United States on June 4. Heintz still remembers his shock at the contrast between the "openness, strong sense of possibility we had experienced in Beijing spring and the reversal of Tiananmen." Because he also lived in Prague in the 1990s, Heintz was influenced by personally observing the contributions of civil society to the political transitions of Eastern Europe.

An underlying goal of the RBF's China philanthropy, initiated during the 1990s, is to empower local Chinese civic organizations—in other words, to nurture "nascent civil society." The RBF uses the programmatic concept "strengthening community leadership to support sustainable development" to encompass activities that build independent citizen networks and organizations, including those that engage youth and promote indigenous philanthropy. When their work began in South China, nongovernmental civil society organizations were weak and politically fragile. In the last several years, the more permissive official Chinese view of these institutions, especially those involved in health and environmental sectors, has apparently contributed to the RBF's relative success in this area.

Zhongshan University's Institute for Civil Society has received the most RBF funding in this sector, and it is generally considered one of China's leading civil society support and advocacy organizations. With a staff of sixteen, it provides resources for nongovernmental organizations, develops models for indigenous philanthropy, and is constantly involved in working with government officials to strengthen trust between the official and unofficial sectors. Visiting Zhongshan in 2006, President Heintz recognized the growing importance of this institute and the centrality of civil society to the RBF's programs. Speaking on the topic "The Role of NGO's in Modern Societies and an Increasingly Interdependent World," Heintz outlined the history of nongovernmental organizations and civil society in the United States and Europe, and he also addressed the China context, calling for "the sustained engagement of Chinese citizens acting through the institutions of civil society," and for the overall Chinese development of a more "vibrant, diverse, and effective nongovernmental sector."[24]

Such advocacy for civil society in China by the president of an American foundation might have been controversial were it not for the fact that the RBF has carefully embedded its focus on civil society within two other sectors: environment and health, and energy and climate change. Its environment and health project endeavors to expand the public knowledge base for understanding the impact of environmental degradation on human health. Because this subject touches on many aspects of society—official regulations, corporate policies, development agendas, and scientific knowledge—the RBF works across all these communities within their South China context. Typical of the RBF's community-based philanthropy, grants are made to raise public awareness and to strengthen the capacity of local institutions to address these issues. In a 2010 review of the work to date, Shenyu Belsky, RBF's China program officer, concludes:

Progress has surpassed expectations. In the past three-plus years, RBF grantees
have helped knit together for the first time an independent network of activists
from government, civil society, academia, and the private sector focused
on addressing China's environmental pollution and its impact on human
communities. Significantly, civil society organizations, with Fund support,
are playing central roles in this work, steadily building their capacity and
establishing credibility and legitimacy in the eyes of both the government and
the public.[25]

The China focus on energy and climate change evolves directly from the
RBF's long-standing U.S. and international leadership in this arena. In China,
the RBF has funded national and international projects as well as local ones.
For example, it has funded a Track II dialogue between senior Chinese and
American leaders organized by the Global Environmental Institute and the
Carnegie Endowment for International Peace. This contributed to the detailed
Memorandum of Understanding to Enhance Cooperation on Climate Change,
Energy, and the Environment, which was signed by both countries in June 2009.
The RBF also funded a number of Chinese nongovernmental organization and
business leaders to attend the December 2009 Copenhagen international climate change conference, one of the first times such Chinese organizations were
represented at an international forum. Much of the RBF's effort in energy and
the environment, however, remains locally based, working with provincial universities, townships, and institutes to assist China's efforts to reduce greenhouse
gas emissions.

These China-based community leadership, health, and energy programs now
garner approximately 12 percent of total RBF funding, a significant increase
from earlier levels. From 2006 through the end of 2009, the RBF expended
$9,188,270 on its China programs. China funding for these four years was
slightly more than all the China funds expended in the previous two decades.[26]
Like the CMB, the RBF has become far more hands-on in its China philanthropy; Belsky, its China program officer, now spends at least half of her time
in China.

With the RBF's emphasis on promoting indigenous Chinese philanthropy,
its staff often evokes the Rockefeller family's long-standing China philanthropy.
In his address at Zhongshan University, President Heintz gave a brief history of
the philanthropic and commercial interests of John D. Rockefeller, emphasizing
that "JDR was determined not just to alleviate symptoms of social problems; he
wanted his philanthropy to address the underlying causes of these conditions."
While mentioning PUMC, Heintz also noted somewhat more relevant aspects of
twentieth-century Rockefeller China philanthropy—"literacy promotion and a
wide variety of rural development initiatives."[27]

CONTINUITY AND CHANGE IN
ROCKEFELLER PHILANTHROPY IN CHINA

The new Rockefeller philanthropy in China reflects both continuity and change. The support for the sciences that was so characteristic of the RF's China programs throughout the twentieth century has ended. This is in large part because of the strides that Chinese science has made during the past three decades, with both Chinese government support and extensive international interaction. Conversely, the medical internationalism of the CMB continues long-standing Rockefeller traditions. Strengthening the capacity of China's institutions remains a common strategy. The RBF's efforts have primarily been focused on grassroots and community organizations, while the CMB and the RF have traditionally worked with China's elite academic and scientific institutions. Even here, there is some change, for the CMB has created a new network of China's regional medical institutions that focus on health care delivery in the poorest western provinces.

The governance of Rockefeller philanthropies related to China has been relatively unchanged since the early twentieth century. More than half a century since JDR 3rd first considered investing some of the CMB's endowment in China, this endowment continues to be managed in the United States and is not invested directly in Chinese equities. Although all three foundations have relied on Chinese advisers, foundation trustees continue to be primarily American citizens, Americans of Asian origin among them. The CMB elected its first Chinese citizen in 2010. In both Lincoln Chen and Shenyu Belsky, the CMB and RBF have chosen Americans of Chinese origin to lead their China programs, perhaps the most significant governance change from the past.

Throughout the era of Rockefeller philanthropic engagement in China, we have seen how American social and intellectual trends have influenced the three foundations' philanthropic agendas. Clearly this continues today. For example, Stephen Heintz emphasized that the RBF's concerns with democratic practice, sustainable development, peace and security, and human advancement are reflected in its U.S. philanthropy as well as its programs in China and elsewhere. Environmental sustainability and the effects of pollution on health are not China-specific issues; they represent popular American priorities as well. Improving the quality and distribution of physicians among underserved populations is the one of the goals of recent U.S. health care reforms as well as the CMB's priorities in China.

Given China's economic competition with the United States today, the continuing American faith that American ideas can make a significant contribution to China's development is striking. Nonetheless, recognizing that their funding has a far more limited impact in China today, all three foundations have narrowed their focus, targeting more policy-oriented areas—China's role in Africa, China's need for equitable health access, and China's sustainable development. The RBF has the most explicit political agenda, but for the CMB, there is also a new willingness to engage in more sensitive and politically related topics. In doing so, these Rockefeller philanthropies have become more representative of the overall American nongovernmental role in China today. Zi Zhongyun notes that targeting China's social policies is common to American philanthropic work in recent decades: "After China opened its doors in the late 1970s, American foundations, led by the Ford Foundation, started work in China immediately under the general premise of promoting reform and working toward China's modernization. . . . Now that the Chinese government played the leading role in all realms, one characteristic of foundation work has been to push for government reform."[28]

Modifications in Rockefeller philanthropic policy do not mean that these traditional Rockefeller philanthropies have suddenly become social or political activist groups in China; both the CMB and RBF, and earlier the RF, work in partnership with Chinese institutions and in the mainstream of American cultural engagement with China. Indeed, working within the constraints of an authoritarian government, both in Republican China and now during the reform era of the People's Republic of China, has been a hallmark of Rockefeller philanthropy. In both periods, there has been sufficient political "space" for these philanthropies to operate with almost complete autonomy and independence, although general approval from relevant ministries of the People's Republic has been required. Indeed, in both eras Rockefeller philanthropists have sought to advise Chinese government agencies on medical education, scientific research, and now environmental policies. As noted early on, the relative success of the Rockefeller agendas has been due, in no small part, to this perceived and real convergence of Chinese and Rockefeller priorities.

Rockefeller philanthropic engagement today demonstrates that China's rise as a global power has not deterred the American desire to participate in, and perchance to shape, China's modern development. There is a new hope that collaborative cultural and scientific relations can help create a common agenda between two competitive powers, an agenda that reflects global concerns. These foundations now hope to collaborate with China as a global partner in addressing health, environmental, and poverty issues. From promoting scientific thinking to taking advantage of China's "plasticity" to encouraging civil society and more equitable health care, today's Rockefeller philanthropists, like their missionary predecessors, have sought to influence the direction of Chinese civilization, to contribute to its modern identity. The terms of reference may have shifted from "changing" China domestically to "engaging" China in the world, but the lure and expectations remain.

Profits from John D. Rockefeller's Standard Oil Company and other investments provided the original philanthropic resources that enabled his son, grandchildren, and great-grandchildren to make their own philanthropic imprimatur. These successor generations have broadened the Rockefeller mission and the

American engagement with China from religion to medicine to science, and more recently to the environment and civil society. Rockefeller wealth also enabled the family to embrace Chinese culture, investing in Asian art for themselves and for the American public.

In 2006 the Asia Society, which most embodies this cultural legacy, marked its fiftieth anniversary by celebrating the Rockefeller family's "passion for Asia." Since it was created by JDR 3rd in the mid-1950s, when no one thought it could be successful, the Asia Society has promoted American understanding of Asia through cultural, educational, and policy programs. With U.S. regional offices in Washington, Houston, Los Angeles, and San Francisco, as well as several international offices in Asia, the society has become an international presence, bringing together corporate, cultural, and political leaders in a wide variety of policy and cultural forums. In the United States, it is especially well known for making the works of contemporary Chinese artists accessible to the American public, providing a base for Track II dialogues on a wide range of policy issues, and improving and expanding the study of the Chinese language in American public schools. With regard to language instruction, the society is now working collaboratively with the Chinese government-funded Confucius Institute to create a hundred model classrooms utilizing nationally recognized best practices.

Like the RF, the CMB, and the RBF, the Asia Society has a relatively recent new president, Vishaka Desai, who was appointed in 2004. She is the first woman and first Asian American to lead the New York–based organization. With board chair Richard Holbrooke and trustee Arthur Ross, Desai led the Asia Society in shifting its long-standing focus from promoting an American understanding of China to promoting a more policy-oriented spotlight on the bilateral relationship. A new Center on U.S.-China Relations was created in 2007 with this mission: "Forging an open and collaborative relationship between the U.S. and China is essential to global peace, balanced economic growth and environmental sustainability." Its first signature program is U.S.-China Cooperation on Energy and Climate, including policy engagement and public education. The policy goal is to promote collaborative mechanisms for Chinese and Americans to work together on one of the most vexing and contentious issues in the bilateral relationship. A new ChinaGreen Web site tracks environmental problems in China. Future programming will include a Web site that tracks and translates what the Chinese are saying about the ever-dynamic United States–China relationship.[29]

Even as this new China Institute engages Americans and Chinese in global issues of mutual concern, the Asia Society continues its cultural programs and has not forgotten its deep Rockefeller roots in Asian culture. At its fiftieth-anniversary celebration, David Rockefeller paid tribute to both his parents and his brother JDR 3rd for the many ways in which the Asia Society and Asian art have expanded Americans' understanding of Asia:

Not only has the Society done much to stimulate thinking about the politics and economics of that vast and increasingly important continent, but the gift of his [John 3rd's] exquisite collection of Asian art has allowed many Americans to develop a better understanding of the achievements of the glorious civilizations that existed there in the past and continue to flourish in the present day. Both John and I first learned of these things because of our parents' trip to Asia in 1921.[30]

Two members of the fourth generation, John (Jay) D. Rockefeller IV and Steven C. Rockefeller, illustrate the wide range of family perspectives on Asia. Titling his contribution to the Asia Society volume "Understanding Asia through Rationalism and Realism," Jay Rockefeller reflects on his years of living in Japan as a college student, but now, as a U.S. senator, he notes that he is more concerned with Asia's political dimension, turning his attention to the importance of China in the world today:

In today's world and even more so in tomorrow's, it is in our best national interest—as well as China's—to find ways in which our strengths complement one another and in which our differences can be resolved constructively. A strong and self-confident China, one that sees itself as a respected and responsible member of the community of nations, will have much to offer the world.[31]

His cousin Steven remembered his childhood visits to the Japanese garden at Kykuit and Abby's garden in Seal Harbor as well as her Buddhist collection:

As a boy I often attended luncheons with my grandparents at Kykuit and the Eyrie, which had a special room devoted to Abby's collection of Buddhist art. . . . The landscape design, the artwork, and the images of the Buddha issued their own silent teaching. . . . Everyone entered these gardens with reverence. No running or loud voices were permitted. We all knew it was a sacred place.

If the old PUMC courtyard is the heart of Rockefeller history in China, as Steven's memories attest, Kykuit and Abby's Chinese garden in Maine represent the Rockefeller family's Asian aesthetic legacy in the United States. In Kykuit itself, the sequential collecting habits of the Rockefeller family can clearly be seen: JDR Jr.'s large and ornate Kangxi porcelain vases, Abby's muted monochromatic Han and Wei Buddhist statuary, and Nelson's dramatic three-glazed Tang camel and guardian figures. The family's much-beloved Tang Dynasty sculpture of a bodhisattva, acquired by John and Abby in 1926 and passed down to Nelson, stands as a dramatic sentinel overlooking the Hudson River.[32] To the north, on Mount Desert Island in Maine, Abby's garden is still cherished and tended by David Rockefeller and his daughter Neva Goodwin (*see figure 6.4*).[33] Open once a week to the public, it is approached through the moss and pine forest by a spirit path, lined with Korean Yi Dynasty figures and entered through a traditional Chinese moon gate. A rose Chinese wall, still topped with JDR Jr.'s controversial gold tiles from the Forbidden City, surrounds an English-style country garden. (When David was in Peking in the 1990s, he ordered some replacement tiles from the imperial kiln that has been reopened to support the recent extensive renovation.) Statuary—Ming Dynasty bronze bodhisattvas and a sixth-century Buddhist votive stele among others—hold their place in shady side gardens. The Asian elements and Western flower garden are not mixed together—each retains its distinct identity within an integrated whole. This was Abby Rockefeller's aesthetic vision, her emulation of a harmonious cultural interplay between East and West. Her garden still summons successive generations. Every summer, family members make pilgrimages to the garden, even though the Rockefeller summer home, the Eyrie, was taken down decades ago.

FIGURE 6.4. Abby Aldrich Rockefeller Garden. Gate with tiles from the Forbidden City. Mount Desert Island, Maine. *Photograph courtesy of The Rockefeller Archive Center.*

Steven himself achieved a different kind of synthesis between East and West in his study of Buddhism. A long-time professor of religion at Middlebury College, he taught courses on Buddhism, eventually writing the book *The Christ and the Bodhisattva*. As he wrote for the Asia Society's commemorative volume:

> Having grown up in an environment where Eastern and Western art and landscape design sit comfortably beside each other, it seems to have been my destiny to wrestle with how certain Eastern and Western traditions are related intellectually and may be connected on the level of faith and spiritual practice. I became convinced, for example, that while Christian faith and love (*agape*) and Buddhist wisdom and compassion (*karuna*) have their unique qualities, they also have much in common, and people with a serious spiritual interest have much to learn from both traditions.[34]

When John D. Rockefeller gave his first $10 to China missions in 1863, he did not anticipate that his great-grandson would seek to reconcile the religious traditions of East and West, nor that his great-great-granddaughter would marry a Chinese citizen and live for a time in Hong Kong. He did live for many years surrounded by his son's collection of Qing Dynasty porcelain, and he did visit his daughter-in-law Abby's garden, but only once. He would probably not be surprised, however, that the global reach of his Standard Oil Company and the Rockefeller Foundation are among the institutions that set in motion the forces of globalization with which we live today.

If it was John D. Rockefeller Sr. whose imaginative scale included a global oil monopoly and a University of Chicago, it was John D. Rockefeller Jr. who became the first global philanthropist. His attention to China predated and outlasted his philanthropic advisers. His China trip in 1921 sparked a host of international philanthropic endeavors. Abby's intimate aesthetic engagement with Chinese art and religion paralleled her husband's institutional role. Together, they inspired family and institutional forces that broadened and deepened the American engagement in China. That their privileged position gave them unprecedented opportunity, and that both family and institutions wielded extraordinary cultural power, is almost beside the point. What if the world's greatest twentieth-century Western power had not sought to include the world's largest Eastern developing country in an international cultural and scientific community? This is where Rockefeller philanthropy made a difference.

In 1928, a front-page story in the *New York Times* by Hallet Abend, a well-known reporter living in Peking, predicted that the Rockefeller China engagement would mark a pivotal turning point in United States–China relations: "It is in work like this, fostered by the Rockefeller Foundation, that most hope for the future is to be found, for in such circles old principles and inhibitions of racial superiority or inferiority fall away in the common devotion to high professional standards and ability and common striving for scientific advancement."[35] Notions of racial and cultural superiority may have declined, but they are certainly difficult to dispel—in both countries. Conversely, "the common devotion to high professional standards . . . and common striving for scientific attainment" became a new value in Sino-American relations. Today, transnational scientific communities are a global reality, binding intellectuals of all kinds together in professional associations and collaborative research with shared normative goals.

As Abend so clearly foresaw, twentieth-century Rockefeller philanthropy—in many countries and through many institutions—was a handmaiden to this development, fortuitously including China early and prominently in its orbit. This was true in both the Nationalist era and in the first decades of American reengagement with the People's Republic of China. American and Chinese scientists, social scientists, natural scientists, and medical scientists have become a part of the intellectual landscape of each other's countries. History reveals that science and technology can divide nations and peoples, but history also demonstrates that these epistemic communities can transcend authoritarian regimes and national boundaries, becoming transnational in scope. These commonalities hold much promise for future collaboration, even as we enter an age of greater competition with China. Raymond Fosdick once wrote: "Science is the patrimony of all mankind." This value is the greatest Rockefeller legacy.

APPENDIXES

Appendix A:
Rockefeller Philanthropic Expenditures for China

Table A1. The Rockefeller Foundation's Expenditures, 1913–51
(in order of size of funding)

CATEGORY	AMOUNT (DOLLARS)	PERCENT
China Medical Board[a]	27,079,015.34	48.84
Peking Union Medical College	17,970,527.31	32.41
Missionary colleges	4,257,385.28	7.68
Fellowships/grants	2,139,753.11	3.86
Chinese hospitals, universities, and institutions	2,024,320.34	3.65
Missionary hospitals and missionary general	1,024,880.90	1.85
Administration/surveys	951,004.13	1.71
Total	55,446,886.41	100

[a]The sum of $22 million is an endowment that has remained invested in the United States by the China Medical Board since 1951.
Source: These data were extrapolated from "The Rockefeller Foundation Payments for Work in China, 1914–1951," 13/133, RG 1, 601, Rockefeller Foundation Archives, Rockefeller Archives Center.

Table A2. The Rockefeller Foundation's Expenditures, 1972–2005
(in order of size of funding)

CATEGORY	AMOUNT (DOLLARS)	PERCENT
Agriculture	14,475,037	37
Population sciences	10,447,646	26
Health	3,798,400	10
Special interests	3,275,500	8
Energy/environment	2,805,178	7
International relations	2,282,785	6
Southeast Asia Regional Program	1,778,938	4
Arts and humanities	720,950	2
Total	39,584,434	100

Note: This includes grants made in the 1970s to organizations involved in exchanges with the People's Republic of China.
Source: Amanda Severeid, "Grantmaking in China," Rockefeller Foundation Paper, 2006, 1.

Table A3. The China Medical Board's Expenditures, 1980–2008
(in order of size of funding)

INSTITUTION	AMOUNT (DOLLARS)	NUMBER OF GRANTS	PERCENT
Peking Union Medical College	22,722,564	62	17
Peking University Health Science Center	18,398,356	60	14
Sun Yat-sen University Medical School	16,779,292	35	13
West China Medical School of Sichuan University	15,459,418	43	12
Xi'an Medical College of Jiaotong University	13,399,971	44	10
Shanghai Medical College of Fudan University	11,375,900	39	9
China Medical University	9,210,050	29	7
Xiangya Medical College of Central South University	7,986,500	29	6
Tibet University Medical College	5,358,577	10	4
Zhejiang University Medical College	4,647,000	14	4
Jiujiang University Medical College	2,568,400	11	2
Ningxia Medical College	1,619,000	5	1
Harbin Medical University	1,015,000	3	1
Total	130,597,598	385	100

Source: These data were provided by Helen Wang, grants administrator, China Medical Board, August 20, 2008.

Table A4. The Rockefeller Brothers Fund's Expenditures, 1984–2010
(in order of size of funding)

CATEGORY	AMOUNT (DOLLARS)	PERCENT
Pivotal Place: Southern China (2005–10)[a]	13,548,270	64.85
Sustainable Development and Sustainable Resource Use Programs (1985–2005)	3,587,800	17.17
Global Security/East Asia (1984–93)	2,535,898	12.14
Special Concerns/China Arts Education (1984–87)	980,000	4.69
Nonprofit Sector/Development of Resources (2001–3)	164,000	.79
Program for Asian Projects (1995–2002)	74,500	.36
Total	20,890,468	100

[a]Environment and Health, Energy and Climate, and Community Leadership
Source: These data were provided by the Rockefeller Brothers Fund, January 2010.

APPENDIX B:
INTERVIEWS WITH PEKING UNION MEDICAL COLLEGE FACULTY AND GRADUATES

Interviewed in May 1984

   Beijing: Huang Jiasi, Wu Jieping, Cheng Xianqiu, Wang Jiwu, Zhong Huilan, Wang Zhengyi, Huang Zhenxiang, Wu Yingkai, Yan Renying, Zhu Futang, Huang Cuiding, Ye Gongshao, Deng Jiadong

   Tianjin: Zhu Xianyi, Shi Xien, Kimm Hyentaik, Yu Songding

   Chengdu: Chen Zhiqian

   Shanghai: Rong Dushan, Zhang Zhubin, Xiong Rucheng, Lin Feiqing

   Guangzhou: Chen Guozhen, He Dianji, Tang Zeguang, Xu Tianlu, Zhang E, Huang Ailian, Huang Shuyuan

Interviewed in September 1987

   Beijing: Gu Fangzhou, Dai Yuhua, Deng Jiadong

Interviewed in May 2001

   Beijing: Ba Denian, Liu Depei

Interviewed in March 2007

   Beijing: Liu Depei, Wang Kean, Peng Mengzhao, Huang Renjian, Wu Mingjiang, Tang Pingzhang, Ma Sui, Tang Xiaofu, Fang Yi, Zhu Yu, Luo Weici, Gao Youhe, Zhang Dechang, Liu Zimin, Dai Yuhua, Zhu Yuanjue, Chen Yuanfang, Lu Zhaoling, Lu Shiyuan

Interviewed in October 2007

   Beijing: Chao Ni, Hu Tiansheng, Wu Weiran, Li Xuewang

Appendix C:
Chinese Names

PINYIN ROMANIZATION (WADE-GILES ROMANIZATION OR IDIOSYNCRATIC USAGE IN PARENTHESES)	CHINESE CHARACTERS
Ba Denian	巴德年
Bing Zhi	秉志
Chen Duxiu	陈独秀
Chen Guozhen	陈国桢
Chen Kehui	陈克恢
Chen Minzhang	陈敏章
Chen Yuanfang	陈元方
Chen Zhangliang	陈章良
Chen Zhiqian (C. C. Chen)	陈志潜
Chen Ziying	陈子英
Deng Jiadong	邓家栋
Deng Xiaoping	邓小平
Ding Wenjiang	丁文江
Duo Duo	多铎
Fang Shishan	方石珊
Fang Xianting	方显廷
Fang Yi	方毅
Fei Xiaotong	费孝通
Feng Yuxiang	冯玉祥
Gu Fangzhou	顾方舟
Guo Bingwen	郭秉文
Guo Moruo	郭沫若
Guo Xianwei	郭宪伟
Han Qide	韩启德
He Cheng	贺诚
He Lian (Franklin Ho)	何廉
Hong Xiuquan	洪秀全
Hu Chuankui	胡传揆
Hu Hongji	胡鸿基

PINYIN ROMANIZATION (WADE-GILES ROMANIZATION OR IDIOSYNCRATIC USAGE IN PARENTHESES)	CHINESE CHARACTERS
Hu Jintao	胡锦涛
Hu Shi (Hu Shih)	胡适
Hu Xiansu	胡先骕
Hu Yaobang	胡耀邦
Hu Zhengxiang	胡正祥
Huang Hua	黄华
Huang Jiasi	黄家驷
Huang Zifang	黄子方
Jiang Jieshi (Chiang Kai-shek)	蒋介石
Jiang Yongzhen	江勇振
Jin Baoshan (P. Z. King)	金宝善
Jin Shuchu (Sohtsu G. King)	金叔初
Jin Xianzhai	金显宅
Kangxi	康熙
Kong Xiangxi (H. H. Kung)	孔祥熙
Li Dequan	李德全
Li Hongzhang	李鸿章
Li Peng	李鹏
Li Ruqi	李汝祺
Li Tingan	李廷安
Li Wenren	李温仁
Li Zicheng	李自成
Li Zongen (C. U. Lee)	李宗恩
Liang Qichao	梁启超
Liang Sicheng	梁思成
Lin Feiqing	林飞卿
Lin Kesheng (Robert K. S. Lim)	林可胜
Lin Qiaozhi	林巧稚
Lin Yifu (Justin Yifu Lin)	林毅夫
Lin Zongyang (C. E. Lim)	林宗扬
Liu Depei	刘德培
Liu Qian	刘谦
Liu Ruiheng (J. Heng Liu)	刘瑞恒

PINYIN ROMANIZATION (WADE-GILES ROMANIZATION OR IDIOSYNCRATIC USAGE IN PARENTHESES)	CHINESE CHARACTERS
Lu Xun	鲁迅
Ma Wenzhao	马文昭
Mao Zedong	毛泽东
Nurhachi (or Nu'erhachi)	努尔哈赤
Qian Duansheng	钱端升
Quan Shaoqing	全绍清
Rong Dushan	荣独山
Shi Meiyu (Mary Stone)	石美玉
Shi Xien	施锡恩
Shi Zhaoji (Alfred Sao-ke Sze)	施肇基
Song Meiling (Soong Mei-ling)	宋美龄
Song Ziwen (T. V. Soong)	宋子文
Sun Zhongshan (Sun Yat-sen)	孙中山
Tan Jiazhen (C. C. Tan)	谈家桢
Tang Zeguang	汤泽光
Wang Jiwu	王季午
Wang Ren	王韧
Wang Zhengting	王正廷
Wang Zuoyue	王作跃
Weng Wenhao	翁文灏
Wu Chaoshu (C. C. Wu)	伍朝枢
Wu Jieping	吴阶平
Wu Ruiping	吴瑞萍
Wu Weiran	吴蔚然
Wu Wenzao	吴文藻
Wu Xian	吴宪
Wu Yingkai	吴英恺
Wu Chaoshu (C. C. Wu)	伍朝枢
Xi Zhongxun	习仲勋
Xiong Rucheng	熊汝成
Xu Shilian (Leonard S. Hsu)	许仕廉
Xu Shichang	徐世昌
Yan Fuqing (F.C. Yen)	颜福庆

PINYIN ROMANIZATION (WADE-GILES ROMANIZATION OR IDIOSYNCRATIC USAGE IN PARENTHESES)	CHINESE CHARACTERS
Yan Huiqing (W. W. Yen)	颜惠庆
Yan Jingqing	严镜清
Yan Jingyao	严景耀
Yan Xishan	阎锡山
Yan Yangchu (James Y. C. Yen)	晏阳初
Yang Chongrui (Marion Yang)	杨崇瑞
Yao Xunyuan	姚寻源
Ye Jiachi	叶嘉炽
Yuan Shikai	袁世凯
Zeng Guofan	曾国藩
Zhang Boling	张伯苓
Zhang Jingyue	张景钺
Zhang Xijun	张锡钧
Zhang Xiruo	张奚若
Zhang Xiaoqian	张孝骞
Zhang Xueliang (ChangHsueh-liang)	张学良
Zhang Yangfen	章央芬
Zhang Zhiqiang	张之强
Zhao Chenggu (Chou T. Q.)	赵承嘏
Zhao Chengxin	赵承信
Zhao Ziyang	赵紫阳
Zhong Huilan	钟惠澜
Zhou Enlai (Chou En-lai)	周恩来
Zhou Peiyuan	周培源
Zhou Shoukai	周寿恺
Zhou Wenzhong	周文中
Zhou Yichun	周诒春
Zhu Futang	诸福堂
Zhu Hengbi	朱恒璧
Zhu Qiqian	朱启钤
Zhu Xianyi	朱宪彝
Zhu Zhanggeng (C. K. Chu)	朱章赓
Zi Zhongyun	资中筠

NOTES

Introduction

1 The combined expenditures of the Rockefeller Foundation, the China Medical Board, and the Rockefeller Brothers Fund in China between 1913 and 2008 were $246,519,386. Using the consumer price index conversion system for multiple benchmark years, this equates to approximately $771 million in 2000 dollars. See appendix A.

2 Akira Iriye, *Cultural Internationalism and World Order* (Baltimore: Johns Hopkins University Press, 1997), 3.

3 Akira Iriye, *Global Community: The Rise of International Organizations in the Making of the Contemporary World* (Berkeley: University of California Press, 2002), 191.

4 Alexandra Munroe, *The Third Mind: American Artists Contemplate Asia, 1860–1989* (New York: Guggenheim Museum, 2009); Warren Cohen, *East Asian Art and American Culture: A Study in International Relations* (New York: Columbia University Press, 1992).

5 Frank Ninkovich, "The Rockefeller Foundation, China and Cultural Change," *Journal of American History* 70 (March 1984): 799–820.

6 E. Richard Brown, "Exporting Medical Education: Professionalism, Modernization and Imperialism," *Social Science and Medicine* 13A (1979): 585–95.

7 Quoted by Joseph Manzione, "'Amusing and Amazing and Practical and Military': The Legacy of Scientific Internationalism in American Foreign Policy, 1945–1963," *Diplomatic History* 24 (Winter 2000): 23.

Chapter 1

1 Wendy O'Neill Wang, *Rockefeller Philanthropy in China: The Oil Prince's Palace and Other Tales from the Middle Kingdom* (New York: Rockefeller Brothers Fund, 2002), 1; James Thomas Gillam, "The Standard Oil in China (1863–1930)," PhD dissertation, Ohio State University, 1987, 1.

2 *Cleveland Morning Leader*, September 3, 1860, Ohio Historical Society, Columbus (hereafter OHS).

3 Ron Chernow, *Titan: The Life of John D. Rockefeller, Sr.* (New York: Random House, 1998), 50.

4 Grace Goulder, *John D. Rockefeller: The Cleveland Years* (Cleveland: Western Reserve Historical Society, 1972), 41.

5 Kenneth Scott Latourette, *A History of Christian Missions in China* (New York: Macmillan, 1929), 251.

6 *Cleveland Newspaper Digest*, September 27, 1864; *Cleveland Morning Leader*, May 23, 1863, OHS.

7 *Cleveland Newspaper Digest*, June 17, 1859, January 14, 1857, March 26, 1859, and October 26, 1859; *Cleveland Morning Leader*, September 25, 1865, and February 21, 1865, OHS.

8 *Cleveland Morning Leader*, September 7, 1860, OHS.

9 Gillam, "Standard Oil in China," 1. There is some dispute about this early date. Gillam references Irvine H. Anderson, *The Standard Vacuum Oil Company and U.S. East Asian Policy, 1933–1941* (Princeton, N.J.: Princeton University Press, 1975), 80; and Ralph W. Hidy and Muriel E. Hidy, *Pioneering in Big Business, 1882–1911* (New York: Harper Brothers, 1955). Neither is conclusive. Michael Hunt, conversely, gives the late 1870s as the beginning of kerosene sales to China. See Michael Hunt, "Americans in the China Market: Economic Opportunities and Economic Nationalism, 1890s–1931," *Business History Review* 51, no. 3 (Autumn 1976): 281. Certainly, any kerosene shipped in 1863 was not part of an organized trade strategy.

10 *Cleveland Newspaper Digest*, September 25, 1865.

11 Gillam, "Standard Oil in China," 66–72.

12 John D. Rockefeller, *Random Reminiscences of Men and Events* (New York: Doubleday, Page, 1909), 63.

13 Gillam, "Standard Oil in China," 372.

14 Chernow, *Titan*, 238–41.

15 Quoted in ibid., 314.

16 Frederick Taylor Gates, *Chapters in My Life* (New York: Free Press, 1977), 162.

17 Rockefeller, *Random Reminiscences*, 177.

18 Chernow, *Titan*, 344, 553–57.

19 John Ensor Harr and Peter J. Johnson, *The Rockefeller Century* (New York: Charles Scribner's Sons, 1988), 61.

20 James B. Simmons to John D. Rockefeller, December 19, 1882, in 35/0617, Rockefeller Business Letters, Record Group (hereafter RG) 1, Rockefeller Family Archives, Rockefeller Archive Center (hereafter RAC).

21 JDR Jr. to Mott, Nov. 12, 1898, 255/75; September 6, 1900, 257/287; September 19, 1900, 257; October 1, 1900, 325/347; April 15, 1901, 065/292; April 25, 1901, 165/362; January 29, 1902, 069-307; February 15, 1902, 261/470, all in Rockefeller Letter Press, RG 1, Rockefeller Family Archives, RAC. See also C. Howard Hopkins, *John R. Mott, 1865–1955: A Biography* (Grand Rapids: William B. Eerdmans, 1979), 116, 137–38, 220.

22 Quoted by Qiusha Ma, "The Rockefeller Foundation and Modern Medical Education in China, 1915–1951," PhD dissertation, Case Western Reserve University, 1995, 68.

23 H. P. Parker to Gates, October 23, 1907; M. O. Eubank to Gates, 1907; Henry C. Mabie to Gates, January 29, 1908, in 24/240, "Proposed Foreign Mission Fund," RG 2, Office of the Messrs. Rockefeller (hereafter OMR), Rockefeller Family Archives, RAC.

24 Burton and Judson to Gates, December 31, 1906, in 24/240, "Proposed Foreign Mission Fund," RG 2, OMR, Rockefeller Family Archives, RAC.

25 Gates to Arthur Smith, June 10, 1907, Rockefeller Letter Press, 276/136-141, RG 1, Rockefeller Family Archives, RAC.

26 JDR Jr. to JDR Sr., March 10, 1908; JDR Jr. to JDR Sr., August 31, 1907; JDR Sr. to JDR Jr., September 11, 1907, all in Burton Commission, 112/8, RG 2, OMR, Rockefeller Family Archives, RAC.

27 Frederick Gates, "The China Medical Board," c. 1924, 3, Gates Papers, 1/10, RAC.

28 Ernest D. Burton, "Journal and Record of Interviews and Observations, University of Chicago, Oriental Education Investigation, 1909," typed mimeograph copy, Missionary Research Library, New York, 503, 514.

29 Quoted by Mary Ferguson, *China Medical Board and Peking Union Medical College: A Chronicle of Fruitful Collaboration* (New York: China Medical Board of New York, 1970), 14.

30 Harr and Johnson, *Rockefeller Century*, 87.

31 Quoted by Raymond Fosdick, *The Story of the Rockefeller Foundation* (New York: Harper Brothers, 1952), 23.

32 John Farley, *To Cast Out Disease: A History of the International Health Division of the Rockefeller Foundation, 1913–1951* (New York: Oxford University Press, 2004), 269–71, 294.

33 This includes funding for the China Medical Board and Peking Union Medical College; see appendix A.

34 Transcript, "China Conference of the Rockefeller Foundation," January 19–20, 1914, in 11/91, Rockefeller Boards, RG 2, OMR, Rockefeller Family Archives, RAC.

35 For a recent study of the impact of these surveys in China, see Daqing Zhang, "Mapping Modern Medicine in China: Impact of Rockefeller Foundation," *Studies in the History of Natural Sciences* 28 (2009): 137–55.

36 Chernow, *Titan*, 476.

37 *New York Times*, June 16, 1915, and August 29, 1920.

38 See Mary Brown Bullock, *An American Transplant: The Rockefeller Foundation and Peking Union Medical College* (Berkeley: University of California Press, 1980), 24–47.

39 See, e.g., JDR Jr. to Wallace Buttrick, April 10, 1916, in 1/23, RG 4, Rockefeller Foundation Archives, RAC.

40 Roger Greene Diary, 1919, Peking Union Medical College Archives, Peking (hereafter PUMC Archives), 67.

41 *New York Times*, June 20, 1921.

42 Dennis Bracale, "The Abby Aldrich Rockefeller Garden: Chinese Heart of Acadia National Park," MLA thesis, University of Virginia, 1998; this includes a list of all their books related to Asia, 122–30. Of particular note is the extensive collection on Buddhism, Chinese porcelain, and Chinese art published before 1921.

43 Raymond Fosdick, *John D. Rockefeller, Jr., A Portrait* (New York: Harper Brothers, 1956), 334–35.

44 Cynthia Bronson Altman, "A Family's Love of Asian Art," in *A Passion for Asia: The Rockefeller Legacy*, edited by Asia Society (New York: Hudson Hills Press, 2006), 69–72; Yiyou Wang, "Art Dealers, the Rockefellers and the Network of Chinese Art in America," Rockefeller Archive Research Report (New York: Rockefeller Archive, 2008).

45 David Rockefeller, *Memoirs* (Random House: New York, 2002), 25.

46 Altman, "Family's Love of Asian Art," 59.

47 Abby Rockefeller to Lucy Aldrich, August 13 and September 13, 1919, in *Abby Aldrich Rockefeller's Letters to Her Sister Lucy* (New York, 1957), 25.

48 Bernice Kerr, *Abby Aldrich Rockefeller: The Woman in the Family* (New York: Random House, 1993), 191–94.

49 Ibid., 571–90.

50 Buttrick to Greene, July 1, 1915, 24/170, CMB Inc., RAC.

51 *New York Times*, July 26, 1908.

52 *New York Times*, August 14, 1915.

53 *New York Times*, August 15, 1915; Noel H. Pugach, "Standard Oil and Petroleum Development in Early Republican China," *Business History Review* 45 (Winter 1971): 452–73; Gillam, "Standard Oil in China," 243.

54 "Second Report of Investigations Re J. D. Rockefeller Jr. Canal Trip," 14/133, Rockefeller Boards, RG2, OMR, Rockefeller Family Archives, RAC.

55 JDR Jr., September 26, 1921, "Oriental Trip, 1921," 39/339, RG 2, OMR, Rockefeller Family Archives, RAC.

56 JDR Jr. to JDR Sr., September 12, 1921, 15/34, RG 2, OMR, Rockefeller Family Archives, RAC.

57 JDR Jr. to S. B. Walker, September 26, 1921, in ibid.

58 JDR Jr. to JDR 3rd, September 10, 1921, 31/287, RG 3, Rockefeller Family Archives, RAC.

59 JDR Jr. to Nelson, September 10, 1921, 15/34, RG 2, OMR, Rockefeller Family Archives, RAC.

60 JDR Jr. to Nelson, September 27, 30/275, RG 5, Rockefeller Family Archives, RAC.

61 Abby to David, September 27, 1921, 39/355, Abby Aldrich Rockefeller Series, RG2, Rockefeller Family Archives, RAC.

62 Abby to John, September 16, 1921; August 27, 1921, in ibid.

63 JDR Jr. to JDR 3rd, November 5, 1921, box 31/287, RG 3, Rockefeller Family Archives, RAC.

64 JDR Jr., "China Diary," 39/339, RG 2, OMR, series II, Personal Papers, Rockefeller Family Archives, RAC.

65 JDR Jr. to JDR Sr., September 19, 1921, 15/134, RG 2, OMR, Rockefeller Family Archives, RAC.

66 Yang Deng, "The Mansion of the Prince of Yu," unpublished document, c. 2000, in the author's possession.

67 Harry Hussey, *My Pleasures and Palaces: An Informal Memoir of Forty Years of Modern China* (Garden City, N.Y.: Doubleday, 1968), 221.

68 Ibid.

69 Ibid., 220.

70 Ibid., 229.

71 Quoted by Ge Ou, *Xiehe Yishi* (Memories of Peking Union Medical College) (Beijing: Shenghuo, Dushu, Xin-zhi Sanlian Shudian, 2007), 30.

72 Quoted in his letter to his father, September 19, 1921.

73 Fosdick, *Story of the Rockefeller Foundation*, 86–87.

74 *Addresses and Papers, Dedication Ceremonies and Medical Conference, Peking Union Medical College* (Concord, N.H.: Rumford Press, 1922), 65.

75 Quoted by Jessica C. E. Gienow-Hect, "*Shame on US*? Academics, Cultural Transfer and the Cold War—A Critical Review," *Diplomatic History* 24, no. 3 (Summer 2000): 476.

76 *Addresses and Papers*, 59.

77 "Mrs. Rockefeller on China," *New York Times*, February 2, 1922.

78 John D. Rockefeller, Jr., "Impressions of China, Jan. 19, 1922," in 2/103, Rockefeller Family Archives, RG 2, OMR, Series Z, RAC.

79 Wang, *Rockefeller Philanthropy in China*, 2.

80 Rockefeller, *Memoirs*, 244.

81 Kerr, *Abby Aldrich Rockefeller*, 197–99.

82 Robert Hatsfield Ellsworth, "Introduction," in *Asian Sculpture in the Abby Aldrich Rockefeller Garden: The David and Peggy Rockefeller Collection* (New York, 1994), 12.

83 Interview with David Rockefeller, February 20, 2008.

84 Quoted by Kerr, *Abby Aldrich Rockefeller*, 238.

85 Abby Rockefeller to Beatrix Farrand, September 24, 1928, 73/752, RG 2, series 1, Rockefeller Family Archives, RAC.

86 David Rockefeller, "Preface," in *Asian Sculpture in the Abby Aldrich Rockefeller Garden*, 9; for the details of Abby's China garden, see Bracale, "Abby Aldrich Rockefeller Garden."

87 JDR Jr. to Roger Greene, September 13, 1928; Greene to JDR Jr., September 24, 1928; JDR Jr. to Farrand, October 15, 1928; Farrand to JDR Jr., November 1, 1928; Farrand to JDR Jr., September 4, 1930, all in 73/752, RG 2, OMR, Rockefeller Family Archives, RAC. Several years later, in 1933, the *New York Times* reported a rumor that JDR Jr. and Henry Ford were paying $20 million for national Chinese art treasures to keep them safe from the Japanese. See *New York Times*, February 8, 1933.

88 *New York Times*, February 8, 1933.

89 Quoted by Liping Bu, *Making the World Like Us: Education, Cultural Expansion and the American Century* (Westport, Conn.: Praeger, 2003), 90.

90 Interview with Steven Rockefeller, November 7, 2008; see his "Great Dialogue, Great Community," Keynote Address, International House 75th Anniversary Gala, May 9, 2006, unpublished speech.

91 Charles A. Keller, "Rockefeller Support for the Industrial Work of the Chinese YMCA," *Rockefeller Archive Center Research Reports*, Spring 1994, 16–18.

92 Charles W. Hayford, *To the People: James Yen and Village China* (New York: Columbia University Press, 1990), 79; Shirley Garrett, *Social Reformers in Urban China: The Chinese Y.M.C.A., 1895–1926* (Cambridge, Mass.: Harvard University Press, 1970), 205 n. 101.

93 Nelson Rockefeller to Harland Cleveland, November 29, 1948, in 6/57, series L, RG 4, Nelson Rockefeller Papers, RAC.

94 Fosdick, *John D. Rockefeller, Jr.*, 219.

95 JDR 3rd, "World Tour 1929," box 6, JDR 3rd Papers, 1, OMR, 6, Trips 1920–60.

96 For extensive correspondence involving JDR Jr., JDR 3rd, Dean Meeks (Yale), James H. Breasted (Chicago), Arthur Woods, and Roger Greene concerning this project, see Cultural Interests, 139/1218, RG 2, OMR, Rockefeller Family Archives, RAC.

97 JDR Jr. to George Vincent, January 5, 1931, in ibid.

98 JDR Jr. to Roger Greene, September 25, 1931, and "Memo for Mr. Howland in connection with study he is to make for us in China, Nov. 1931," both in ibid.

99 Greene to JDR Jr., July 29, 1931, in ibid.

100 JDR Sr. to JDR Jr., November 18, 1921, 15/134, RG 2, OMR, Rockefeller Family Archives, RAC.

101 China Press, "John D. Rockefeller, Jr. Is Honored by Chinese Businessmen at Tiffin," September 29, 1921, 15/139, RG 2, OMR, R, Rockefeller Family Archives, RAC.

102 Ibid.

103 Akira Iriye, *Cultural Internationalism and World Order* (Baltimore: Johns Hopkins University Press, 1997), 3.

104 Frederick Gates to Chamberlain and Burton, February 15, 1910, 112/8, Burton Commission, RG 2, OMR, Rockefeller Family Archives, RAC.

105 Mari Yoshihara, *Embracing the East: White Women and American Orientalism* (New York: Oxford University Press, 2003).

106 Sherman Lee, "The Mr. and Mrs. John D. Rockefeller, 3rd Collection: A Personal Recollection," in *Treasures of Asian Art: The Asia Society's Mr. and Mrs. John D. Rockefeller, 3rd Collection*, edited by Denise Patry Leidy (New York: Abbeville Press, 1994), 7.

107 I am grateful to Steven Rockefeller for drawing this credo to my attention.

108 Franklin C. McLean, "Report to the China Medical Board and the Board of Trustees of the Union Medical College," 8, 14/126, RG 2, OMR, Rockefeller Boards, China Medical Board, PUMC, Rockefeller Family Archives, RAC.

CHAPTER 2

1 I have borrowed this chapter title from the excellent study edited by Marcos Cueto, *Missionaries of Science: The Rockefeller Foundation and Latin America* (Bloomington: Indiana University Press, 1994).

2 In addition to my own research, this judgment is based on the monographic studies of China's science and social sciences during the Republican era, which are cited in this chapter. Of particular importance are the works on biology by Laurence Schneider, on chemistry by James Reardon-Anderson, on the social sciences by Yung-chen Chiang, on public health by Ka-che Yip, on economics by Paul Trescott, and on medical education by Ma Qiusha.

3 Ruth Hayhoe, *China's Universities, 1895–1995: A Century of Cultural Conflict* (Hong Kong: University of Hong Kong Press, 1999), 42, 52; E-Tu Zen Sun, "The Growth of the Academic Community, 1912–1949," in *The Cambridge History of China*, vol. 13, part 2, edited by John King Fairbank and Albert Feuerwerker (Cambridge: Cambridge University Press, 1986), 361–420.

4 Hongshan Li emphasizes the role of the U.S. and Chinese governments in managing the Boxer program and Qinghua College; see Hongshan Li, *U.S.-China Educational Exchange: State, Society, and Intercultural Relations, 1905–1950* (New Brunswick, N.J.: Rutgers University Press, 2008).

5 Ruth Rogaski, *Hygienic Modernity in Treaty-Port China* (Berkeley: University of California Press, 2004); Carol Benedict, *Bubonic Plague in Nineteenth-Century China* (Stanford, Calif.: Stanford University Press, 1996).

6 G. H. Choa, *"Heal the Sick" Was Their Motto: The Protestant Medical Missionaries in China* (Hong Kong: Chinese University Press, 1990), 220.

7 Soma Hewa and Philo Hove, eds., *Philanthropy and Cultural Context: Western Philanthropy in South, East and Southeast Asia in the 20th Century* (Lanham, Md.: University Press of America, 1997), 6.

8 Bridie Jane Andrews, "The Making of Modern Chinese Medicine, 1895–1937," PhD dissertation, University of Cambridge, 1996, illustrates how the assimilation of Western medicine comes via late-nineteenth-century and early-twentieth-century Chinese intellectuals, not the missionary movement.

9 William Welch, "Medicine in the Orient," in *Addresses and Papers by William Henry Welch*, vol. 3 (Baltimore: Johns Hopkins University Press), 81. See also William Welch, *Diary #2*, 24 in William Welch Papers, Johns Hopkins University.

10 Frederick Gates, "The China Medical Board," unpublished paper, c. 1924, Gates Papers, 1/10, Rockefeller Archives Center (hereafter RAC). For the complex relationship between Gates and the China Medical Board, see John S. Baick, "Cracks in the Foundation: Frederick T. Gates, the Rockefeller Foundation, and the China Medical Board," *Journal of the Gilded Age and Progressive Era* 3, no. 1 (January 2004): 59–89.

11 Frederick Gates to Mr. Rockefeller and Mr. Debevoise, "World Philanthropy," January 7, 1927, Gates Papers, 4/79, RAC.

12 John D. Rockefeller Jr. to the Missionary Societies, March 15, 1915, 24/233, Record Group (hereafter RG) 1.1, 601, Rockefeller Foundation Archives, RAC.

13 Zhongyun Zi, "The Rockefeller Foundation and China," unpublished paper, 1995; Qiusha Ma, "The Rockefeller Foundation and Modern Medical Education in China, 1915–1951," PhD dissertation, Case Western Reserve University, 1995.

14 Henry Houghton served as PUMC director from 1921 to 1928 and 1937 to 1946, and Roger Greene served as the China Medical Board's director from 1915 to 1934 and acting PUMC director from 1929 to 1934.

15 February 5 (no year), Houghton to Greene, "Ten-Year Program," #170, Peking Union Medical College Archives, Peking (hereafter PUMC Archives).

16 Ibid.

17 John Bowers, *Western Medicine in a Chinese Palace: Peking Union Medical College, 1917–1951* (New York: Macy Foundation, 1972), 166–68.

18 Quoted by Ge Ou, *Xiehe Yishi* (Memories of Peking Union Medical College) (Beijing: Shenghuo, Dushu Xinxhi Sanlian Shudian, 2007), 234. Kidney disease is often bilateral, and the fact that Liang lived for four more years suggests that the wrong kidney was not removed. The PUMC's surgeon's report provided a detailed explanation of the surgery, rejecting the claim of surgical error. See "Files of Liang Qichao Case," #600, PUMC Archives. Much of the controversy arose after Liang's death in 1929, when his surgeon, PUMC's Liu Juiheng, had become head of the Guomindang's National Health Administration and was advocating against traditional medicine.

19 Quoted by Ma, "Rockefeller Foundation," 197.

20 "Fellowships for Study in America or Europe, 1915–1928," 42/346a, RG 1, 601 E, CMB, Rockefeller Foundation Archives, RAC; Rockefeller Foundation Fellowship History File, "Fellows from the Peoples Republic of China, 1915–1949," computer printout dated March 28, 1975.

21 Darwin H. Stapleton, "The Rockefeller Foundation and the Transfer and Diffusion of Scientific Instrumentation to China, 1915–1949," paper presented at the Twenty-Second International Congress in History of Science, Peking, July 2005.

22 "The Rockefeller Foundation Payments for Work in China, 1914–1951," 13/133, RG 1, 601, Rockefeller Foundation Archives, RAC. For an evaluation of the work with missionary hospitals, see Roger Greene, "China Medical Board, 1915–1919," #485, PUMC Archives.

23 Ka-che Yip, *Health and National Reconstruction in Nationalist China: The Development of Modern Health Services, 1928–1937* (Ann Arbor, Mich.: Association of Asian Studies, 1995), 132–61.

24 See correspondence in National Medical Association of China, 63/1541, RG 4.1.2, Rockefeller Foundation Archives, RAC.

25 Gates, "World Philanthropy."

26 Michael Hunt, *The Making of a Special Relationship; The United States and China to 1914* (New York: Columbia University Press, 1983), 293

27 Ge Ou, *Xiehe Yishi*, 98, 101.

28 Isadore Snapper, *Chinese Lessons to Western Medicine: A Contribution to Geographical Medicine from the Clinics of Peiping Union Medical College* (New York: Interscience Publishers, 1941); Bowers, *Western Medicine in a Chinese Palace*, 77–150.

29 Marjorie King, *China's American Daughter: Ida Pruitt (1888–1985)* (Hong Kong: Chinese University Press, 2006), 49–64.

30 Kaiyi Chen, "Quality versus Quantity: The Rockefeller Foundation and Nurses' Training in China," *Journal of American–East Asian Relations* 5 (Spring 1996): 77–104; John Watt, "Breaking into Public Service: The Development of Nursing in Modern China, 1870–1949," *Nursing History Review* 12 (2004): 67–96.

31 Socrates Litsios, "The Rockefeller Foundation's Struggle to Correlate Its Existing Medical Program with Public Health Work in China," November 2007, unpublished paper. Litsios details the conflicts between Grant and the International Health Board over the China program.

32 Andrews, "Making of Modern Chinese Medicine"; Rogaski, *Hygienic Modernity*.

33 For Grant, see Mary Brown Bullock, *An American Transplant: The Rockefeller Foundation and Peking Union Medical College* (Berkeley: University of California Press, 1980), chap. 6.

34 Liping Bu, "From Private Lives to Public Knowledge: Statistical Analysis of Health and Death in Beijing, 1925–1934," paper given at a meeting of the Asian Studies Association, April 2008.

35 E.g., see Hu Hongji (Shanghai), Jin Baoshan (Nanjing), Quan Shaoqing (Tianjin), and Huang Zifang (League of Nations' Health Organization).

36 C. C. Chen, *Medicine in Rural China: A Personal Account* (Berkeley: University of California Press, 1989).

37 James Reardon-Anderson, *The Study of Change: Chemistry in China, 1840–1949* (New York: Cambridge University Press, 1991), 120.

38 Paul Monroe, "Report on the Pre-Medical School Situation Made to the Trustees of the Peking Union Medical College," 14/129, RG 3, 2 O, Rockefeller Foundation Archives, RAC.

39 Jessie Lutz, *China and the Christian Colleges, 1850–1959* (Ithaca, N.Y.: Cornell University Press, 1971), 171–78; Laurence Schneider, *Biology and Revolution in Twentieth Century China* (Lanham, Md.: Rowman & Littlefield, 2003), 65.

40 Marilyn Bailey Ogilvie and Clifford J. Choquette, "Western Biology and Medicine in Modern China: The Career and Legacy of Alice M. Boring (1883–1955)," *Journal of the History of Medicine and Allied Sciences* 48 (April 1993): 199, 203.

41 Philip West, *Yenching University and Sino-Western Relations, 1916–1952* (Cambridge, Mass.: Harvard University Press, 1976), 112; Schneider, *Biology and Revolution*, 67–78; interview with Gary Toenniessen, Rockefeller Foundation, April 11, 2008.

42 Schneider, *Biology and Revolution*, 38.

43 Ibid., 33–63.

44 Reardon-Anderson, *Study of Change*, 140.

45 Ibid., 140–51. Wu's son, Ray Wu (1928–2008), a U.S. leader in molecular biology and genetic engineering, led in the reestablishment of United States–China scientific relations after 1979, including serving as an important adviser to PUMC.

46 William Haas, *China Voyager: Gist Gee's Life in Science* (Armonk, N.Y.: M. E. Sharpe, 1996), 160–62, 173–93; Jia Sheng, "The Origins of the Science Society of China, 1914–1937," PhD dissertation, Cornell University, 1995; Zuoyue Wang, "Saving China through Science: The Science Society of China, Scientific Nationalism and Civil Society in Republican China," *Osiris* 17 (2002): 291–322.

47 For examples of the frequent and detailed Mason-Gunn correspondence, see Gunn to Mason, March 23, 1935; Mason to Gunn, June 27, 1935; Gunn to Mason, September 13, 1935; Mason to Gunn, October 13, 1935, in 14/144, RG 1, 601, Rockefeller Foundation Archives, RAC.

48 Laurence S. Schneider, "The Rockefeller Foundation, the China Foundation, and the Development of Modern Science in China," *Social Science of Medicine* 16 (1982): 1217.

49 Laurence D. Stifel, Ralph K. Davidson, and James S. Coleman, "Agencies of Diffusion: A Case Study of the Rockefeller Foundation," in *Social Sciences and Public Policy in the Developing World* , edited by Laurence D. Stifel, Ralph K. Davidson, and James S. Coleman (Lexington, Mass.: D. C. Heath, 1982), 58–59.

50 Chung-hsing Sun, "The Development of the Social Sciences in China before 1949," PhD dissertation, Columbia University, 1987, 222. For more on the IPR, see John N. Thomas, *The Institute of Pacific Relations: Asian Scholars and American Politics* (Seattle: University of Washington Press, 1974).

51 For reviews of the history of the social sciences in China, see Yung-chen Chiang, *Social Engineering and the Social Sciences in China, 1919–1949* (New York: Cambridge University Press, 2001); Sun, "Development of the Social Sciences."

52 Stifel, Davidson, and Coleman, "Agencies of Diffusion," 61.

53 West, *Yenching University*, 111.

54 Chiang, *Social Engineering*, 78–103. For the influence of Yanjing on Fei Xiaotong, see David Arkush, *Fei Xiaotong and Sociology in Revolutionary China* (Cambridge, Mass.: Harvard University Press, 1981), 28–36.

55 Chiang, *Social Engineering*, 88.

56 Paul B. Trescott, "American Philanthropy and the Development of Academic Economics in China before 1949," in *Philanthropy and Cultural Context*, ed. Hewa and Hove, 157–81. For a comparison with Rockefeller support for economics in Europe, see Earlene Craver, "Patronage and the Directions of Research in Economics: The Rockefeller Foundation in Europe, 1924–38," *Minerva* 24 (1986): 205–22.

57 Stifel, Davidson, and Coleman, "Agencies of Diffusion," 61.

58 Chiang, *Social Engineering*, 113.

59 Trescott, "American Philanthropy," 158.

60 Randall Stross, *The Stubborn Earth: American Agriculturalists on Chinese Soil, 1898–1937* (Berkeley: University of California Press, 1986), 156, 147–60.

61 John Lossing Buck, "Development of Agricultural Economics at the University of Nanking, Nanking, China, 1920–1946," *Cornell International Agricultural Development Bulletin* 25, September 1973; Trescott, "American Philanthropy," 168–75.

62 Trescott, "American Philanthropy," 174.

63 Raymond Fosdick, *The Story of the Rockefeller Foundation* (New York: Harper Brothers, 1952), 240.

64 Zi Zhongyun, "The Rockefeller Foundation and China," unpublished paper.

65 David Stevens, "Humanities—Program and Policy: Past Program and Proposed Future Program," from Trustee Meeting, April 11, 1935. 2/9, RG 3, 911, Rockefeller Foundation Archive, RAC.

66 David Stevens to Selskar Gunn, June 22, 1933, 1/1/ RG3, 911, Rockefeller Foundation Archive, RAC.

67 Frank Ninkovich, "The Rockefeller Foundation, China and Cultural Change," *Journal of American History* 70 (March 1984): 799–820; the citation here is on 813.

68 For a complete bibliography, see "A Bibliography of Scholarship at the Rockefeller Archive Center, 1975–2007," RAC. Selected examples follow: For the International Health Division, see John Farley, *To Cast Out Disease: A History of the International Health Division of the Rockefeller Foundation* (New York: Oxford University Press, 2004); for the League of Nations Health Organization, see Paul Weindling, "Philanthropy and World Health: The Rockefeller Foundation and the League of Nations Health Organization," *Minerva* 35 (1997): 269–81; for Latin America, see Cueto, *Missionaries of Science;* for Europe, see Donald Fisher, "The Rockefeller Foundation and the Development of Scientific Medicine in Great Britain," *Minerva* 16 (1978): 22–39; for South Asia, see Soma Hewa, *Colonialism, Tropical Disease and Imperial Medicine: Rockefeller Philanthropy in Sri Lanka* (Lanham, Md.: University Press of America, 1995); and for Thailand, see Peter J. Donaldson, "Foreign Intervention in Medical Education: A Case Study of the Rockefeller Foundation's Involvement in a Thai Medical School," *International Journal of Health Services* 6 (1976): 251–70.

69 Weili Ye, *Seeking Modernity in China's Name: Chinese Students in the United States, 1900–1927* (Stanford, Calif.: Stanford University Press, 2001); Y. C. Wang, *Chinese Intellectuals and the West, 1872–1949* (Chapel Hill: University of North Carolina Press, 1966).

70 For the evolution of Rockefeller patronage networks for the natural sciences in the United States, see Robert E. Kohler, *Partners in Science: Foundations and Natural Scientists, 1900–1945* (Chicago: University of Chicago Press, 1991).

71 Chiang, *Social Engineering*, 213.

72 Letter to the author, January 9, 2009.

73 Selskar Gunn, "Report on Visit to China, June 9th to July 30th, 1931," 12/129, RG 1.1, 601, Rockefeller Foundation Archives, RAC.

74 Timothy B. West, *The Power of Position: Beijing University, Intellectuals, and Chinese Political Culture, 1898–1929* (Berkeley: University of California Press, 2004), 219.

75 "The Rockefeller Foundation Payments for Work in China, 1914–1951," in 13/133, Rockefeller Foundation Archives, RG 1, 601, RAC.

76 Quotes from Gunn's Diary cited by Paul B. Prescott, *Jingji Xue: The History of the Introduction of Western Economic Ideas into China, 1850–1950* (Hong Kong: Chinese University Press, 2007), 229.

77 Selskar Gunn, *China Report*, 12/129, RG 1.1, 601, Rockefeller Foundation Archives, RAC.

78 Xu Xiaoqun, *Chinese Professionals and the Republican State: The Rise of Professional Associations in Shanghai, 1912–1937* (Cambridge: Cambridge University Press, 2001).

79 Ye, *Seeking Modernity*, 51–80.

80 Chiang, *Social Engineering*, 214.
81 *Peiping Chronicle*, May 25, 1937, copy located in 138/993, CMB Inc., RAC.
82 "JDR Sr. Memorial Held at PUMC," in ibid.
83 Cable to JDR 3rd, in ibid.

CHAPTER 3

1 For the trip details, see John Ensor Harr and Peter J. Johnson, *The Rockefeller Century* (New York: Charles Scribner's Sons, 1988), 275–96.
2 Zhongyun Zi, *The Destiny of Wealth: An Analysis of American Philanthropic Foundations from a Chinese Perspective* (Dayton: Kettering Foundation Press, 2007), 170.
3 Nancy Bernkopf Tucker, *Patterns in the Dust: Chinese-American Relations and the Recognition Controversy, 1949–1950* (New York: Columbia University Press, 1983).
4 Raymond Fosdick, *The Story of the Rockefeller Foundation* (New York: Harper Brothers, 1952), 283.
5 Akira Iriye, *Cultural Internationalism and World Order* (Baltimore: Johns Hopkins University Press, 1997), 92.
6 JDR 3rd, "Diary 1929," 86/104, 105, Record Group (hereafter RG) 5, 1, 6, Rockefeller Family Archives, Rockefeller Archives Center (hereafter RAC).
7 Ibid., 109. The diary suggests that Yan and Feng were together at this time, but that is not clear from the historical record.
8 Ibid., 140.
9 Ibid., 147.
10 Ibid., 150.
11 Hsai Sheng, president, PUMC Students' Association, to Henry Houghton, June 10, 1925; Roger Greene to George Vincent, July 15, 1925; July 22, 1925, in "Files of the May 30th Movement," #549, PUMC Archives, Peking.
12 Ibid., 145.
13 Ibid., 135.
14 James Thomas Gillam, "The Standard Oil in China (1863–1930)," PhD dissertation, Ohio State University, 1987, chap. 6. A recent Chinese study of Standard Oil does not mention the agreement between the GMD and Standard Oil, but it does detail the many disputes over treaty interpretations. See Wu Lingjun, "Standard Oil Company's Trade Negotiation with China, 1870–1930/33," *Guoli zhengzhi daxue lishi xuebao* 17 (May 2000): 229–61.
15 See, e.g., Greene to Vincent, June 15, 1927, #527, Peking Union Medical College Archives, Peking (hereafter PUMC Archives).
16 Quoted by Warren I. Cohen, *The Chinese Connection: Roger S. Greene, George E. Sokolsky and Thomas W. Lamont and American East-Asian Relations* (New York: Columbia University Press, 1978), 144.
17 Gillam, "Standard Oil in China," 299.
18 JDR 3rd, "Diary," 145.
19 Ibid., 119.
20 See JDR Jr. to Henry Houghton, December 21, 1938, 138/993, CMB Inc., RAC.
21 *Minutes of the China Medical Board, 1928–1947*, copies located at the CMB office, Cambridge, Mass. For the continuing tension between PUMC, the CMB, and the Rockefeller Foundation, see Mary Brown Bullock, *An American Transplant: The Rockefeller Foundation and Peking Union Medical College* (Berkeley: University of California Press, 1980); and Mary Ferguson, *China Medical Board and Peking Union Medical College: A Chronicle of Fruitful Collaboration* (New York: China Medical Board of New York, 1970).
22 "Report to the China Medical Board by its special Committee of One appointed to study the advisability and feasibility of the Board's investing funds in China," Minutes of the CMB, November 14, 1934.
23 Ferguson, *China Medical Board*, 82–114; Bullock, *American Transplant*, 48–77.
24 JDR Jr. to Henry Houghton, December 21, 1938, and October 2, 1940, 138/993, CMB Inc., RAC.
25 James C. Thomson Jr., *While China Faced West: American Reformers in Nationalist China, 1928–1937* (Cambridge, Mass.: Harvard University Press, 1969); John Hersey, *The Call* (New York: Alfred A. Knopf, 1986).
26 "Sun Yat-sen," unpublished paper, probably written by Mary Ferguson, in author's possession.
27 Greene to Vincent, June 10 and 27, and July 29, 1927; 71/1697, RG 4, CMB, Rockefeller Foundation Archives, RAC.
28 Ka-che Yip, *Health and National Reconstruction in Nationalist China: The Development of Modern Health Services, 1928–1937* (Ann Arbor, Mich.: Association of Asian Studies, 1995), 47.
29 Ibid., 40. See also C. C. Chen, *Medicine in Rural China: A Personal Account* (Berkeley: University of California Press, 1989), chap. 2.
30 John Grant, "State Medicine: A Logical Policy for China," *National Medical Journal of China* 14 (1928): 65–80.
31 See Bullock, *American Transplant*, chapter on John Grant, 134–61.
32 Greene to Vincent, August 16, 1929, #721, PUMC Archives.
33 John Grant, "Reminiscences," Columbia University Oral Project, 66; Grant to J. Heng Liu, December 3, 1929, Roger Greene Papers, Harvard University. Yip does not contradict Grant but points out that Rajchman had first visited China in 1926, Yip, *Health and National Reconstruction*, 53–54.

34 John R. Watt, "J. Heng Liu and ABMAC," unpublished paper, provides details on Liu's activities after 1945.

35 Yip, *Health and National Reconstruction*, 183.

36 "Recommendations for the P.U.M.C.—April 1935," translation of the document received from the Ministry of Education, 1, 61/429, CMB Inc., RAC.

37 JDR 3rd to Alan Gregg, August 20, 1935, in ibid.

38 Bridie Jane Andrews, "The Making of Modern Chinese Medicine, 1895–1937," PhD dissertation, University of Cambridge, 1996, 194.

39 Xiaoqun Xu, *Chinese Professionals and the Republican State: The Rise of Professional Associations in Shanghai, 1912–1937* (Cambridge: Cambridge University Press, 2001), 129–54, 190–214.

40 Selskar M. Gunn, "Report on Visit to China," June 9th to July 30th, 1931," 12/129, RG 1.1, 601, Rockefeller Foundation Archives, RAC.

41 Selskar M. Gunn to Max Mason, May 29, 1933, in ibid.

42 James Thomson, *While China Faced West*, 58–75.

43 Rockefeller Foundation, *Annual Report, 1935* (New York: Rockefeller Foundation, 1935), 321.

44 Gunn to Mason, May 29, 1933, 12/125, RG 1.1, 601, Rockefeller Foundation Archives; Gunn to Mason, March 25, 1935, 14/143, RG 1.1, 601 Rural Reconstruction, Rockefeller Foundation Archives, RAC.

45 Mayling Soong Chiang to Selskar Gunn, February 5, 1937, 12/125, RG 1.1, 601, Rockefeller Foundation Archives, RAC.

46 Gunn to Fosdick, February 23, 1937, 14/146, RG 1, 601, Rockefeller Foundation Archives, RAC.

47 Thomson, *While China Faced West*.

48 Raymond Fosdick to John D. Rockefeller Jr., July 30, 1937, and July 31, 1937, RAC. Copies of letters in the author's possession.

49 Selskar Gunn, "Report on China Program as Presented by Mr. Gunn to the Trustees, April 6, 1938," 12/126, RG 1, 601.1, Rockefeller Foundation Archives, RAC.

50 John D. Rockefeller Jr. to Sumner Welles, March 16, 1942; JDR Jr. to Raymond Fosdick, September 15, 1942; and Raymond Fosdick to JDR Jr., September 17, 1942, 13/120, RG 2, OMR, Rockefeller Family Archives, RAC.

51 Harr and Johnson, *Rockefeller Century*, 408.

52 See the letters in Cultural Interests, 57/588, RG 5, 2 E, Rockefeller Family Archives, RAC.

53 "Introductory Remarks by John D. Rockefeller Jr. at the Reception for Madame Chiang Kai-shek at Madison Square Garden, Tuesday Evening, March 2, 1943," 4/196, RG 2, Office of the Messrs. Rockefeller (hereafter OMR), Z, Rockefeller Family Archives, RAC.

54 Zi, *Destiny of Wealth*, 169–71.

55 "Minutes of Meeting of Joint Planning Committee held October 9, 1945," 124/898, CMB Inc., RAC.

56 "JHW's (Joseph H. Willits) and RFE (Roger F. Evans) Memorandum: Policy Re China," January 5, 1944, 13/134, RG 1, 601, Rockefeller Foundation Archives, RAC.

57 "JHW's and RFE to Senior staff, 'Policy Re China,'" January 4, 1944, in ibid.

58 "Minutes of Meeting of Interdivisional Committee on China," October 10, 1945, in ibid.

59 JDR Jr. to Fosdick, November 26, 1942.

60 C. U. Lee, "Memorandum on the C.M.B. and the P.U.M.C," c. 1944, #722, PUMC Archives.

61 Ma Wenzhao to Alan Gregg, February 27, 1947, 387/289, RG 2, 601, Rockefeller Foundation Archives, RAC.

62 "Report of the Commission Sent by the Rockefeller Foundation to China to Study the Problem of the Development of Medicine and Public Health," November 15, 1946, 12/127, RG 1, 601, Rockefeller Foundation Archives, RAC, 7.

63 Raymond Fosdick, "Memorandum dated October 21 from RBF to Dr. Gregg, Dr. Loucks and Dr. Burwell," in ibid.

64 Ibid, 5.

65 See Fosdick to Winthrop Aldrich, chair of the Rockefeller Foundation Board, January 2, 1947, in ibid.

66 Rockefeller Foundation, *Annual Report, 1947* (New York: Rockefeller Foundation, 1947), 5–6. The total appropriations budget for 1947 was $23,413,615, and $20 million was transferred from the Rockefeller Foundation's capital fund to meet the overall budget requirements of 1947.

67 Rockefeller Foundation, *Annual Report, 1947*, 24, 22.

68 "Officers' Conference, Tuesday, January 7, 1947," 5/39, RG 3, Series 904, Rockefeller Foundation Archives, RAC.

69 JDR 3rd to H. C. Peterson, June 2, 1947, 87/738, RG 5, Series 1, OMR Files, Rockefeller Family Archives, RAC.

70 JDR 3rd to JDR Jr., August 12, 1947; Fosdick to JDR 3rd, July 13, 1947, all in ibid.

71 JDR 3rd China Notebook, 1947, 88/743, RG 5, series 1, Rockefeller Family Archives, RAC.

72 Ibid.

73 Ibid.

74 Ibid.

75 JDR 3rd to Blanchette Rockefeller, September 18 and October 5, 1947, 12/100, RG 53, Blanchette H. Rockefeller Papers, series 2, RAC.

76 "China—National Institutes of Health, 1949 Estimates," 5/52a, RG 1, 601, Rockefeller Foundation Archives, RAC.

77 Robert Watson to George Strode, May 23, 1949, 6/57, RG 1, 601, Rockefeller Foundation Archives, RAC.

78 Robert Watson to George Strode, February 18, 1949, 463/3106, RG 2, 601, Rockefeller Foundation Archives, RAC.

79 Marshall Balfour to George Strode, February 25, 1949, 6/57, RG 1, 601, Rockefeller Foundation Archives, RAC.

80 Watson to Balfour, March 10, 1949, 13/138, RG1, 601, Rockefeller Foundation Archives, RAC.

81 Frank Ninkovich, "The Rockefeller Foundation, China and Cultural Change," *Journal of American History* 70 (March 1984): 817.

82 John Farley, *To Cast Out Disease; A History of the International Health Division of the Rockefeller Foundation, 1913–1951* (New York: Oxford University Press, 2004), 270.

83 JHW (Willits) to RBF (Fosdick), September 22, 1947, 3, 387/2510, RG 2–1947, 601, Rockefeller Foundation Archives, RAC. Willits quotes a report from Roger Evans (emphasis in original).

84 Rodney Koeneke, *Empires of the Mind: I. A. Richards and Basic English in China, 1929–1979* (Stanford, Calif.: Stanford University Press, 2004).

85 Fahs to David Stevens, June 26, 1948, 12/182, RG 1, 601, Rockefeller Foundation Archives, RAC.

86 CBF (Fahs), "Humanities Program in China," December 16, 1948, 2/15, RG 1.2, 600, Rockefeller Foundation Archives, RAC.

87 "Minutes of Meeting of Executive Committee of China Medical Board, Inc.," December 27, 1948, in CMB Minutes, 1948.

88 Strode to Watson, March 1, 1949. See also Watson to Balfour, March 10, 1949, and Watson to Strode, May 23, 1949.

89 JDR 3rd to JDR Jr., July 29, 1949, 32/295, RG 5, series 1–OMR Files, Rockefeller Family Archives, RAC.

90 JDR Jr. to JDR 3rd, August 1, 1949, 32/298, RG 5, series 1–OMR Files, Rockefeller Family Archives, RAC.

91 Raymond B. Fosdick to Ambassador Philip Jessup, August 29, 1949, in 35/327, RG 5, series 1–OMR Files, Rockefeller Family Archives, RAC.

92 Fosdick to Jessup, October 25, 1949, in ibid. For a discussion of the work of the Jessup review, see Nancy Bernkopf Tucker, *Patterns in the Dust*, 168–72.

93 C. U. Lee to Philo Parker, October 13, 1949, #722, PUMC Archives.

94 CMB Inc. Minutes, November 14, 1949.

95 Ferguson, *China Medical Board*, 226.

96 JDR Jr. to JDR Sr., September 19, 1921, 15/134, RG 2, OMR, Rockefeller Family Archives, RAC.

97 JDR Jr. to Raymond Fosdick, January 2, 1935, 62/465, RG 3, 2 H, Rockefeller Family Archives, RAC.

98 Frank Dikotter, *The Age of Openness: China before Mao* (Berkeley: University of California Press, 2008).

CHAPTER 4

1 This chapter is based, in part, on formal interviews with PUMC graduates and faculty conducted mainly in 1984, 1987, and 2007. I have listed the date of all interviews but primarily identified the names of deceased individuals. A complete list of the individuals interviewed is given in appendix B.

2 C. U. Lee to JDR 3rd, June 7, 1948, #722, Peking Union Medical College Archives (hereafter PUMC Archives).

3 See Mary Brown Bullock, "Zhou Peiyuan and Scientific Nationalism," in *Remapping China: Fissures in Historical Terrain*, edited by Gail Hershatter, Emily Honig, Jonathan N. Lipman, and Randall Stross (Stanford, Calif.: Stanford University Press, 1996), 210–23.

4 Mary Ferguson, *China Medical Board and Peking Union Medical College: A Chronicle of Fruitful Collaboration* (New York: China Medical Board of New York, 1970), 227. The letter is dated April 4, 1952.

5 Mary Brown Bullock, *An American Transplant: The Rockefeller Foundation and Peking Union Medical College* (Berkeley: University of California Press, 1980), 214.

6 Interview with Zhong Huilan, Peking, March 1984.

7 Jessie Lutz, *China and the Christian Colleges, 1850–1959* (Ithaca, N.Y.: Cornell University Press, 1971), 473–85.

8 Interview, Peking, March 2007.

9 Bullock, *American Transplant*, 212.

10 Ibid.

11 Lutz, *China and the Christian Colleges*, 212.

12 Jiasi Huang, "Medical Education in China," in *Medical Education in Asia: A Symposium* (New York: China Medical Board of New York, 1981), 81. The four different names were China Union Medical College (1952–57); China Medical College (1959–70); Capital Medical College (1979–85); and, since 1985, Peking Union Medical College. Note that the college was closed periodically during this period. During the Cultural Revolution, the PUMC hospital was called the Anti-Imperialist Hospital.

13 Historic Display, PUMC, March 2007.

14 Ge Ou, *Xiehe Yishi* (Memories of Peking Union Medical College) (Beijing: Shenghuo, Dushu Xinzhi Santian Shudian, 2007), 98.

15 See, e.g., *Zhongguo xiehe daxue renwu huicui* (PUMC elites); *(Qunxing cuican: Yuanxiao bufen zhuanjia ji liejie*

dangzheng lingdao jianjie (Bright stars: Introduction of PUMC experts, and past and current party and government administrators); Jiasi Huang, "An Analysis of the 'PUMC Phenomenon,' in Medical Education Development in China," in *China Medical Board, 75th Anniversary Celebration* (New York: China Medical Board, 2004), 21–27.

16 Huang, "Analysis of the 'PUMC Phenomenon,'" 23.

17 Cao Bingkun, *Huashuo Lao Xiehe* (The Old PUMC) (Baoding: Hebei Publishing House, 2004). Many of the chapters were compiled from an earlier 1987 publication.

18 Peter M. Haas, "Introduction: Epistemic Communities and International Policy Coordination," *International Organization* 46 (Winter 1992): 3.

19 Han Qide, "Remarks," in *China Medical Board, 75th Anniversary Celebration*, 45.

20 *Chen Zhiqian xiansheng danchen 100 zhounian* (Tribute to Dr. C. C. Chen) (Chengdu: Sichuan University Press, 2004), 2.

21 Interview with Chen Guozhen, Guangzhou, May 1984.

22 Bullock, *American Transplant*, chap. 6, 134–61.

23 When I interviewed PUMC graduates, I sought information on their classmates as well. These data, coupled with data from PRC medical journals cited in the epilogue of my book *An American Transplant*, provided post-1950 career information on almost all the PUMC graduates. The accuracy was confirmed by comparing it with an official 1997 PUMC data set, *Zhongguo Xiehe Yike Daxue: Biye Tongxue lu* (Peking Union Medical College: An Alumni Roster) (Peking: PUMC Press, 1997).

24 Loo Chih-teh to the author, November 20, 1972.

25 Huang, "Medical Education in China." Examples of others who were leaders of their medical schools include Zhu Xianyi, Tianjin Medical University; Chen Guozhen and Zhou Shoukai, Zhongshan Medical College; Wang Jiwu, Zhejiang Medical College; and Li Wenren, Fujian Medical College.

26 Interviews with PUMC graduates in Tianjin, 1984.

27 Interviews with PUMC graduates in Shanghai, 1984.

28 Interviews with PUMC graduates in Guangzhou, 1984.

29 John Bowers, *Western Medicine in a Chinese Palace: Peking Union Medical College, 1917–1951* (New York: Macy Foundation, 1972), 131.

30 Interview with Zhu Futang, Peking, March 1984.

31 Interview with Zhong Huilan, Peking, March 1984.

32 Bullock, *American Transplant*, 216.

33 AnElissa Lucas, *Chinese Medical Modernization: Comparative Policy Continuities, 1930s–1980s* (New York: Praeger, 1982), 99.

34 C. C. Chen, *Medicine in Rural China: A Personal Account* (Berkeley: University of California Press, 1989), 127.

35 Interviews with Chen, Chengdu, May 1984; and correspondence with the author 1980–96.

36 *Chen Zhiqian xiansheng danchen 100 zhounian.*

37 See Lucas, *Chinese Medical Modernization*, 73–76, 136–39; and Ka-che Yip, *Health and National Reconstruction in Nationalist China: The Development of Modern Health Services, 1928–1937* (Ann Arbor, Mich.: Association of Asian Studies, 1995), 186–92.

38 Interview with Chen Zhiqian, Chengdu, May 25, 1984.

39 Chen Zhaobin, "The Major Thinking of Professor Chen Zhiqian in 'Dingxian Model,'" and "The Necessity and Significance of Naming the 'Dingxian Model' as the 'Chen Model,'" both *Xiandai Yufang Yixue* (Modern Preventive Medicine) 31, no. 5 (2004): 651–55.

40 Interviews with Liu Depei, Jesse Huang, and Tang Xiaofu, Peking, March 2007.

41 PUMC, *Zhongguo Xiehe Yike Daxue: Biye Tongxue lu*, 1997.

42 Lucas, *Chinese Medical Modernization*, 97.

43 For the 100 Flowers Movement and the backlash at PUMC, see Roderick MacFarquhar, *The Hundred Flowers* (London: Stevens and Sons, 1960), 126–27; and Bullock, *American Transplant*, 220.

44 C. E. Lim to Harold Loucks, December 12, 1958, in 1/14, Harold Loucks Collection, Rockefeller Archive Center (hereafter RAC).

45 Interview with Jiasi Huang, May 9, 1984.

46 Interview with Jesse Huang, Peking, June 2009.

47 David M. Lampton, *The Politics of Medicine in China: The Policy Process, 1949–1977* (Boulder, Colo.: Westview Press, 1977), 106, 113.

48 Liu Depei and Liu Qian, *Waike yisheng Huang Jiasi* (Surgeon Huang Jiasi) (Peking: PUMC Press, 2006), 107.

49 Huang Jiasi interview. Huang died of a heart attack several days later.

50 C. E. Lim to Harold Loucks, August 14, 1959, and August 15, 1973, Loucks Collection, 1/14, RAC.

51 Liu and Liu, *Waike yisheng Huang Jiasi*, 107.

52 Ibid., 114.

53 Interviews with Huang, Deng, and Wu, March 1984.

54 This is from a PUMC seventieth-anniversary publication.

55 Ibid.

56 E. Grey Dimond, "Peking Union Medical College: Born-Again Elitism," *Pharos*, Spring 1988, 19. I attended this anniversary celebration.

57 Aaron D. Levine, "Trends in the Movement of Scientists between China and the United States and Implications

for Future Collaboration," paper prepared for the National Science Foundation Committee on Science Policy with the People's Republic of China, 2006, 10–12.

58 Interviews with PUMC students, March 2007.

59 Clyde Wu to the author, August 20, 2008.

60 Lesley Gray, *The China Medical Board: History of Institutions Sponsored by the China Medical Board* (New York: China Medical Board, 2003), 80.

CHAPTER 5

1 JDR 3rd, "Remarks and Introduction of Senator Edward M. Kennedy at the National Conference of the National Committee on United States–China Relations, Inc. at the New York Hilton on March 20, 1969," 9/84, Record Group (hereafter RG) 5, Series 2, Rockefeller Family Archives, Rockefeller Archive Center (hereafter RAC).

2 John Ensor Harr and Peter J. Johnson, *The Rockefeller Century* (New York: Charles Scribner's Sons, 1988), 447, 6.

3 JDR 3rd, "Remarks."

4 Frank A. Ninkovich, *The Diplomacy of Ideas: U.S. Foreign Policy and Cultural Relations, 1938–1950* (New York: Cambridge University Press, 1981).

5 Harr and Johnson, *Rockefeller Century*, 506.

6 Ibid.

7 "Speech of H. E. Cox of Georgia," August 1, 1951. For the Rockefeller Foundation response, see "Answers of the Rockefeller Foundation Dated October 31, 1952 to 'Questionnaire Submitted by the Select Committee of the House of Representatives of the Congress of the United States,'" both in 14/89, RG 3.2, 900, Rockefeller Foundation Archives, RAC.

8 Recent research refutes an earlier contention that the RF withdrew its support from the IPR because of the congressional inquiry. See Lawrence T. Woods, "The Rockefeller Foundation's Support of the Institute of Pacific Relations," in *Rockefeller Archive Center Research Reports*, Spring 1996, 16–18.

9 Takeshi Matsuda, *Soft Power and Its Perils: U.S. Cultural Policy in Early Postwar Japan and Permanent Dependency* (Washington, D.C., and Stanford, Calif.: Woodrow Wilson Center Press and Stanford University Press, 2007), 5.

10 JDR 3rd, "Objective and Focus of My Asian Interest," November 17, 1953, 35/327, RG 5, Rockefeller Family Archives, RAC.

11 Asia Society, *A Passion for Asia: The Rockefeller Legacy* (New York: Asia Society and Hudson Hills Press, 2006), 22–33.

12 Asian Cultural Council, *Asian Cultural Council, 40 Years* (New York: Asian Cultural Council, 2004), 24.

13 James S. Coleman and David Court, *University Development in the Third World: The Rockefeller Experience* (Oxford: Pergamon, 1993), 12–24.

14 JDR 3rd to Agnes Pearce, September 28, 1953; to Harold Loucks, August 30, 1955, December 31, 1956; December 9, 1958, all in 2/11, RG 5, 2, Rockefeller Family Archives, RAC. Laurie Norris, *The China Medical Board: 50 Years of Programs, Partnerships, and Progress, 1950–2000* (New York: China Medical Board, 2003), 61; Richard Pearce to JDR 3rd, October 15, 1953; to JDR Jr., November 17, 1953, in 20/12, RG 3, Rockefeller Foundation Archives, RAC.

15 JDR Jr. to Harold Loucks, January 11, 1954, 12/105, RG 3, Office of the Messrs. Rockefeller (hereafter OMR), Rockefeller Family Archives, RAC; see also Alan Gregg to Loucks, December 17, 1953, 1/8, Loucks Collection, RAC.

16 "Future Policy and Programs," 1954, 12/105, RG 3, OMR, Rockefeller Family Archives, RAC.

17 M. C. Balfour to John C. Bugher, September 27, 1956; DR (?) to JCB, October 1, 1956, both in 2/17, RG 1.2, 600, Rockefeller Foundation Archives, RAC.

18 "Future Policy and Programs."

19 Norris, *China Medical Board*, 43, 64–65.

20 "Future Policy and Programs."

21 Ibid., 1–2.

22 Francis X. Sutton, "American Philanthropy in Educational and Cultural Exchanges with the People's Republic of China," in *Educational Exchanges: Essays on the Sino-American Experience*, edited by Joyce K. Kallgren and Denis Fred Simon (Berkeley: Institute of East Asian Studies, University of California, 1987), 96–118.

23 "Summary of Governor Rockefeller's Position on Mainland China," 2/12, RG 4, G.1, Rockefeller Family Archives, RAC; Nelson Rockefeller, "Foreign Policy: News Conferences, 1968," Philadelphia, May 1, 1968, in 1/1, RG 4, series G, Rockefeller Family Archives, RAC.

24 John Ensor Harr and Peter J. Johnson, *The Rockefeller Conscience: An American Family in Public and in Private* (New York: Charles Scribner's Sons, 1991), 203.

25 Henry Kissinger, *White House Years* (Boston: Little, Brown, 1979), 715.

26 Interview with David Rockefeller, February 20, 2008; David Rockefeller, *Memoirs* (New York: Random House, 2002), 247–58.

27 David Rockefeller, "From a China Traveler," *New York Times*, August 10, 1973.

28 Henry Kissinger to JDR 3rd, August 22, 1972, and June 4, 1973, both in 445, RG 5, series 5.4, Rockefeller Family Archives, RAC.

29 Huang Hua to JDR 3rd, December 25, 1974. See also JDR 3rd to Huang Hua, January 2, 1973, July 18, 1973, and October 1, 1973, all in ibid.

30 Interview with Jan Berris, March 2010.

31 Sherman E. Lee, "Words of Commemoration," in *Treasures of Asian Art: The Asia Society's Mr. and Mrs. John D. Rockefeller 3rd Collection*, by Denise Patry Leidy (New York: Abbeville Press, 1994).

32 Interview with Ralph Samuelson, March 6, 2007; Asian Cultural Council, *Grant Recipients and Project Participants, 1963–2004* (New York: Asian Cultural Council, 2004).

33 John Knowles, "China Diary," unpublished Rockefeller Foundation report, 17.

34 "Rockefeller Foundation News Release of Luncheon for Chinese Medical Delegation, October 18, 1972," in Ibid., Appendix II, 178.

35 John Knowles to Dr. Kissinger, February 5, 1973, in "China Diary," appendix III.

36 Ibid., 179–81.

37 Sheldon Segal, "China Notes, January 19–February 1, 1979," 17. Notes given to the author by James P. Grant.

38 Segal to Chang, June 27, 1978, in Sheldon Segal Papers, uncataloged, RAC.

39 Ibid., January 22, 1979, 4.

40 Interview with Sheldon Segal, September 25, 2006.

41 Rockefeller Foundation, *Annual Report, 1981* (New York: Rockefeller Foundation, 1980), 18.

42 Richard Lyman to the author, March 2, 1992.

43 Amanda Severaid, "Grantmaking in China," Rockefeller Foundation Paper, 2006, 3.

44 Frank Ninkovich, "The Trajectory of Cultural Internationalism," in *Educational Exchanges*, ed. Kallgren and Simon, 15–16.

45 Kenneth Prewitt, "The Rockefeller Foundation and China," presentation at a meeting of the National Committee on U.S.-China Relations, February 25, 1991. From my notes of the meeting.

46 Peter Geithner, "The Ford Foundation and China," presentation at a meeting of the National Committee on U.S.-China Relations, February 25, 1991.

47 The heading above is a quotation from Segal to C. Y. Chang, June 27, 1978, in Segal Papers.

48 Interview with Segal, Dean H. Hammer and Shain-dow Kung, *Biotechnology in China* (Washington, D.C.: Committee on Scholarly Communication with the People's Republic of China, National Academies Press, 1989), 44. This institute merged with two others and is today the Institute of Genetics and Developmental Biology.

49 Severaid, "Grantmaking in China," 7.

50 Sheldon J. Segal, "Biomedical Research Needs and Possibilities in the People's Republic of China," unpublished paper, Segal Papers, c. 1980, 7.

51 Interview with Segal.

52 Segal, "Biomedical Research Needs and Possibilities," 2.

53 Matthew Connelly, *Fatal Misconception: The Struggle to Control World Population* (Cambridge, Mass.: Harvard University Press, 2008), 339–48.

54 Severaid, "Grantmaking in China," 4–6; Ake Hooker and Walt Bogdanich, "Tainted Chinese Drug Scandal Linked to U.S. Abortion Pill," *New York Times,* January 31, 2008. Note that the facility that produces RU-486 was not implicated in this article.

55 Herbert L. Smith, "Introducing New Contraceptives in Rural China: A Field Experiment," *Annals of the American Academy of Political and Social Science* 599 (May 2005): 246–71; Severaid, "Grantmaking in China," 4–5.

56 Laurence Schneider, *Biology and Revolution in Twentieth Century China* (Lanham, Md.: Rowman & Littlefield, 2003); the quotation is on 103; see also 74–75, 100–104, 188, 250.

57 J. C. O'Toole, G. H. Toenniessen, T. Murashige, R. R. Harris, and R. W. Herdt, "The Rockefeller Foundation's International Program on Rice Biotechnology," unpublished paper, Rockefeller Foundation, 2001.

58 Severaid, "Grantmaking in China," 9.

59 Interview with Gary Toenniessen, April 11, 2007; Valerie J. Karplus and Xingwang Deng, *Agricultural Biotechnology in China: Origins and Prospects* (New York: Springer, 2008).

60 Peter Goldmark, "President's Review," in *Annual Report, 1989* (New York: Rockefeller Foundation, 1989), 7.

61 Severaid, "Grantmaking in China," 12.

62 Hammer and Kung, *Biotechnology in China*, 71.

63 I have been a member of the CMB since 1981 and the chair since 2005. This section is based primarily on materials in the public domain. The views expressed here are my own and do not necessarily represent those of the CMB.

64 Patrick Ongley, "Considerations," May 25, 1970, 1/7, Loucks Collection, RAC.

65 "Peking Union Medical College Claim," December 5, 1979, CMB Docket, 79057.

66 Norris, *China Medical Board*, 96.

67 Ibid., 105.

68 Author's telephone interview with Robert Buchanan, February 2010.

69 Norris, *China Medical Board*, 118–25. The subsequent discussion of Sawyer and Schwarz's tenure as CMB president is primarily based on ibid., 173–232; and M. Roy Schwarz, "President's Report: Nine Years as President," unpublished report, China Medical Board of New York, June 13, 2006.

70 Andrzej Wojtczak and M. Roy Schwarz, "Minimum Essential Requirements and Standards in Medical Educa-tion," *Medical Teacher* 22 (2000): 555–59.

71 Zhongyun Zi, *The Destiny of Wealth: An Analysis of American Philanthropic Foundations from a Chinese Perspec-tive* (Dayton: Kettering Foundation Press, 2007), 182–92. For recent figures, see Ford Foundation, "The Ford Foundation and China," printed brochure, 2008.

72 Harr and Johnson, *Rockefeller Conscience*, 519–25, 556–57.

73 Rockefeller Brothers Fund, *Annual Report, 1980* (New York: Rockefeller Brothers Fund, 1980), 9.

74 Rockefeller Brothers Fund, *Annual Report, 1985* (New York: Rockefeller Brothers Fund, 1985).

75 "RBF Grants, China, Global Security/East Asia," in *RBF Briefing Book*, compiled by Rockefeller Brothers Fund, 1992; Shiping Zheng, "Sino-American Educational Exchanges and International Relations Studies in China," in *Bridging Minds across the Pacific: U.S.-China Educational Exchanges, 1978–2003*, edited by Cheng Li (Lan-ham, Md.: Lexington Books, 2005).

76 Peter Riggs, "Toward Future RBF Grantmaking in Asia: Defining a Pivotal Place," in *RBF Briefing Book*, com-piled by Rockefeller Brothers Fund, October 2003, 6.

77 Ibid.

78 Peter Riggs, "Rockefeller Brothers Fund East Asia Sustainable Resource Use Program," in *RBF Briefing Book*, compiled by Rockefeller Brothers Fund, October 1998, 16.

79 Rockefeller Brothers Fund, *Annual Report, 1989* (New York: Rockefeller Brothers Fund, 1989), 10.

80 Rockefeller Foundation, *Annual Report, 1997* (New York: Rockefeller Foundation, 1997), 4.

CHAPTER 6

1 I attended this ceremony as chair of the China Medical Board.

2 Zhongyun Zi, *The Destiny of Wealth: An Analysis of American Philanthropic Foundations from a Chinese Perspec-tive* (Dayton: Kettering Foundation Press, 2007), 271.

3 "The Rockefeller (China) Research and Development Center," 2007. Author's notes from seminar in Peking, March 21, 2008. See www.rockefeller.org.cn.

4 I visited Jiujiang in March 2007.

5 Joseph Levenson, *Confucian China and Its Modern Fate: A Trilogy* (Berkeley: University of California Press, 1968), vol. 3, 76.

6 Mary Ferguson, *China Medical Board and Peking Union Medical College: A Chronicle of Fruitful Collaboration* (New York: China Medical Board of New York, 1970), 40.

7 Liu Qian, *1917–2007 Hurrah for PUMC* (Peking: PUMC Press, 2007), 2.

8 Richard Rockefeller, "Remarks at PUMC 90th Anniversary," October 14, 2007.

9 Wendy O'Neill Wang, "Remarks at History Seminar, PUMC 90th Anniversary," October 14, 2007.

10 Chen Yuanfeng, "A Glance Back," presentation at PUMC's ninetieth-anniversary celebration, October 14, 2007, unpublished speech.

11 Liu Depei, "PUMC's Past, Present and Future," presentation at PUMC's ninetieth-anniversary celebration, October 14, 2007, unpublished speech.

12 Franklin McLean, "Report to the China Medical Board," 8.

13 Interview with Janet Maughan, Rockefeller Foundation, April 12, 2007.

14 Rockefeller Foundation, Grant Search "China," http://www.rockfound.org/grants/GrantSearch.aspx?ke ywords=China&AllDates=1&month; Amanda Severaid, "Grantmaking in China," Rockefeller Founda-tion Paper, 2006, 10–13; Amanda Severaid, email message to the author, April 10, 2008; James Nyoro, "China's Engagement in Africa: Key Findings and Recommendations," Rockefeller Foundation, 2009, http://www.rockefellerfoundation.org/news/publications/chinas-engagement-africa-key-findings.

15 Rockefeller Foundation, "What We Do," http://www.rockefellerfoundation.org/what-we-do.

16 Ibid.

17 Rockefeller Foundation, "Grants & Grantees," http://www.rockfound.org/grants.

18 Lincoln Chen, "China Medical Board Strategy Paper," September 28, 2007, 3.

19 China Medical Board, "Biennial Report, 2007–2008." China Medical Board, 2008, http://*www.chinamedical-board.org/docs/BiennialReport1Dec08_000.pdf*.

20 *The Lancet*, October 20, 2008, and March 27, 2010.

21 *The Lancet*, "Press Release," October 20, 2008.

22 Stephen B. Heintz, "An RBF Pivotal Place in Asia," in *RBF Briefing Book*, compiled by Rockefeller Brothers Fund, 2004, 27–32.

23 Interview with Stephen Heintz, New York City, March 2007.

24 Stephen Heintz, "The Role of NGO's in Modern Societies and an Increasingly Interdependent World," paper presented at Annual Conference of the Institute of Civil Society, Zhongshan University, Guangzhou, January 14, 2006, 11.

25 Shenyu G. Belsky, "Pivotal Place: Southern China: Southern China Program Review: 2006–2009," unpub-lished paper, March 2010.

26 Rockefeller Brothers Fund, "Grants and Grantees, South China," http://www.rbf.org/grantsdatabase/grantsda-tabase_list.htm?page_num=3&program=1895.

27 Heintz, "Role of NGOs," 4.
28 Zi, *Destiny of Wealth*, 215.
29 Telephone interview with Vishaka Desai, May 7, 2010; Asia Society Web site, www.asiasociety.org.
30 David Rockefeller, "An Enduring Gift," in *A Passion for Asia: The Rockefeller Legacy*, edited by Asia Society (New York: Hudson Hills Press, 2006), 40.
31 John D. Rockefeller IV, "Understanding Asia through Rationalism and Reason," in *A Passion for Asia*, ed. Asia Society, 42.
32 I am grateful to Cynthia Altman, the curator of Kykuit, for giving me a tour in March 2008. See *A Passion for Asia*, ed. Asia Society, 118.
33 David Rockefeller gave me a tour of the garden in August 2009. See *A Abby Rockefeller Garden: History, Garden, Sculpture* (published privately, 2009).
34 Steven C. Rockefeller, "Manjusri and Abby's Gardens," in *A Passion for Asia*, ed. Asia Society, 45.
35 Hallett Abend, "Great Health Work Goes on in Peking," *New York Times*, February 12, 1928.

BIBLIOGRAPHY

Abby Aldrich Rockefeller's Letters to Her Sister Lucy. New York, published privately, 1957.

Addresses and Papers, Dedication Ceremonies and Medical Conference, Peking Union Medical College. Concord, N.H.: Rumford Press, 1922.

Amreith, Sunil S. *Decolonizing International Health: India and Southeast Asia, 1930–65.* New York: Palgrave Macmillan, 2006.

Andrews, Bridie Jane. "The Making of Modern Chinese Medicine, 1895–1937." PhD dissertation, University of Cambridge, 1996.

Arkush, David. *Fei Xiaotong and Sociology in Revolutionary China.* Cambridge, Mass.: Harvard University Press, 1981.

Asia Society. *A Passion for Asia: The Rockefeller Legacy.* New York: Hudson Hills Press, 2006.

Baick, John S. "Cracks in the Foundation: Frederick T. Gates, the Rockefeller Foundation, and the China Medical Board." *Journal of the Gilded Age and Progressive Era* 3, no. 1 (January 2004): 59–89.

Benedict, Carol. *Bubonic Plague in Nineteenth-Century China.* Stanford, Calif.: Stanford University Press, 1996.

Berman, Edward H. *The Influence of the Carnegie, Ford and Rockefeller Foundations on American Foreign Policy.* Albany: State University of New York Press, 1982.

Borowy, Iris, ed. *Uneasy Encounters: The Politics of Medicine and Health in China 1900–1937.* Berlin: Peter Lang, 2009.

Bowers, John. *Western Medicine in a Chinese Palace: Peking Union Medical College, 1917–1951.* New York: Macy Foundation, 1972.

Bracale, Dennis. "The Abby Aldrich Rockefeller Garden: Chinese Heart of Acadia National Park." MLA thesis. University of Virginia, 1998.

Brown, E. Richard. "Exporting Medical Education: Professionalism, Modernization and Imperialism." *Social Science & Medicine* 13A (1979): 585–95.

Bu, Liping. *Making the World Like Us: Education, Cultural Expansion and the American Century.* Westport, Conn.: Praeger, 2003.

Buck, Peter. *American Science and Modern China, 1876–1936.* Cambridge: Cambridge University Press, 1980.

Bullock, Mary Brown. "American Exchanges with China, Revisited." In *Educational Exchanges: Essays on the Sino-American Experience,* edited by Joyce K. Kallgren and Denis Fred Simon. Berkeley: Institute of East Asian Studies, 1987.

———. *An American Transplant: The Rockefeller Foundation and Peking Union Medical College.* Berkeley: University of California Press, 1980.

———. "Zhou Peiyuan and Scientific Nationalism." In *Remapping China: Fissures in Historical Terrain,* edited by Gail Hershatter, Emily Honig, Jonathan N. Lipman, and Randall Stross. Stanford, Calif.: Stanford University Press, 1996.

Cao, Bingkun. *Huashuo Lao Xiehe* (The Old PUMC). Baoding: Hebei Publishing House, 2004.

Chen, C. C. *Medicine in Rural China: A Personal Account.* Berkeley: University of California Press, 1989.

Chen, Kaiyi. "Quality Versus Quantity: The Rockefeller Foundation and Nurses' Training in China." *Journal of American East-Asian Relations* 5 (Spring 1996): 77–104.

———. *Seeds from the West: St. John's Medical School, Shanghai, 1880–1952.* Chicago: Imprint Publications, 2001.

Chen, Zhaobin. "The Major Thinking of Professor Chen Zhiqin in 'Dingxian Model' as the "Chen Model." *Xiandai yufang yixue* (Modern Preventive Medicine) 31, no. 5 (2004): 654–55.

————."The Necessity and Significance of Naming the 'Dingxian Model' as the 'Chen Model'." *Xiandai yufang yixue* (Modern preventive medicine) 31, no. 5 (2004): 651–55.

Chen Zhiqian xiansheng danchen 100 zhounian (Tribute to Dr. C. C. Chen). Chengdu: Sichuan University Press, 2004.

Chernow, Ron. *Titan: The Life of John D. Rockefeller, Sr.* New York: Random House, 1998.

Chiang, Yung-chen. *Social Engineering and the Social Sciences in China, 1919–1949.* New York: Cambridge University Press, 2001.

Choa, G. H. *"Heal the Sick" Was Their Motto: The Protestant Medical Missionaries in China.* Hong Kong: Chinese University Press, 1990.

Cody, Jeffrey W. *Building in China: Henry K. Murphy's "Adaptive Architecture," 1914–1935.* Seattle: University of Washington Press, 2001.

Cohen, Warren I. *The Chinese Connection: Roger S. Greene, George E. Sokolsky and Thomas W. Lamont and American East-Asian Relations.* New York: Columbia University Press, 1978.

————. *East Asian Art and American Culture: A Study in International Relations.* New York: Columbia University Press, 1992.

————. *Pacific Passage: The Study of American-East Asian Relations on the Eve of the Twenty-First Century.* New York: Columbia University Press, 1996.

Coleman, James S., and David Court. *University Development in the Third World: The Rockefeller Experience.* Oxford: Pergamon, 1993.

Connelly, Matthew. *Fatal Misconception: The Struggle to Control World Population.* Cambridge, Mass.: Harvard University Press, 2008.

Craver, Earlene. "Patronage and the Directions of Research in Economics: The Rockefeller Foundation in Europe, 1924–38." *Minerva* 24 (1986): 205–22.

Cueto, Marcos, ed. *Missionaries of Science: The Rockefeller Foundation and Latin America.* Bloomington: Indiana University Press, 1994.

Cunningham, Andrew, and Bridie Andrews, eds. *Western Medicine as Contested Knowledge.* Manchester: Manchester University Press, 1997.

Dikotte, Frank. *The Age of Openness: China before Mao.* Berkeley: University of California Press, 2008.

Dimond, E. Grey. "Peking Union Medical College: Born-Again Elitism." *Pharos* 19 (Spring 1988).

Donaldson, Peter J. "Foreign Intervention in Medical Education: A Case Study of the Rockefeller Foundation's Involvement in a Thai Medical School." *International Journal of Health Services* 6 (1976): 251–70.

Elman, Benjamin A. *A Cultural History of Modern Science in China.* Cambridge, Mass.: Harvard University Press, 2006.

————. *On Their Own Terms: Science in China, 1550–1900.* Cambridge, Mass.: Harvard University Press, 2005.

Ernst, Joseph W., ed. *"Dear Father"/"Dear Son": Correspondence of John D. Rockefeller and John D. Rockefeller, Jr.* New York: Fordham University Press, 1994.

Farley, John. *To Cast Out Disease: A History of the International Health Division of the Rockefeller Foundation (1913–1951).* Oxford: Oxford University Press, 2004.

Ferguson, Mary. *China Medical Board and Peking Union Medical College: A Chronicle of Fruitful Collaboration.* New York: China Medical Board of New York, Inc., 1970.

Fisher, Donald. "The Rockefeller Foundation and the Development of Scientific Medicine in Great Britain." *Minerva* 16 (1978): 22–39.

Fosdick, Raymond. *John D. Rockefeller, Jr., A Portrait.* New York: Harper Brothers, 1956.

————. *The Story of the Rockefeller Foundation.* New York: Harper Brothers, 1952.

Garrett, Shirley. *Social Reformers in Urban China: The Chinese Y.M.C.A., 1895–1926.* Cambridge, Mass.: Harvard University Press, 1970.

Gates, Frederick Taylor. *Chapters in My Life.* New York: Free Press, 1977.

Gienow-Hect, Jessica C. E. "'Shame on US'? Academics, Cultural Transfer and the Cold War—A Critical Review." *Diplomatic History* 24 (Summer 2000):, 465–95.

Gillam, James Thomas. "The Standard Oil in China (1863–1930)." PhD dissertation, Ohio State University, 1987.

Goulder, Grace. *John D. Rockefeller: The Cleveland Years.* Cleveland: Western Reserve Historical Society, 1972.

Grant, John. "State Medicine: A Logical Policy for China." *National Medical Journal of China* 14 (1928): 65–80.

Gray, Lesley. *The China Medical Board: History of Institutions Sponsored by the China Medical Board*. New York: China Medical Board, 2003.

Haas, Peter M. "Introduction: Epistemic Communities and International Policy Coordination." *International Organization* 46 (Winter 1992).

Haas, William. *China Voyager: Gist Gee's Life in Science*. Armonk, N.Y.: M. E. Sharpe, 1996.

Hammer, Dean, and Shain-dow Kung. *Biotechnology in China*. Washington, D.C.: National Academies Press, 1989.

Han, Qide. "Remarks." In *China Medical Board, 75th Anniversary Celebration*. New York: China Medical Board, 2004.

Harr, John Ensor, and Peter J. Johnson. *The Rockefeller Century; Three Generations of America's Greatest Family*. New York: Charles Scribner's Sons, 1988.

———. *The Rockefeller Conscience: An American Family in Public and in Private*. New York: Charles Scribner's Sons, 1991.

Hayford, Charles W. *To the People: James Yen and Village China*. New York: Columbia University Press, 1990.

Hayhoe, Ruth. *China's Universities, 1895–1995: A Century of Cultural Conflict*. Hong Kong: University of Hong Kong Press, 1999.

Hayhoe, Ruth, and Marianne Bastid, eds. *China's Education and the Industrialized World: Studies in Cultural Transfer*. Armonk, N.Y.: M. E. Sharpe, 1987.

Hewa, Soma. *Colonialism, Tropical Disease and Imperial Medicine: Rockefeller Philanthropy in Sri Lanka*. Lanham, Md.: University Press of America, 1995.

Hewa, Soma, and Philo Hove, eds. *Philanthropy and Cultural Context: Western Philanthropy in South, East and Southeast Asia in the 20th Century*. Lanham, Md.: University Press of America, 1997.

Hidy, Ralph W., and Muriel E. *Pioneering in Big Business: History of Standard Oil Company (New Jersey), 1882–1911*. New York: Harper Brothers, 1955.

Hooker, Ake, and Walt Bogdanich. "Tainted Chinese Drug Scandal Linked to U.S. Abortion Pill." *New York Times*, January 31, 2008.

Hopkins, C. Howard. *John R. Mott, 1865–1955*. Grand Rapids: William B. Eerdmans, 1979.

Hunt, Michael. "Americans in the China Market: Economic Opportunities and Economic Nationalism, 1890s–1931." *Business History Review* 51 (Autumn 1976): 271–308.

———. *The Making of a Special Relationship: The United States and China to 1914*. New York: Columbia University Press, 1983.

Hussey, Harry. *My Pleasures and Palaces: An Informal Memoir of Forty Years in Modern China*. Garden City, N.Y.: Doubleday, 1968.

Iriye, Akira. *Cultural Internationalism and World Order*. Baltimore: Johns Hopkins University Press, 1997.

———. *Global Community: The Role of International Organizations in the Making of the Contemporary World*. Berkeley: University of California Press, 2002.

Jiang, Xiao-yang. "Cross-Cultural Philanthropy as a Gift Relationship: The Rockefeller Donors and Chinese Recipients, 1913–1921. PhD dissertation, Bowling Green State University, 1995.

Kallgren, Joyce K., and Denis Fred Simon, eds. *Educational Exchanges: Essays on The Sino-American Experience*. Berkeley: Institute of East Asian Studies, 1987.

Karl, Barry D., and Stanley N. Katz. "Foundations and Ruling Class Elites." *Daedalus*, Winter 1987, 1–36.

———. "The American Private Philanthropic Foundation and the Public Sphere, 1890–1930." *Minerva* 19 (Summer 1981): 235–70.

Karplus, Valerie J., and Xing Wang Deng. *Agricultural Biotechnology in China: Origins and Prospects*. New York: Springer, 2008.

Keller, Charles A. "Rockefeller Support for the Industrial Work of the Chinese Y.M.C.A." *Rockefeller Archive Center Research Reports*, Spring 1994.

Kerr, Bernice. *Abby Aldrich Rockefeller: The Woman in the Family*. New York: Random House, 1993.

King, Marjorie. *China's American Daughter: Ida Pruitt (1888–1985)*. Hong Kong: Chinese University Press, 2006.

Kirby, William C. "The Internationalization of China: Foreign Relations at Home and Abroad in the Republican Era." *China Quarterly* 50 (June 1997): 433–58.

Kissinger, Henry. *White House Years*. Boston: Little, Brown, 1979.

Koenke, Rodney. *Empires of the Mind: I.A. Richards and Basic English in China, 1929–1979.* Stanford: Stanford University Press, 2004.

Kohler, Robert E. *Partners in Science: Foundations and Natural Scientists, 1900–1945.* Chicago: University of Chicago Press, 1991.

Lampton, David. *The Politics of Medicine in China: The Policy Process, 1949–1977.* Boulder, Colo.: Westview Press, 1977.

Latourette, Kenneth Scott. *A History of Christian Missions in China.* New York: Macmillan, 1929.

Lee, Sherman. "The Mr. and Mrs. John D. Rockefeller 3rd Collection: A Personal Recollection." In *Treasures of Asian Art: The Asia Society's Mr. and Mrs. John D. Rockefeller, 3rd Collection,* edited by Denise Patry Leidy. New York: Abbeville Press, 1994.

Levenson, Joseph. *Confucian China and Its Modern Fate: A Trilogy.* Berkeley: University of California Press, 1968.

Levine, Aaron D. "Trends in the Movement of Scientists between China and the United States and Implications for Future Collaboration." Unpublished paper.

Li, Hongshan. *U.S.-China Educational Exchange: State, Society, and Intercultural Relations, 1905–1950.* New Brunswick, N.J.: Rutgers University Press, 2008.

Litsios, Socrates. "Selskar Gunn and China: The Rockefeller Foundation's "Other" Approach to Public Health." *Bulletin of the History of Medicine* 79 (2005): 295–318.

Liu, Depei, and Liu Qian. *Waike yisheng Huang Jiasi* (Surgeon Huang Jiasi). Peking: PUMC Press, 2006.

Lu, Yiyi. "Luokefeile Jijinhui de Zhongguo Xiangmu, 1913-41" (The Rockefeller Foundation's Patronage of Science in China, 1913–41). *Zhongguo Keji Shiliao* (China Historical Materials of Science and Technology) 19, no. 2 (1998): 24–28.

Lucas, AnElissa. *Chinese Medical Modernization: Comparative Policy Continuities, 1930s–1980s.* New York: Praeger, 1982.

Lutz, Jessie. *China and the Christian Colleges, 1850–1959.* Ithaca, N.Y.: Cornell University Press, 1971.

Ma, Qiusha. "The Rockefeller Foundation and Modern Medical Education in China, 1915–1951." PhD dissertation, Case Western Reserve University, 1995.

MacFarquhar, Roderick. *The Hundred Flowers.* London: Stevens and Sons, 1960.

Manzione, Joseph. "'Amusing and Amazing and Practical and Military': The Legacy of Scientific Internationalism in American Foreign Policy, 1945–1963." *Diplomatic History* 24 (Winter 2000): 21–56.

Matsuda, Takeshi. *Soft Power and Its Perils: U.S. Cultural Policy in Early Postwar Japan and Permanent Dependency.* Washington, D.C., and Stanford, Calif.: Woodrow Wilson Center Press and Stanford University Press, 2007.

Nelson, Waldemar A. *The Golden Donors: A New Anatomy of the Great Foundations.* New York: E. P. Dutton, 1985.

Nevins, Allan. *Study in Power: John D. Rockefeller, Industrialist and Philanthropist.* 2 vols. New York: Charles Scribner's Sons, 1953.

Ninkovich, Frank A. *The Diplomacy of Ideas: U.S. Foreign Policy and Cultural Relations, 1938–1950.* New York: Cambridge University Press, 1981.

———."Requiem for Cultural Internationalism," *History of Education Quarterly* 26 (Summer 1986): 249–55.

———."The Rockefeller Foundation, China, and Cultural Change." *Journal of American History* 70 (March 1984): 799–820.

Ninkovich, Frank A., and Liping Bu, eds. *The Cultural Turn: Essays in the History of U.S. Foreign Relations.* Chicago: Imprint Publications, 2001.

Norris, Laurie. *The China Medical Board: 50 Years of Programs, Partnerships, and Progress, 1950–2000.* New York: China Medical Board, 2003.

Ogilvie, Marilyn Bailey, and Clifford J. Choquette. "Western Biology and Medicine in Modern China: The Career and Legacy of Alice M. Boring (1883–1955)." *Journal of the History of Medicine and Allied Sciences* 48 (April 1993): 198–215.

O'Neill, Wendy. *Rockefeller Philanthropy in China: The Oil Prince's Palace and Other Tales from the Middle Kingdom.* New York: Rockefeller Brothers Fund, 2002.

Ou, Ge. *Xiehe Yishi* (Memories of Peking Union Medical College). Beijing: Shenghuo, Dushu, Xinzhi Sanlian Shudian, 2007.

Page, Benjamin B., and David A. Valone. *Philanthropic Foundations and the Globalization of Scientific Medicine and Public Health.* Lanham, Md.: University Press of America, 2007.

Parmar, Inderjeet. "'To Relate Knowledge and Action': The Impact of the Rockefeller Foundation on Foreign Policy Thinking during America's Rise to Globalism, 1939–1945." *Minerva* 40 (Fall 2002): 235–62.

Pugach, Noel H. "Standard Oil and Petroleum Development in Early Republican China." *Business History Review* 45 (Winter 1971): 452–73.

Pyenson, Lewis. *Cultural Imperialism and Exact Sciences: German Expansion Overseas, 1900–1930.* New York: Peter Lang, 1985.

Qunxing cuican: Yuanxiao bufen zhanjia ji lijie dangzeng lingdao jianjie (Introduction of some PUMC experts and past and current party and government administrators). Peking: PUMC Press, no date.

Reardon-Anderson, James. *The Study of Change: Chemistry in China, 1840–1959.* New York: Cambridge University Press, 1991.

Rockefeller, David. "From a China Traveler." *New York Times*, August 10, 1973.

———. *Memoirs.* New York: Random House, 2002.

Rockefeller, John D. *Random Reminiscences of Men and Events.* New York: Doubleday, Page, 1909.

Rogaski, Ruth. *Hygienic Modernity in Treaty-Port China.* Berkeley: University of California Press, 2004.

Rosenberg, Emily S. *Spreading the American Dream: American Economic and Cultural Expansion, 1890–1945.* New York: Hill & Wang, 1982.

Schneider, Laurence. *Biology and Revolution in Twentieth Century China.* Lanham, Md.: Rowman & Littlefield, 2003.

———. "The Rockefeller Foundation, the China Foundation, and the Development of Modern Science in China." *Social Science of Medicine* 16 (1982): 1217–21.

Schneider, William H., ed. *Rockefeller Philanthropy and Modern Biomedicine: International Initiatives from World War I to the Cold War.* Bloomington: Indiana University Press, 2002.

Sheng, Jia. "The Origins of the Science Society of China, 1914–1937." PhD dissertation, Cornell University, 1995.

Shepherd, Chris. "Imperial Science: The Rockefeller Foundation and Agricultural Science in Peru, 1940–1960." *Science as Culture* 14 (June 2005): 113–37.

Smith, Herbert L. "Introducing New Contraceptives in Rural China: A Field Experiment." *Annals of the American Academy of Political and Social Science* 599 (May 2005): 246–71.

Snapper, Isadore. *Chinese Lessons to Western Medicine: A Contribution to Geographical Medicine from the Clinics of Peiping Union Medical College.* New York: Interscience Publishers, Inc., 1941.

Stapleton, Darwin W. "The Rockefeller Foundation and the Transfer and Diffusion of Scientific Instrumentation to China, 1915–1949." Paper presented at Twenty-Second International Congress on History of Science, Beijing, July 2005.

Stifel, Laurence D., and Ralph K. Davidson, and James S. Coleman. "Agencies of Diffusion: A Case Study of the Rockefeller Foundation." In *Social Sciences and Public Policy in the Developing World.* Lexington, Mass.: D. C. Heath, 1982.

Stross, Randall. *The Stubborn Earth: American Agriculturalists on Chinese Soil, 1898–1937.* Berkeley: University of California Press, 1986.

Sun, Chung-hsing. "The Development of the Social Sciences in China before 1949." PhD dissertation, Columbia University, 1987.

Sutton, Francis X. "American Philanthropy in Educational and Cultural Exchanges with the People's Republic of China." In *Educational Exchanges: Essays on the Sino-American Experience*, edited by Joyce K. Kallgren and Denis Fred Simon. Berkeley: Institute of East Asian Studies, University of California, 1987.

Tankard, Judith B. *Beatrice Farrand: Private Gardens, Public Landscapes.* New York: Monacelli Press, 2009.

Tchen, John Kuo Wei. *New York before Chinatown: Orientalism and the Shaping of American Culture, 1776–1882.* Baltimore: Johns Hopkins University Press, 1999.

Thomas, John N. *The Institute of Pacific Relations: Asian Scholars and American Politics.* Seattle: University of Washington Press, 1974.

Thomson, James C., Jr. *While China Faced West: American Reformers in Nationalist China, 1928–1937.* Cambridge, Mass.: Harvard University Press, 1969.

Tomlinson, John. *Cultural Imperialism: A Critical Introduction.* London: Pinter, 1991.

Toole, J. D., et al. "The Rockefeller Foundation's International Program on Rice Biotechnology," 2001. Unpublished Rockefeller Foundation paper.

Trescott, Paul B. "American Philanthropy and the Development of Academic Economics in China before 1949." In *Philanthropy and Cultural Context: Western Philanthropy in South, East and Southeast Asia in the 20th Century*, edited by Soma Hewa and Philo Hove. Lanham, Md.: University Press of America, 1997.

———. *Jingji Xue: The History of the Introduction of Western Economic Ideas into China, 1850–1950*. Hong Kong: Chinese University Press, 2007.

Tucker, Nancy Bernkopf. *Patterns in the Dust: Chinese-American Relations and the Recognition Controversy, 1949–1950*. New York: Columbia University Press, 1983.

Wang, Y. C. *Chinese Intellectuals and the West, 1872–1949*. Chapel Hill: University of North Carolina Press, 1966.

Wang, Yiyou. *Art Dealers, the Rockefellers and the Network of Chinese Art in America*. Rockefeller Archive Research Report. New York: Rockefeller Archive, 2008.

Wang, Zuoyue. "Saving China through Science: The Science Society of China, Scientific Nationalism and Civil Society in Republican China." *Osiris* 17 (2002): 291–322.

Watt, John. "Breaking into Public Service: The Development of Nursing in Modern China, 1870–1949. *Nursing History Review* 12 (2004): 67–96.

———. "J. Heng Liu and ABMAC." Unpublished paper.

Weindling, Paul. "Philanthropy and World Health: The Rockefeller Foundation and the League of Nations Health Organization." *Minerva* 35 (1997): 269–81.

West, Philip. *Yenching University and Sino-Western Relations, 1916–1952*. Cambridge, Mass.: Harvard University Press, 1976.

Wojtczak, Andrzej, and M. Roy Schwarz. "Minimum Essential Requirements and Standards in Medical Education." *Medical Teacher* 22 (2000):, 555–59.

Woods, Lawrence T. "Rockefeller Philanthropy and the Institute of Pacific Relations: A Reappraisal of Long-Term Mutual Dependency." *International Journal of Voluntary and Nonprofit Organizations* 10, no. 2 (1999): 151–66.

Wu, Lingjun. "Standard Oil Company's Trade Negotiations with China, 1870–1930/33." *Guoli zhengzhi daxue lishi xuebao* 17 (May 2000): 229–61.

Xu, Xiaoqun. *Chinese Professionals and the Republican State: The Rise of Professional Associations in Shanghai, 1912–1937*. Cambridge: Cambridge University Press, 2001.

Ye, Weili. *Seeking Modernity in China's Name: Chinese Students in the United States, 1900–1927*. Stanford, Calif.: Stanford University Press, 2001.

Yip, Ka-che. *Health and National Reconstruction in Nationalist China: The Development of Modern Health Services, 1928–1937*. Ann Arbor, Mich.: Association of Asian Studies, 1995.

Yoshihara, Mari. *Embracing the East: White Women and American Orientalism*. New York: Oxford University Press, 2003.

Zhongguo Xiehe Yike Daxue: Biye Tongxue lu (Peking Union Medical College: An Alumni Roster). Peking: PUMC Press, 1997.

Zhongyun, Zi. *The Destiny of Wealth: An Analysis of American Philanthropic Foundations from a Chinese Perspective*. Dayton: The Kettering Press, 2007

———. "The Rockefeller Foundation and China." Unpublished English version of "Luokefeile Jijinhui Yu Zhongguo." *Meiguo Yanjiu* (China) 10 (1996): 58–89.

INDEX

Note: Index entries containing "JDR" refer to John D. Rockefeller. Italic page numbers indicate illustrations.